A Reference Gra

of Tamazight

A Comparative Study of the Berber Dialects of Ayt Ayache and Ayt Seghrouchen

Ernest T. Abdel-Massih

MPublishing
University of Michigan Library
and
Center for Near Eastern and North African Studies
University of Michigan
Ann Arbor
2011

Published in 2011 by MPublishing
University of Michigan Library

This volume is reprinted from the 1971 edition by arrangement with the Center for Near Eastern and North African Studies, University of Michigan

MPublishing
4186 Shapiro
919 South University
Ann Arbor, MI 48109
lib.pod@umich.edu

ISBN 978-1-60785-222-3

A Reference Grammar

of Tamazight

Map of Morocco

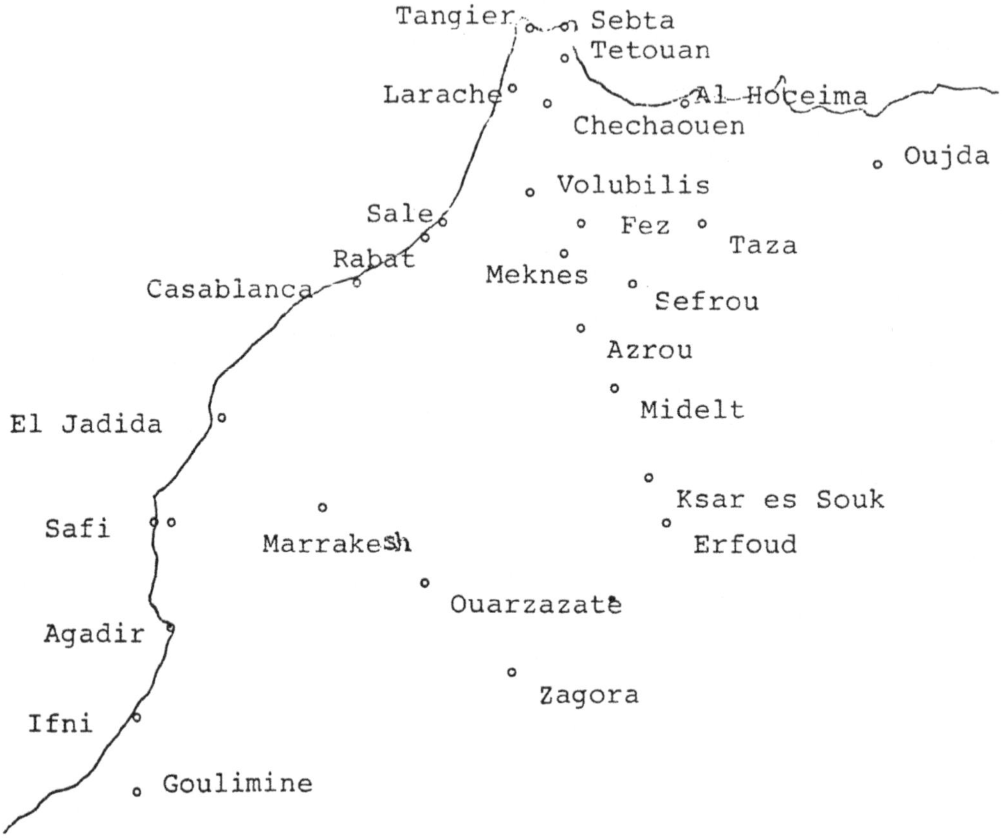

DISTANCES FROM CASABLANCA IN MILES

Al Hoceima	338	Marrakesh	149
Agadir	330	Meknes	146
Azrou	189	Midelt	267
Chechaouen	205	Ouarzazate	273
El Jadida	62	Oujda	403
Erfoud	403	Rabat	58
Fez	183	Safi	158
Goulimine	453	Tangier	236
Larache	180	Taza	257
		Tetuan	248

Foreword

The preparation of this volume and the accompanying one, _A Course in Spoken Tamazight_, was initiated and supported by the University of Michigan Center for Near Eastern and North African Studies as part of its general program of research and training on the languages and cultures of North Africa. A series of studies in anthropology, history and political science are in preparation, as well as instructional materials on Moroccan Arabic.

We are indebted to the Ford Foundation, which is in no way responsible for the specific consequences, for the grants to the Center that have made this work possible. We are most grateful for the tolerance of the people and government of Morocco in accommodating, and often actively assisting, the work of our faculty and students.

W.D. Schorger
Director

Acknowledgements

This book and its companion, A Course in Spoken Tamazight, were made possible by the cooperation of a number of individuals. In particular, I would like to express my appreciation to Mr. Mohammed Raamouch whose comments and constructive remarks were a great help to me in the formulation of the grammar of Ayt Ayache. Thanks are also due to Mr. Mohammed Guerssel who, by his linguistic competence and insightful observations, contributed greatly to the comparative notes on the two dialects.

In addition, I would like to express my thanks to Professor William D. Schorger, who, as Director of the Center for Near Eastern and North African Studies at the University of Michigan, initiated the program of research on North African languages and linguistics. The Center defrayed the costs of research assistants, field trips, typists, tapes and tape recordings, as well as, providing me with the time and opportunity to carry out the field research and the analysis.

I owe an especial debt to my colleagues Professor Ernest N. McCarus and Professor Gene M. Schramm who gave their time freely for linguistic discussions during the early stages of the research that led to the formulation of this present work; I am grateful to them for their many creative suggestions.

Also, I wish to extend thanks to Professor Lionel Galand of L'Ecole Nationale des Langues Orientales Vivantes, Paris, for his helpful comments on an earlier draft of the units, particularly the

Ayt Ayache materials.

And I am also grateful to Professor J. Bynon of the School of Oriental and African Studies, University of London for his enlightening discussions on the problems of Tamazight phonology and word boundary.

I am deeply grateful to my wife, Cecile, whose patience, constant encouragement and deep understanding have sustained my efforts throughout the work on this book.

Ann Arbor, Michigan
January, 1971

E.T.A.

Introduction

This book grew out of the great need for a short reference grammar of the Berber language in general and of the Tamazight dialect in particular that could be used by college students in an elementary course. The first version of the present grammar (1966) concentrated on the phonology and the morphology of the Ayt Ayache dialect of Tamazight and was used in an experimental class organized at the University of Michigan. The second version was completed in 1968, Work of the grammar of Ayt Seghrouchen Tamazight began in December 1968. The formulation of the comparative notes came after the completion of the grammar of the two affiliated dialects.

The language of this book is Tamazight, a dialect of Berber, spoken in the Middle Atlas Mountains of Morocco. Berber is spoken mainly in North Africa (Libya, Tunisia, Algeria and Morocco) and in Siwa (UAR). It is also spoken by the Tuareg groups in Muritania and the countries of the Sahara (Mali, Niger and Chad). Berber, a branch of the Afro-Asiatic family of languages is exclusively an unwritten language. It is divided into some three hundred or more distinct local dialects. The number of the speakers of

Berber have been estimated to be 5,000,000[1] to 7,000,000[2] and over 10,000,000[3]. Berber speakers are discontinuously distributed from the Siwa Oasis in Egypt to the Atlantic Ocean and from the Niger River to the Mediterranean Sea. (See the map on p. vi for the distribution of the Berber dialects in general and the map on p. vii for the distribution of the Berber dialects particularly in Morocco.) It is possible to distinguish four basic dialect groups of Berber:

I. Tamazight, a dialect of the Middle Atlas Mountains in Central Morocco. Among the speakers of Tamazight (which number approximately 2,000,000) are the following groups (tribes, subtribes):

Beni Ouarain, Ait Morghi, Ait Alaham, Ait Youb, Marmoucha, Ait Seghrouchen, Ait Youssi, Beni Mguild, Zaiane, Zemmour, Ait Rbaa, Ait Seri, Beni Mtir, Guerouane, Ait Segougou, Ait Morghad, Ait Ayache, Ait Hadiddou, Ait Izdeg, Ait Sikhmane, Ait Atta.

II. Tashelhit (or Shilha), dialect of the High and Anti-Atlas and the Sous Valley in Southern Morocco. There are approximately 2,000,000 speakers of this dialect.

---

1 Encyclopedia of Islam, vol. I, Fasciulus 19, Leiden, Netherlands, 1959, p. 1177.

2 Ju. N. Zavadovskij, Berberski jazyk (The Berber Language), Moscow, 1967, p. 7.

3 Encyclopedia Britannica, vol. 3, Encyclopedia Britannica Inc., Wm. Benton, Chicago, 1970, p. 496.

III. Zenatiya, a dialect of about 2,000,000 speakers.

Zenatiya distinguishes the following sub-groupings:

a) Rifian or Tarifit (spoken by about 0.5 million Rifians in Northern and Northeastern Morocco)

b) Kabyli (spoken by about 1,300,000 speakers), dialect of the Kabyle tribes in the Kabyle Mountains of Algeria

c) Zenatiya Mzabian (spoken by about 25,000 speakers in Mzab by the Mzabites of Ghardaia)

d) Shawia or Tashawit (spoken by about 150,000 speakers in the Aures Mountains of Algeria)

IV. Tamashek, dialect of the Tuareg groups in Muritania and the open Sahara.

Many speakers of Berber in North Africa are bilingual, with Arabic being their second language. Many of the men speak Berber, Arabic and French, while the women are more conservative.

The main focus of the language of this book is the Tamazight dialects of Ayt Ayache and Ayt Seghrouchen. Ayt Ayache is a tribe composed of twenty-two villages along the Ansegmir River, at the foot of Ayachi Mountain, about thirty kilometers west of the town of Midelt. The limit on the east is National Highway No. 21, on the south the Ayt Yahya tribe at Road No. 3420 and on the north and west the Beni Mguild tribe at Road No. 3422.

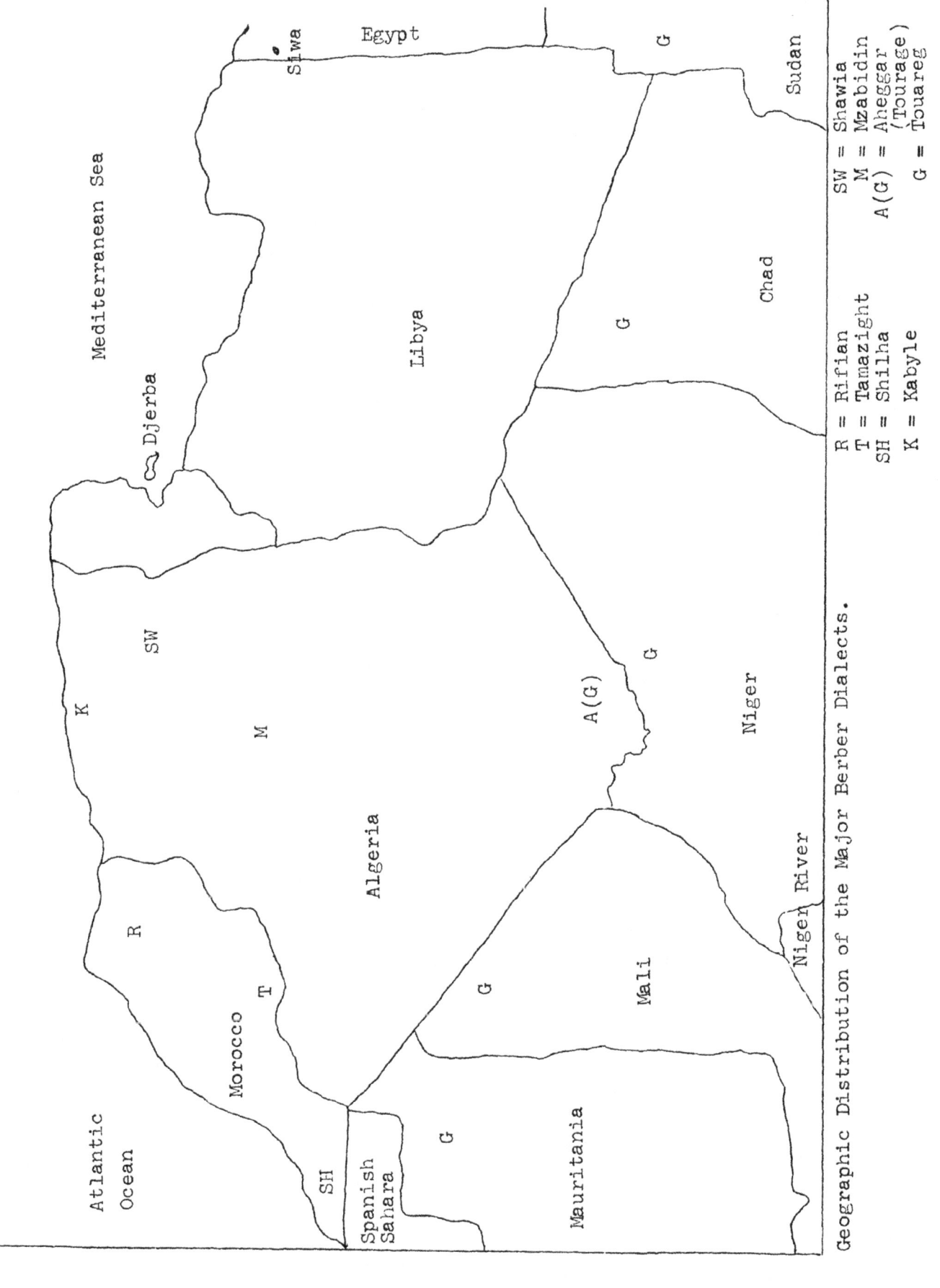

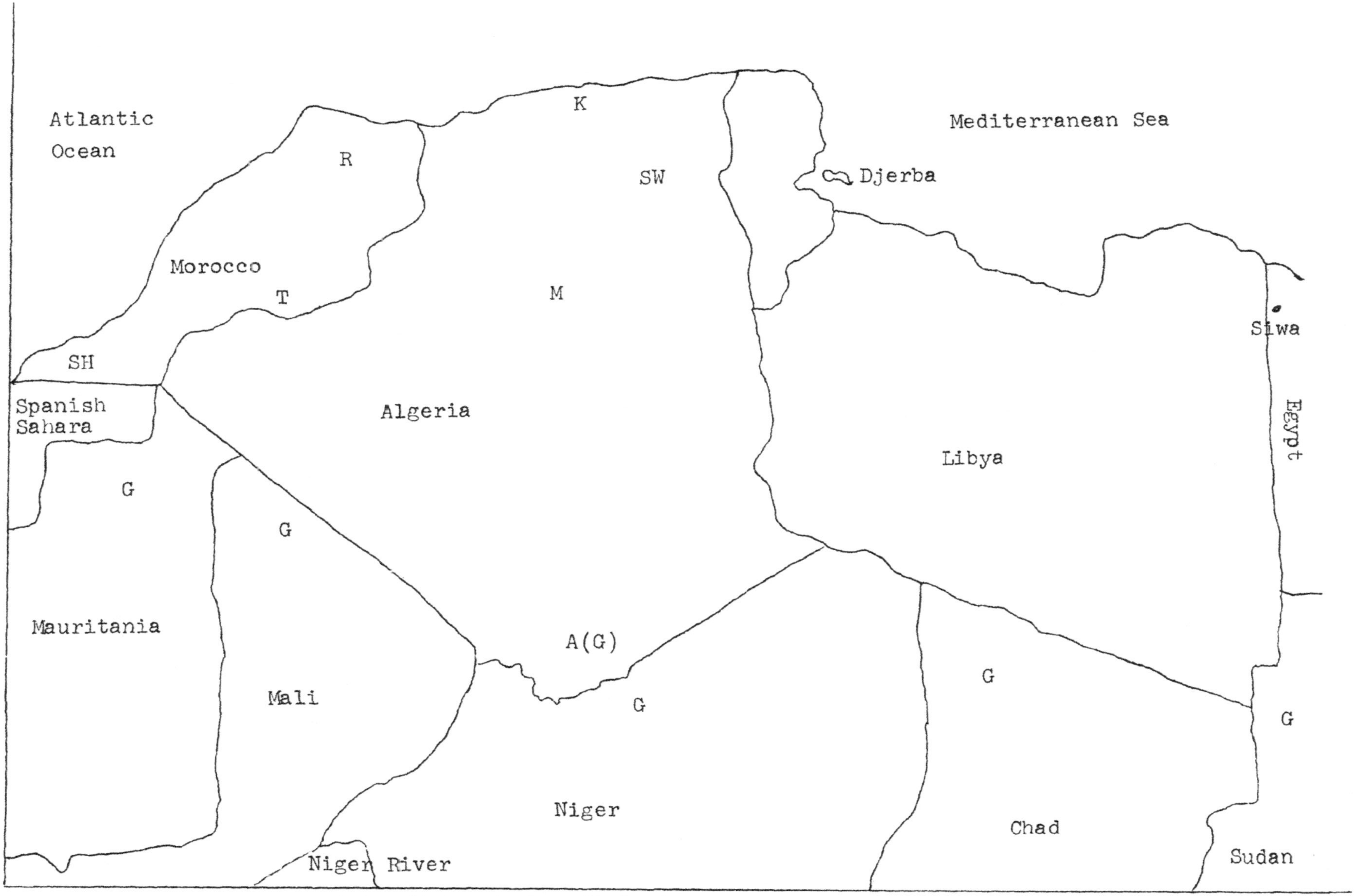

Geographic Distribution of the Major Berber Dialects.

R = Rifian
T = Tamazight
SH = Shilha
K = Kabyle
SW = Shawia
M = Mzabidin
A(G) = Aheggar (Tourage)
G = Touareg

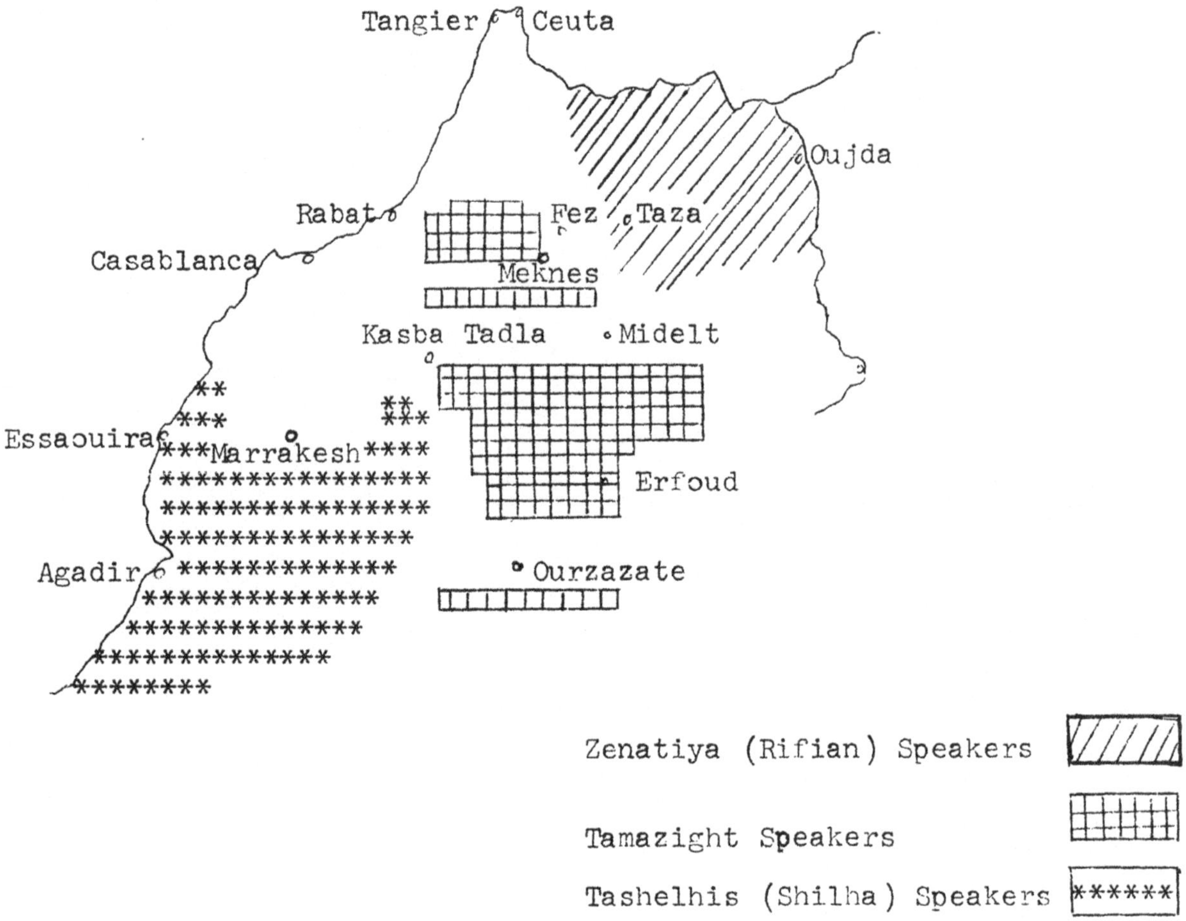

Geographic Distribution of Berber Dialects in Morocco

Ayt Ayache Tamazight is mutually intelligible with the speech of neighboring tribes. Ayt Seghrouchen is a much larger tribe than Ayt Ayache. It is divided into three major sub-tribes: (1) Ayt Seghrouchen of Sidi Ali, known as Ayt Seghrouchen of Tichikout, (2) Ayt Seghrouchen of Imouzzer and (3) Ayt Seghrouchen of Talesinnt. The limits of the Ayt Seghrouchen of Sidi Ali are the Beni Ouarain to the north, Ayt Youssi to the south, Ayt Seghrouchen of Imouzzer and Beni Mguild to the west and southwest and Oulad El-Haj to the east. Ayt Seghrouchen of Imouzzer lies about 30 kilometers south of Fez, surrounded by Ayt Youssi, Beni Mtir and the town of Sefrou. The limits of Ayt Seghrouchen of Talesinnt are Oulad El-Haj, Ayt Yafelmane, the town of Midelt and Beni Guil. Both Ayt Ayache and Ayt Seghrouchen live by farming and by tending and rearing sheep. The main handicraft industry is tapestry.

Berber literature is, of course, mainly oral. It is this lack of written documents that makes the tracing of the history of the language somewhat difficult. However, attempts were made very early to record the language, using various writing systems. The oldest inscriptions come to us from Tunisia and Algeria and are over 2,000 years old. They are written in a consonantal system which resembles that of contemporary Tuareg. The national Berber alphabet is that of the Tuareg tribes, known as Tifinagh; it is composed of strokes, arcs, and dots as well as combinations of these. In this system, individual words are not separated and one can write from left to right or from right to left, from top to bottom ot from bottom to top. The Tuaregs call the symbols Tafineqq (singular) and Tifinagh (plural). The Tuaregs have no manuscripts, strictly speaking, only short notes on pots, bracelets, shields, etc. The only Berber texts we have are written in Arabic script. These are mainly religious texts used for instruction in Islam.

Following is a simplified table with samples of the Libyan inscriptions and Tuareg (Tifinagh), both ancient and contemporary inscriptions, with the corresponding Arabic script and phonetic equivalents.

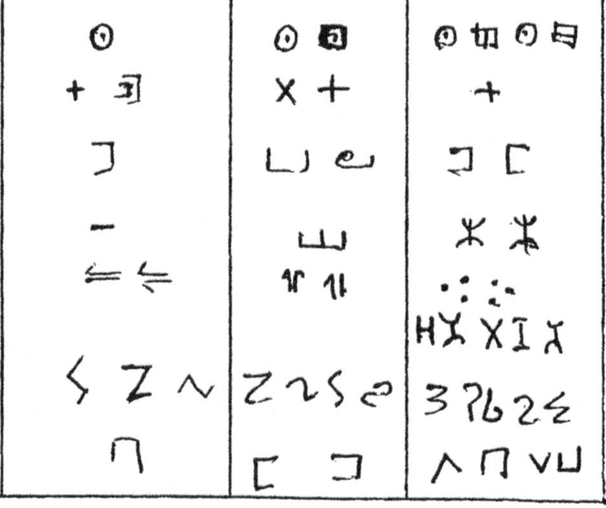

Phonetic Equiv.	Libyan	Tuareg (Tifinagh)		Corresponding Arabic Script
		ancient	contemp.	
b	⊙	⊙ ▣	⊙ ⊞ ⊙ ⊟	ب
t	+ ⋾	X +	+	ت
m	⌐	⊔ ꭢ	⌐ ⊏	م
z	—	⊔⊔	⋇ ⋇	ز
k	⇐ ⇐	⋔ ⋔	∴ ∴	ك
ž			HX XIX	ج
y	⟨ Z ∧	Z ⋂ S ꭢ	3 ? 6 2 ⋞	ي
d	⋂	⊏ ⊐	∧ ⋂ ∨⊔	د

Table of Berber and Arabic Script

This book is intended to be used mainly as a reference grammar for the dialect of Ayt Ayache, but, more importantly, it can serve as a source for the comparative study of the two dialects: Ayt Ayache and Ayt Seghrouchen. The order of presentation of the morphology of the dialects is arbitrary and, therefore, is not binding for the user.

At the beginning of each chapter appears a short summary of the contents of that section. Comparative notes on the two dialects sometimes appear at the end of a chapter (e.g., I. Phonology, II. The Numerical System, III. Pronominal Systems, IV. The Noun, VI. The Verb). However, in Chapter V. "Particles", a full discussion of each of the different groups of particles is given for Ayt Seghrouchen following that of Ayt Ayache. This is due to the great lexical difference between the two dialects in this domain.

Chapter VII. "Sentences" lists examples consisting of 157 pairs of sentences to exemplify the different structures of the two dialects. The first member of each pair of sentences is from Ayt Ayache, the second from Ayt Seghrouchen.

In studying the grammatical point in issue, often the user will find numerous examples listed. This serves a dual purpose: the exemplification of the grammatical point under discussion and the provision of additional lexical items.

It is hoped that this book may serve as a reference grammar for its twin, A Course in Spoken Tamazight (Center for Near Eastern and North African Studies, the University of Michigan, 1971), for indeed they complement one another. Usage of both texts is indispensable for mastery of Tamazight.

Ann Arbor, Michigan

January 1971 E.T.A.

TABLE OF CONTENTS

Foreword.. v
Acknowledgements.. vi
Introduction.. viii

I. Phonology

I.1 Consonants and Vowels of Tamazight, Ayt Ayache...... 2
I.1.1 Explanation of Phonological Terms.................. 2
I.1.2 Pronunciation of Consonants and Semi-Vowels......... 5
I.2 Vowels.. 11
I.3 Structure of the Syllable............................. 15
I.4 Stress.. 17
Notes on the Phonology in Ayt Seghrouchen(A.S.)........... 19

II. The Numerical System

II.1 Cardinal Numbers..................................... 22
II.2 Ordinal Numbers...................................... 29
II.3 Fractions.. 31
Notes on the Numerical System in Ayt Seghrouchen(A.S.).... 33

III. Pronominal Systems

III.1 Personal Pronouns................................... 35
III.1.1 Independent Forms................................. 35
III.1.2 Emphatic Personal Pronouns........................ 35
III.2 Possessive Pronouns................................. 36
III.2.1 Independent Set................................... 36
III.2.1.1 Masculine....................................... 36
III.2.1.2 Feminine.. 36
III.2.2 Possessive Pronominal Suffixes.................... 37
III.2.2.1 Suffixed to Nouns Ending in Consonant........... 37
III.2.2.2 Suffixed to Nouns Ending in Vowel............... 39
III.2.2.3 Used with Kinship Terms......................... 40
III.3 Pronominal Affixes for Verbs and Prepositions...... 44
III.3.1 Affirmative....................................... 46
III.3.1.1 With Intransitive Verbs:Indirect Objects........ 46
III.3.1.2 With Transitive Verbs:Direct Objects............ 49
III.3.2 Negative.. 52
III.3.2.1 With Intransitive Verbs:Indirect Objects........ 52
III.3.2.2 With Transitive Verbs:Direct Objects............ 55

III.3.3 Interrogative.. 58
III.3.3.1 With Intransitive Verbs:Indirect Objects........ 58
III.3.3.2 With Transitive Verbs:Direct Objects............ 61
III.3.4 Negative Interrogative.............................. 63
III.3.4.1 With Intransitive Verbs:Indirect Objects........ 63
III.3.4.2 With Transitive Verbs:Direct Objects............ 66
III.4 Demonstrative Pronouns(Independent Set)......... 69
III.4.1 Singular.. 69
III.4.2 Plural.. 69
III.4.3 Demonstrative Pronominal Suffixes.............. 69
III.4.3.1 /-a#/, /-in:#/............................. 69
III.4.3.2 /-d: /...................................... 70
III.4.3.3 /-n:a/...................................... 70
III.4.4 The Demonstrative ha,han......................... 71
III.4.4.1 ha + Personal Pronouns.......................... 71
III.4.4.2 hat.. 72
III.5 Relative Pronouns.................................. 72
III.5.1 Subject.. 72
III.5.2 Object... 74
III.6 Indefinite Pronouns................................ 74
III.6.1 Proximate Indefinite Pronouns.................... 74
III.6.2 Remote Indefinite Pronouns....................... 75
III.6.3 Every, Each... 76
Notes on the Pronominal System in Ayt Seghrouchen(A.S.)... 77

IV. Grammar of the Noun

IV.1 Introduction... 87
IV.2 Basic and Derived Noun Stems and Nouns........... 88
IV.2.1 Basic Noun Stems and Nouns....................... 88
IV.2.2 Derived Noun Stems and Nouns..................... 92
IV.3 Definiteness, Gender and Number.................. 92
IV.3.1 Definite/Indefinite................................ 92
IV.3.2 Gender and Number.................................. 93
IV.3.2.1 Noun Affixes...................................... 93
IV.3.2.1-a Masculine Singular Prefixes.................. 93
IV.3.2.1-b Masculine Plural Prefixes.................... 94
IV.3.2.1-c Feminine Singular Affixes.................... 95
IV.3.2.1-d Feminine Plural Affixes...................... 96
IV.4 Plural Nouns... 97
IV.4.1 Masculine Plurals.................................. 97
IV.4.1.1 External Plurals(Sound Plurals)................. 97
IV.4.1.2 Internal Plurals(Broken Plurals)................ 104
IV.4.1.3 Mixed Plurals..................................... 107
IV.5 Feminine Plurals...................................... 109
IV.5.1 External Plurals(Sound Plurals).................. 109
IV.5.2 Internal Plurals(Broken Plurals)................. 111
IV.5.3 Mixed Plurals.. 112

IV.6 Miscellaneous.. 114
IV.6.1 Plurals with /id-/ (m,f) and /ist:/ (f)............ 114
IV.6.2 Plurals with /ayt-/ (m)............................ 115
IV.6.3 Plurals of Different Roots......................... 115
IV.6.4 Diminutives.. 115
IV.6.5 Augmentative....................................... 116
IV.6.6 Collective Nouns................................... 116
IV.6.6.1 Singular Collective Nouns........................ 116
IV.6.6.2 Plural Collective Nouns.......................... 117
IV.6.7 Noun of Unity...................................... 117
IV.6.8 Composed Nouns..................................... 118
IV.7 Construct State of the Noun.......................... 119
IV.7.1 Changes occuring in Masculine Nouns................ 119
IV.7.2 Changes occuring in Feminine Nouns................. 120
IV.7.3 Conditions for Construct State..................... 121
Notes on the Noun in Ayt Seghrouchen(A.S.)................ 126

V. Particles

V.1 Interrogative Particles(Ayt Ayache).................. 132
V.2 Interrogative Particles(Ayt Seghrouchen)............. 137
V.3 Conjunctions... 141
V.3.1 Ayt Ayache... 141
V.3.2 Ayt Seghrouchen.................................... 143
V.4 Prepositions... 145
V.4.1 Ayt Ayache... 145
V.4.2 Ayt Seghrouchen.................................... 147
V.5 Presentational Particles............................. 149
V.6 Vocative Particles................................... 150
V.7 Conditional Particles................................ 150

VI. Grammar of the Verb

VI.1 Basic and Derived Verb Stems........................ 153
VI.1.1 Basic Verb Stems................................... 153
VI.1.2 Derived Verb Stems................................. 153
VI.2 Verb Affixes.. 153
VI.2.1 Movable Affixes.................................... 154
VI.2.2 Fixed Affixes...................................... 155
VI.3 Classification of Verb Stems........................ 160
VI.3.1 The Different Ablauts.............................. 161
VI.3.1.1 Zero Ablaut /Ø/.................................. 161
VI.3.1.2 [Ø:i/a] Ablaut................................... 163
VI.3.1.3 Predictable Ablauts.............................. 165
VI.3.1.3-a [Ø:i] Ablaut................................... 165
VI.3.1.3-b [a:u] Ablaut................................... 165
VI.3.1.4 Metathesis....................................... 165
VI.3.1.5 Predictable Changes in the Sub-class/d:u/ - /iri/.. 166
VI.3.2 Classes and Sub-classes of the Verb Stem Types..... 167
VI.3.2.1 Ablauted and Unablauted Types.................... 167
VI.3.2.2 Classes of the Ablauted Type..................... 168
VI.3.2.3 Classes of the Unablauted Type................... 169

VI.3.2.4 Sub-classification of Verb Stems.................. 169
VI.3.3 Illustrative Examples of Verb Conjugations......... 170
VI.4 Derivational Processes............................ 174
VI.4.1 Introduction...................................... 174
VI.4.2 Derivation of the Habitual VH of Unaugmented Stem.. 176
VI.4.3 Causative Stem Derivation......................... 179
VI.4.4 Recprocal Verb Stem Derivation.................... 179
VI.4.5 Passive Berb Stem Derivation...................... 181
VI.4.6 Derived Noun Stems and Nouns...................... 182
VI.4.6.1 Introduction.................................... 182
VI.4.6.2 Noun Stem Derivation............................ 182
VI.4.7 Temporal and Modal Derivation..................... 186
VI.4.7.1 Introduction.................................... 186
VI.4.7.2 Derivation of Imperative Structures............. 187
VI.4.7.3 Derivation of Past Tense and Its Different Modes... 192
VI.4.7.4 Derivation of Future Tense and Its Different Modes. 195
VI.4.7.5 Derivation of Present Tense and Its Different Modes 197
VI.4.7.6 Derivation of the Aorist........................ 199
VI.4.7.7 Derivation of the Participles.................... 200
VI.4.7.8 Summary of Rules for Temporal,Modal and Participle Derivations.................................... 203
VI.5 Morphophonemic Sketch............................. 207
VI.5.1 Introduction...................................... 207
VI.5.2 General Rules of Verb Morphophonemics.............. 207
VI.5.3 Examples.. 210
Notes on the Verb in Ayt Seghrouchen(A.S.)................ 216
Introduction to Verb Sample Appendix A(Ayt Ayache)......... 240
Verb Sample Appendix A (Ayt Ayache)....................... 245
List of Verbs (Ayt Ayache)................................ 262
Verb Sample Appendix B (Ayt Seghrouchen).................. 283

VII. Sentences

A.1 Verbless:Affirmative.................................. 287
A.2 Verbless:Interrogative................................ 289
A.3 Verbless: Negative.................................... 291
A.4 Verbless: Negative-Interrogative....................... 292
B.1 Verbal:Affirmative.................................... 293
B.1.1 Sentences having one Verb........................... 293
B.1.2 Sentences having two Verbs.......................... 300
B.2 Verbal:Interrogative.................................. 308
B.3 Verbal:Negative....................................... 311
B.4 Verbal:Negative-Interrogative......................... 314
C. Imperative Structures.................................. 315

TABLES, FIGURES AND ILLUSTRATIONS

Map of Morocco.. ii
Geographic Distribution of the Major Berber Dialects...... xi
Geographic Distribution of Berber Dialects in Morocco..... xii
Table of Berber and Arabic Script......................... xiv

Tables and Figures of Chapter I: Phonology

Table 1.- Tamazight Consonants and Semi-Vowels............ 4
Table 2.- Tamazight Vowels................................ 4
Figure 1.- Diagram of the Organs of Speech................ 3
Figure 2.- Tongue position for /t/........................ 9
Figure 3.- Tongue position for /ṭ/........................ 9
Figure 4.- Tongue position for /s/........................ 10
Figure 5.- Tongue position for /ṣ/........................ 10
Table 3.- Tamazight Vowel Allophones...................... 12

Tables and Figures of Chapter VI: The Verb, in Ayt Ayache

Table 1.- Second Person Imperative Suffixes (A.A.)........ 158
Table 2.- Hortatory Suffixes (A.A.)....................... 158
Table 3.- Ayt Ayache /-PNG-/ Affixes...................... 159
Table 4.- Person-Number-Gender Paradigms for Unablauted Stems (A.A.)................................ 171
Table 5.- Person-Number-Gender Paradigms for [Ø:O] Ablauted Stems (A.A.)................................ 172
Table 6.- Person-Number-Gender Paradigms for [Ø:i/a] Ablauted Stems (A.A.)....................... 173
Tables 7-13.- Imperative Structures (A.A.)............... 190-192
Tables 14-17.- Past Tense Structures (A.A.).............. 193-194
Tables 18-21.- Future Tense Structures (A.A.)............ 196-197
Tables 22-25.- Present Tense Structures (A.A.)........... 198-199
Table 26.- Aorist Structures (A.A.)...................... 200
Tables 27-29.- Participles (A.A.)........................ 201-202

Tables of Comparative Notes to Chapter VI (Ayt Seghrouchen)

Table 1.- Second Person Imperative Suffixes (A.S.)........ 217
Table 2.- Hortatory Suffixes (A.S.)....................... 217
Table 3.- -PNG- Affixes (A.S.)............................ 217
Tables 4-11.- Conjugations of Unablauted Stems (A.S.)..... 220-223
Tables 12-23.- Conjugations of Ø:O Ablauted Stems (A.S.).. 224-229
Tables 24-27.- Conjugations of i/a Ablauted Stems (A.S.).. 230-231
Tables 28-31.- Conjugations of i/u Ablauted Stems (A.S.).. 232-233
Tables 32-35.- Conjugations of a-u Ablauted Stems (A.S.).. 234-235
Tables 36-39.- Conjugations of a-i Ablauted Stems (A.S.).. 236-237

I. Phonology

This section discusses the phonology of Ayt Ayache (A.A.) Tamazight citing examples to illustrate the different phonological features of this dialect. At the very end of this section a few notes on the phonology of Ayt Seghrouchen (A.S.) are included. The two dialects are very much alike in their phonological systems except for the fact that /k/ and /g/ are fricatives in Ayt Ayache whereas they are stops in Ayt Seghrouchen

I. Phonology

I.1 Tamazight, Ayt Ayache dialect, has the following consonants:
/btd kgq šž xγ mnlr ḥʕh/ (See Table 1)
and the following vowels:
/i u a/ (See Table 2)

I.1.1 The terms used in Table 1 are here explained in terms of the articulators that help produce the different sounds. These are followed by explanations of the terms voiced and voiceless, lax and tense, labialized and finally flat. It is also suggested that the student refer to Figure 1. for a better understanding of these terms.

Bilabial: lower lip and upper lip
Labio-dental: lower lip and upper teeth
Dental: apex of tongue and upper teeth
Alveolar: apex of tongue and alveolar ridge
Alveo-palatal: apex of tongue and front part of palate
Palatal: tongue blade and palate
Post palatal: tongue blade and back of palate
Velar: tongue dorsum and velum
Uvular: tongue dorsum and uvula
Pharyngeal: root of the tongue and pharynx (constriction)
Glottal: produced in the larynx by constriction of the two vocal chords
Voiced (vd): during the production of voiced sounds the vocal chords are closed
Voiceless (vl): during the production of voiceless sounds the vocal chords are open
Lax: a speech sound produced with little muscular tension in the speech organs; e.g. /b/
Tense: a speech sound produced with great muscular tension in the speech organ; e.g. /b:/

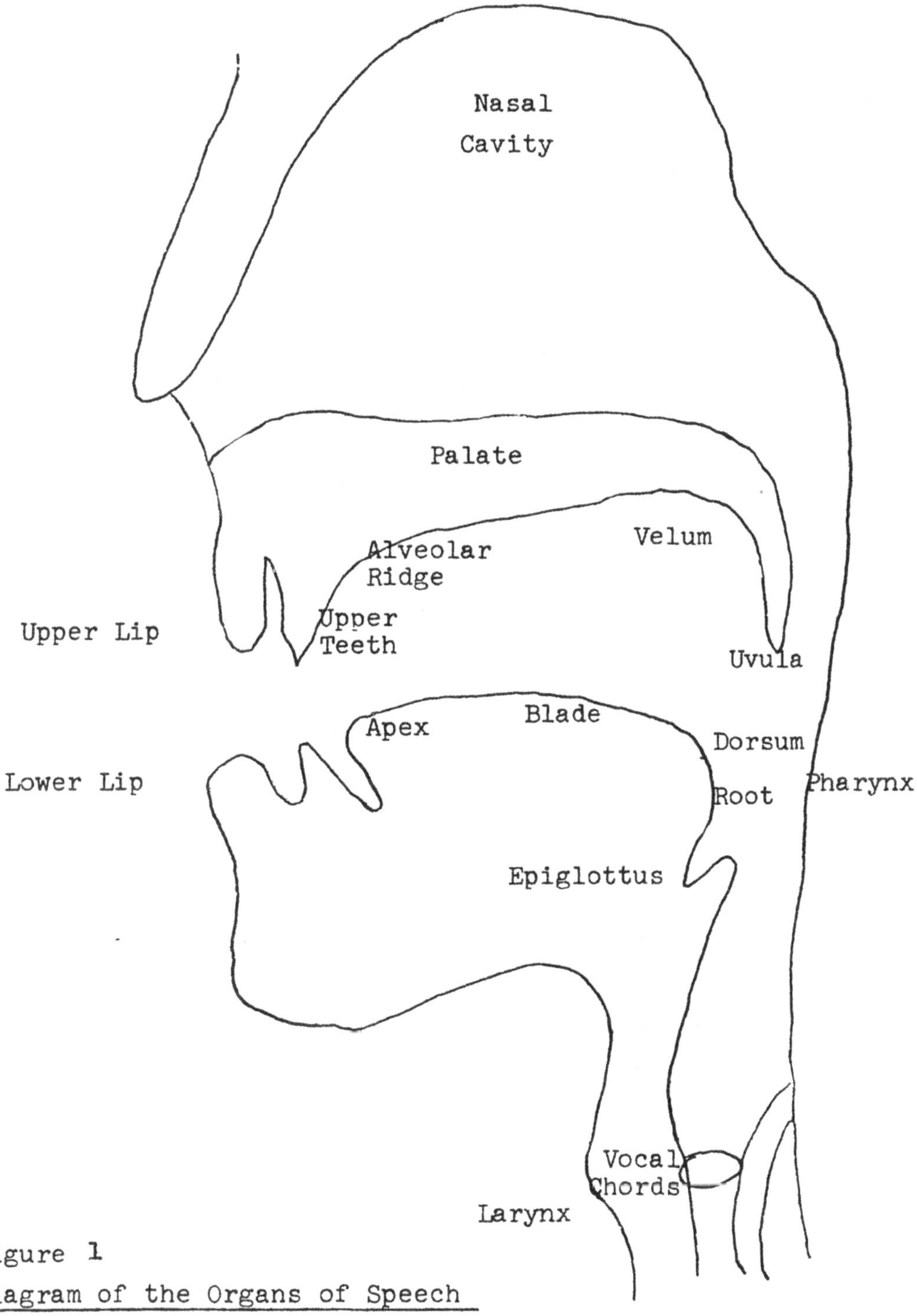

Figure 1

Diagram of the Organs of Speech

		Bilabial	Labio-Dental	Dental	Alveolar	Alveo-palatal	Palatal	Post palatal	Velar	Uvular	Pharyngial	Glottal
Stop	vl.			t				k		q		ʔ
	vd.	b		d				g				
Fric.	vl.		f	s		š				x	ḥ	h
	vd.			z		ž				ɣ	ʕ	
Nasal		m			n							
Lateral				l								
Flap					r							
Semi-Vowel							y		w			

Table I: Tamazight Consonants and Semi-Vowels

	Front	Central	Back
High	i		u
Low		a	

Table 2: Tamazight Vowels

Labialized: a speech sound produced with added lip rounding; e.g., /q̣/ = [q̑] or [q^{w}].

Flat: a speech sound produced by pressing the blade of the tongue against the palate so that the articulation is velarized rather than dental; e.g. /ṭ/

I.1.2 Remarks on the pronunciation of the consonants and semi-vowels of Ayt Ayache Tamazight:

a) /b t d f s š l z ž m n h w y /

Group (a) are to varying degrees the same as in English . However the following slight differences are here noted for this Berber dialect:

1. /b/ which is a voiced bilabial stop can sometimes be heard as voiced bilabial fricative [β] by very few speakers; e.g., /lbab/ [lβæβ] 'the door'

2. /t/ has more puff with the air release than is the case in English; e.g.: /tafunast/ [t^{h}æfunæsth]'cow'

3. On the other hand, we would like to note that /š/ is pronounced as in English "she", e.g., /ša/ 'some'. /ž/ is pronounced as in English "measure"; e.g. /žhd/ 'to be strong'. /h/ is pronounced as in English "he", e.g. /dhn/ 'to rub ointment'. Finally /l/ in Tamazight is pronounced as English "clear" [l]; i.e., when preceding a vowel in English as in "lazy" or "late", but not like dark [l] in English, i.e. when following a vowel as in "feel". Tamazight /l/ is like the first [l] in English "level" but not the second one; e.g. Tamazight /lalal/ 'no' where all the three l's are pronounced like the first [l] in English "level".

b) /k g q x γ ḥ ʕ r/ [1] (for Comparative Notes on this chapter see pp. 19-70)

Group (b) do not exist in English.

1. Of group (b) /k/ and /g/ are fricatives in Ayt Ayache (though they are stops in other dialects of Berber as well as in English; e.g.; /irkm/ 'it (m.) boiled', /iga/ 'he did'.

2. /q x γ ḥ ʕ / are all back consonants known as "gutterals". Their place of articulation is uvular (/q x γ /) and pharyngeal (/ḥ ʕ /).

3. /q/ is a voiceless uvular stop that is produced by the tongue dorsum (back) forming a stop against the uvula. Notice that the place of articulation for Berber /q/ is further back than that of English /k/: e.g., /taqdurt/ 'a pot'.

4. /x/ is a voiceless velar fricative. Its place of articulation is uvular. To pronounce /x/ produce English /k/ then move the dorsum (back of the tongue) back and produce a fricative; this produces /x/. This will sound like the "ch" in German doch, lachen and nach; e.g., /xali/ 'my maternal uncle'.

5. /γ/ is a voiced velar fricative. It has the same place and manner of articulation as /x/. Try to produce English /g/ then move the dorsum of your tongue back and produce the fricative /γ/. Let us call /γ/ the "gargling" sound; e.g., /iγus/ 'he burnt'.

6. /ḥ/ is a voiceless pharyngeal fricative. As we know pharyngeal sounds are produced by a constric-

tion of the root of the tongue against the pharynx. This is not an easy sound for non-natives. It is advisable to practice pronouncing /ḥ/ by producing a vigorous constriction of the pharynx slightly below and behind the extreme edge of the velum. This can be achieved by drawing the body of the tongue back toward the posterior wall of the pharynx with considerable force. Try this and it should produce /ḥ/. Let us call this sound the "panting" sound; e.g., /ḥml/ 'to flood'.

7. /ʕ/ is a voiced pharyngeal fricative. If you try to pronounce the English vowel "a" as in "father" with your tongue pressed down, you will hear /ʕ/ which we will call the "bleating" sound; e.g., /lʕil/ 'the boy'.

8. /r/ is a flap, i.e., a sound that is produced by the very rapid viberation of the tip of the tongue (apex); e.g., /ira/ 'he wanted'.

<u>Flàtness, Labialization and Tenseness</u>

a) The domain of <u>flatness</u>, i.e., that of emphatic* consonants (also velarized and pharyngealized are terms used in this connection) is the syllable. We call /ṭ ḍ ṣ ẓ ḷ ṛ / a primary Tamazight "emphatic" set, the occurence of which affects other non-emphatic segments** to become

---

* Emphatic articulation refers to the pressing of the blade of the tongue against the palate in formation of some consonant sounds; the articulation is then velarized rather than dental or pharyngealized rather than velar.

** The term segment refers to a minimal portion of speech consisting of a spoken language item known as a consonant or a vowel.

emphatic. This latter set is here termed secondary emphatic set. Notice that in pronouncing the plain non-emphatic consonant the position of the tip of the tongue is dental for, let us say /t/ and the back of the tongue is depressed whereas in pronouncing its emphatic counterpart /ṭ/, the tip of the tongue is touching the alveolar ridge and the back of the tongue is raised up toward the velum. Also, note that in the case of the pronunciation of an emphatic consonant the lip muscles are contracted and the lips are extended ventrally whereas they are relaxed when pronouncing the plain consonants. (See figures 2 and 3 for /t/,/ṭ/ and figures 4 and 5 for /s/, /ṣ/).

<u>Examples of emphatic/non-emphatic consonants</u>:

/tizi/	a pass
/ṭiẓi/	pubic hair
/bdu/	to begin
/bḍu/	to share
/tzur/	she is fat
/tẓuṛ/	she visited holy places

b) <u>Labialization</u> is a feature of the back consonants /k g q x γ /. It is manifested as simultaneous lip rounding when producing any of the above mentioned consonants. Thus /q̣/ or /q̂/ is pronounced as $[q^w]$.[2] Labialization is an important feature for /k g q/ but not for /x γ/: e.g.,

/s:ḳ:ṛ/	sugar
/nk:r/	we got up

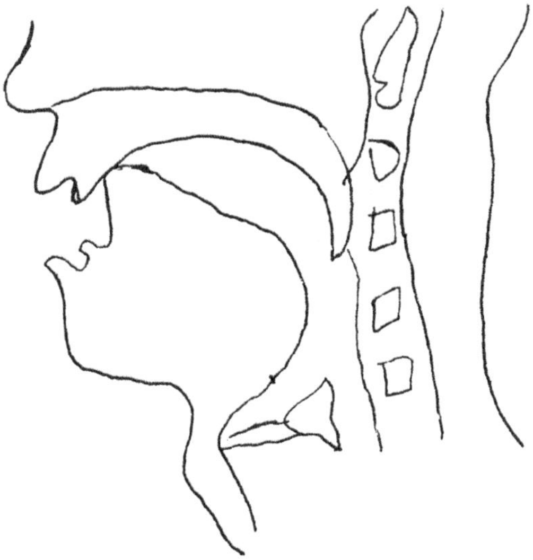

Figure 2: tongue position for /t/

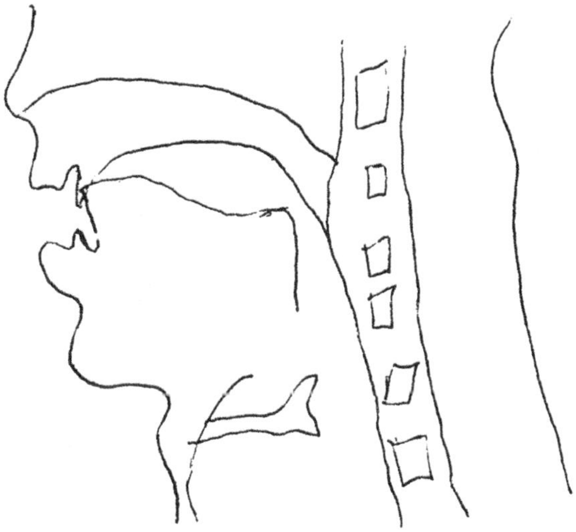

Figure 3: tonguc position for /ṭ/

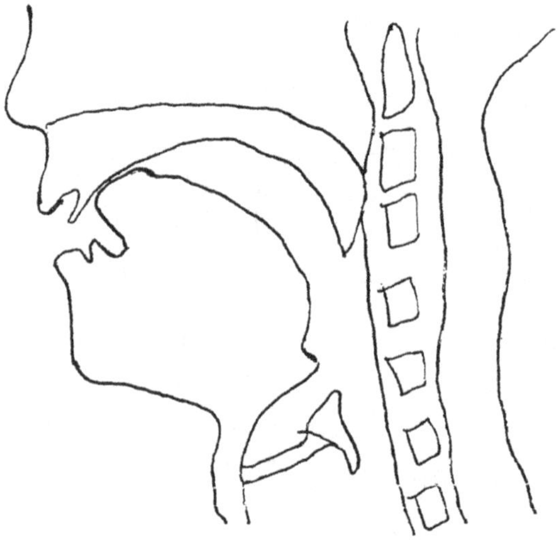

Figure 4: tongue position for /s/

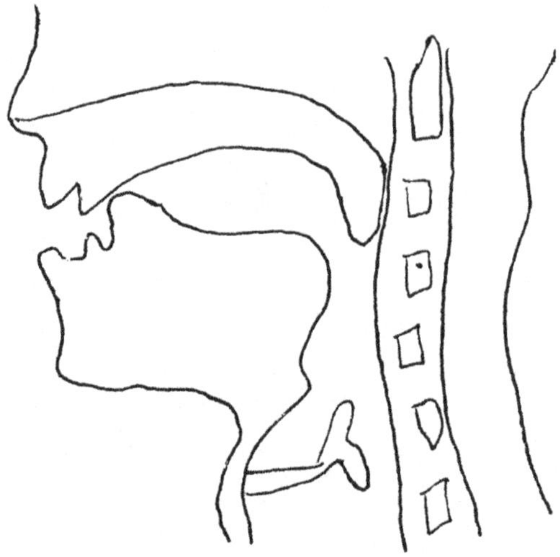

Figure 5: tongue position for /ṣ/

/ag:a/	he is
/ag̣:a/	a burden
/n:q:rt/	he shook it (m.) off
/n:q̣:ṛt/	silver
/lɣš:/~ /lɣ̣š:/	cheating
/ax̣m:as/ ~ /axm:as/	share-cropper

c) A tense* (also fortis) consonant in general is produced with more force than its lax (also lenis) counterpart.[3] The intensity and aspiration which are characteristic of the tense consonants give them a syllabic quality (i.e. maximum degree of sonority in the syllable) so that /b:/ is heard as [^{ə}bb]** or [^{I}bb]; this is transcribed in most other systems that treated Berber phonology /ebb/ or /əbb/ or/ĕbb/. In our system of transcription this will be realized as /b:/ and pronounced as [^{ə}bb] except when proceeded by a vowel, e.g.

/d:u/	[^{ə}ddu̬]	to go
/id:a/	[ɪddæ]	he went

I.2. Vowels

Tamazight has three vowels: /i u a/ (See Table 2). Allophones of the three vowels are shown in Table 3. The marking convention shown in Table 3 is to be understood as follows:

---

* Tense or fortis here refers to a consonant pronounced with stronger articulation and greater tension on the muscles of the articulator, and usually, aspiration. Lax or lenis here refers to a consonant pronounced with lesser muscular tension in the speech organ and weaker, laxer articulation and, usually, no aspiration.

** a raised up vowel -[^{ə}], [^{ɨ}], [^{Ĭ}] denotes that is a purely phonetic non-constrastive element.

[+] denotes the presence of a particular feature (e.g. [+ front] or [+high]) for a certain segment.

	i	ɨ	ɪ, e	u	ʊ, o	æ	æ̇	a
Front	+		+ +			+		
Centralized		+					+	
Back				+	+ +			+
High	+	+		+				
Lowered			+ +		+ +			
Low						+	+	+

Table 3: Tamazight Vowel Allophones

i	as in English "beat", "eat", "feet"
ɨ	does not commonly occur in English
ɪ	as in English "bit", "fit"
e	similar to the initial vowel part of the English words "eight", "ace"
u	as in English "food", "boot", "sue"
ʊ	as in English "book", "wood"
o	roughly as in English "coat"
æ	as in English "sat", "hat", "mat"
æ̇	does not commonly occur in English but corresponds roughly to vowel in "cut"
a	corresponds roughly to the English vowel in "father"

Henceforth the following notations will be used:

C = /b f t d s z s z k g q /

H = /h ḥ w y /

L = / l r m n /

X = C, H and L

γ, x = /γ x/
X = C, H, L, γ and x
V = / a i u /

Diacritics /./ and /:/ may be added and thus give, for example, /C̣/ and /C̣:/ representing /ṭ/ and /ṭ:/ respectively.

In the formulation of phonological rules the following conventions are used:

A----> B	A is rewritten as (or replaced by) B
(A)B or B(A)	A is optionally present, B is obligatorily present
$\begin{Bmatrix} A \\ B \end{Bmatrix}$	Either A or B occurs in this position
A--> B/____C	A is rewritten
A--> B/C___	A is rewritten as B after C

Vowel Allophones (# denotes word boundary, e.g. /-a# and #a-/ mean final and initial /a/ respectively)

1. /i/ ------> [i] $/ \begin{Bmatrix} \#\_\_\_X \\ X\_\_\_X \end{Bmatrix}$

ini	to say
sdid	to be thin

2. /i/-------> [ɨ] $/ \begin{Bmatrix} \#\_\_\_X{:} \\ X{:}\_\_\_ \end{Bmatrix}$

id:a	he went
td:id	you (s.) went

3. /i/-------> $\begin{Bmatrix} [\text{ɪ}] \\ [\text{e}] \end{Bmatrix} / \begin{Bmatrix} \_\_\_ \begin{Bmatrix} \text{C̣} \\ \gamma \\ x \end{Bmatrix} \\ \begin{Bmatrix} C \\ x \end{Bmatrix} \_\_\_ \end{Bmatrix}$

smiḍ	to be cold
zwiγ	to be red
bxin	to be black

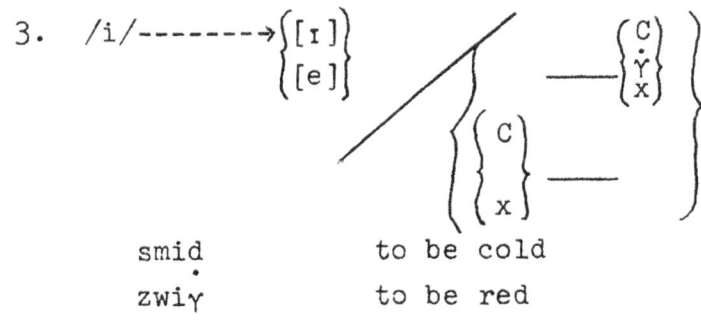

4. /i/ ---------> [ɪy] / χ ____ #

is:frḥi	he made me happy
is:fhmi	he made me understand

5. /u/----------> [u] $/ \left\{ \begin{matrix} \# \_\_\_ \chi \\ \chi(:) \_\_\_ \chi \end{matrix} \right\}$

umsγ	I painted
ufiγ	I found
idrus	It (m) is little
ifs:us	It (m) is light

6. /u/ --------->[ʊ]
[o] $/ \left\{ \begin{matrix} \_\_\_ \left\{ \begin{matrix} \text{C̣} \\ \gamma \\ x \end{matrix} \right\} \\ \left\{ \begin{matrix} \text{C̣} \\ \gamma \\ x \end{matrix} \right\} \_\_\_ \end{matrix} \right\}$

iḍuṛ	he turned
at:bḍud	you (s) will share
adimγur	he will grow up
lxuḍrt	vegetables

7. /u/ --------->[ʊw] / χ(:) ____ #

bdu	to begin
f:u	to dawn

8. /a/ --------->[æ] $/ \left\{ \begin{matrix} \# \_\_\_ \chi(:) \\ \chi(:) \_\_\_ \chi \end{matrix} \right\}$

azn	to send
sal	to ask
n:aγ	to fight

9. /a/ --------> [æ̇] / χ(:)____#

da	here
la	no
hn:a	to be peaceful

10. /a/ --------> [ɑ] / { ____C̣ ; C̣____ }

ḥaḍr	to be present
ṭalb	to demand

I.3 Structure of the Syllable

If /X/ is followed by /X/ without an intervening /V/ there is a predictable transition. Transition between /X/ and /X/ is heard as Vocalic and is represented here by a superscript schwa [^{ə}] to show that it is a phonetic element (schwa occurs as the first speech sound formation in English "about" or as the last speech sound formation in English "sofa"). Thus a word such as /frḥγ / "I was happy" is phonetically [#f^{ə}rḥ^{ə}γ #] consisting of two syllables. [^{ə}] is realized as [ɨ] before front consonants (e.g. /b, t, d.../) and as [ə] before back consonants (e.g. /k, x.../). It is also heard as voiced before voiced consonants (e.g. /b, g.../) and as voiceless before voiceless consonants (e.g. /f, t .../).

The rules governing the predictability of [^{ə}] may be stated as follows:

1. / #X(:)#/ -----> [#^{ə}X(:)#]

/g/	[^{ə}g]	'to be, to do'
/š/	[^{ə}š]	'to give'
/g̣:/	[^{ə}g̣:]	'to knead'
/k:/	[^{ə}k:]	'to pass'

2. $/\#X\ X\ (:)\#/ \dashrightarrow \left\{ \begin{array}{ll} [\#X_1^{ə}X_2(:)\#] & / \ X_1 \text{ is not L} \\ [\#^{ə}X_1X_2\#] & \\ [\#X_1X_2\#] & / \ X_1 \text{ is L} \end{array} \right\}$

/ts/	$[t^{ə}s]$	'to laugh'
/šl/	$[\dot{\check{s}}^{ə}\dot{l}]$	'to spend a day'
/bd:/	$[b^{ə}d:]$	'to stand up'
/ns/	$[^{ə}ns]$ $[n^{ə}s]$	'to spend the night'
/ls/	$[^{ə}ls]$ $[l^{ə}s]$	'to get dressed'

3. $/\#X_1:X_2\#/ \longrightarrow [\#^{ə}X_1:^{ə}X_2\#]$

/f:r/	$[^{ə}f:^{ə}r]$	'to hide'
/f:γ/	$[^{ə}f:^{ə}γ]$	'to go out'
/l:m/	$[^{ə}l:^{ə}m]$	'to spin'

4. $/\#X_1X_2X_3\#/ \dashrightarrow \left\{ \begin{array}{ll} [\#X_1X_2^{ə}X_3\#] & / \ X_1X_2 \text{ are not } \left\{\begin{array}{c} L \\ H \end{array}\right\} \\ \left\{\begin{array}{l} [\#^{ə}X_1X_2{}^{ə}X_3\#] \\ [X_1{}^{ə}X_2{}^{ə}X_3] \end{array}\right\} & / \left\{\begin{array}{c} X_1 \\ X_3 \end{array}\right\} \text{ is } \left\{\begin{array}{c} L,H \\ H,L \end{array}\right\} \\ [\#X_1{}^{ə}X_2{}^{ə}X_3\#] & / \ X_2X_3 = \left\{\begin{array}{c} L \\ H \end{array}\right\} \end{array} \right\}$

/xdm/	$[xd^{ə}m]$	'to work'
/dbγ/	$[db^{ə}γ]$	'to dye'
/xdʕ/	$[xd^{ə}ʕ]$	'to deceive'
/zʕf/	$[zʕ^{ə}f]$	'to get mad'
/hdm/	$[^{ə}hd^{ə}m]$ $[h^{ə}d^{ə}m]$	'to demolish'
/hbl/	$[^{ə}hb^{ə}l]$ $[h^{ə}b^{ə}l]$	'to become silly'
/nfḥ/	$[^{ə}nf^{ə}h]$ $[n^{ə}f^{ə}ḥ]$	'to sniff tobacco'
/ʕdl/	$[^{ə}ʕd^{ə}\dot{l}]$ $[ʕ^{ə}d^{ə}l]$	'to repair'
/ḍmn/	$[ḍ^{ə}m^{ə}n]$	'to guarantee'
/ḟhm/	$[\dot{f}^{ə}h^{ə}m]$	'to understand'
/fṙḥ/	$[f^{ə}r^{ə}ḥ]$	'to be happy'

5. $/\#X_1X{:}_2X_3\#/ \longrightarrow [\#X_1{}^{ə}X{:}^{ə}_2X_3\#]$

/fs:r/	$[f^{ə}s:^{ə}r]$	'to spread'
/sn:d/	$[s^{ə}n:^{ə}d]$	'to lean against'

/xm:m/ [xᵊm:ᵊm] 'to think'
/wk:l/ [wᵊk:ᵊl] 'to appoint as representative'

The postulation of the phonetic syllable shown above supports the transcription of the data of this grammar where three (or more) non-vocalic segments appear next to each other: e.g., /tbṛmnt/ "you (f.p.) turned" which is here represented phonetically as [tᵊbᵊṛ:ᵊmᵊnt].

Words with the structure XVX, VXX, or XV consist of one syllable: e.g., /sal/ "to ask", /šib/ "to become white-haired", /ʕum/ "to swim", /af/ "to find", /amẓ/ "to take", /fa/ "to yawn". Words consisting of vowels and consonants follow the same rules shown above: e.g., /dat:ḥaḍar/ "she is present" is phonetically [dat:ᵊḥaḍaṛ] i.e. consists of three syllables; /ʕaḍ:ṛ/ "to meet" has two syllables [ʕaḍ:ᵊṛ]. Note that /t:/ and /d:/ are not represented as [ᵊt:]and [ᵊḍ:] as was stated before since they are preceded by a vowel.

I.4. Stress

Word stress in Tamazight is a non-contrastive feature. The occurence of word stress is predictable: primary stress falls on the last vowel of the word (i.e. /V/ or [ᵊ]).

Examples:

/sál/	'to ask'
/ʕáwn/	'to help'
/šk:á/	'to doubt'
/slíl/	'to rinse'
/ʕúm/	'to swim'
/ámẓ/	'to take'
/áf/	'to find'
/rár/	'to return'
/bdú/	'to begin'

/adiníγ/	'I will say'
/ndawá/	'we cured'
/tfafád/	'you (s.) woke up'
/isál/	'he asked'
/dayt:ḥaḍáṛ/	'he is present'

The above statement applies to words that phonemically do not contain a vowel /V/. As stated above, /bd:/ is phonetically [bᵊd:], /frḥ/ is phonetically [frᵊḥ] and /fs:r/ is phonetically [fᵊs:ᵊr]. In these cases, word primary stress is on the [ᵊ] of the last syllable.

Examples:

/bd:/	[bᵊ́d:]	'to stand up'
/ls/	[lᵊ́s]	'to dress'
	[ᵊ́ls]	
/f:r/	[ᵊf:ᵊ́r]	'to hide'
/frḥ/	[frᵊ́ḥ]	'to be happy'
/ndr/	[nᵊdᵊ́r]	'to moan'
	[ᵊndᵊ́r]	
/fs:r/	[fᵊs:ᵊ́r]	'to explain'
/tfs:rnt/	[tᵊfᵊs:ᵊrᵊ́nt]	'you (f.p.) explained'

* * *

Notes on the Phonology of Ayt Seghrouchen (A.S.) Dialect of Tamazight

1 /k/ and /g/ are stops in Ayt Seghrouchen. They are prononounced the same as English /k/ and /g/.

Examples:

kl:f	to entrust
lgir:u	cigarettes

2 Lax /q̣/, /ḳ/ and /g̣/ do not occur in A.S.

3 /k:/ and /g:/ are tense counterparts of the stops /k/ and /g/ in A.S.

Examples:

ik:r	he stood up
ang:aru	the last

* * *

Additional Notes on the Phonology of Ayt Seghrouchen

The following phonological features are characteristic of Ayt Seghrouchen.

(a) For some speakers the sequence /-lt-/ is pronounced as a side fricative, i.e. pronouncing /-lt-/ producing friction with air escaping at both sides of the tongue. This, however, occurs in few words.

Examples:

ultma	sister
xalti	my maternal aunt
altu	not yet

(b) Following a tense /k:/ or /g:/, the vowel /u/ has a centralized allophone [ü].

Examples:

l:ayg:ur	he goes
sk:ura	Sekoura (name of a village)

II. The Numerical System

This section discusses the Cardinal and the Ordinal Numerals in Ayt Ayache with enough examples to illustrate the structure of constructs with numerals. It also discusses Fractions. The very few differences that occur in Ayt Seghrouchen concerning the Numerical System are noted at the end of this section.

II. The Numerical System

II.1 Cardinal Numerals

A. 1 - 3 (The Berber Numerals)[1] (for Comparative Notes on this chapter see p. 33)

yun	one (m)
yut	one (f)
sin	two (m)
snat	two (f)
šrad	three (m)
šrat:	three (f)

1 - 3 (The Arabic Numerals)

waḥd	one
tnayn	two
tlata	three

Remarks:

(1) The Arabic numerals 1 - 3 are used only for counting in order without naming things (they are INVARIABLE) and in combination with the tens, e.g. 21, 33, 72, etc. The Berber numerals are used elsewhere.

(2) The Berber numerals (1 - 3) answer such questions as:

šḥal l:wašun ay γuṛš ? How many children do you have?

- yul:ˤil (<yun lˤil) One boy.
- siyšir:an (<sin nišir:an) Two boys.
- šrad išir:an (<šrad nišir:an) Three boys.
- {yut ntrbat: ~ yut:rbat:} (<yut ntarbat:) One girl.
- snat ntšir:atin (<snat ntišir:atin) Two girls.

tšir:atin (<tišir:atin) is referred to as c.s. (construct state of the noun), see Grammar of the Noun.

or šḥal aya ? How much is this?

šḥal ayin: ? How much is that?

- siw:ar:yal: (<sin nar:yal:) Two rials.
- šrad war:yal: (<šrad nar:yal:) Three rials.

or šhal ntfunasin ay γuṛš ? How many cows do you have?

- yut ntfunast (<yut ntafunast) One cow.
- snat ntfunasin (<snat ntifunasin) Two cows.
- šrat: ntfunasin (<šrat: ntifunasin) Three cows.

Berber Numerals 1 - 3		
Num 1 (+ Gender)	+(n) + Noun (sg) c.s.	(+ Gender)
Num 2-3 (+ Gender)	+ n + Noun (pl) c.s.	(+ Gender)

Examples:

yun + n + lʕil ⟶	yul:ʕil	a boy (one boy)
yut + n + tad:art ⟶	yut ntad:art	a house (one house)
sin + n + lk:isan ⟶	sil:k:isan	two glasses
snat + n + tad:rwin ⟶	snat ntad:rwin	two houses
šrad + n + lk:isan ⟶	šrad l:k:isan	three glasses
šrat: + n + tad:rwin ⟶	šrat: ntad:rwin	three houses

B. 4 - 10

ṛbʕa	4
xmsa	5
st:a	6
sbʕa	7
tmanya	8
tsʕa	9
ʕšṛa	10

Num. 4 - 10 + n + Noun (pl) c.s. (m/f)
invariable

Examples:

ṛbʕa + n + ar:yal: ⟶	ṛbʕa w:ar:yal:	four rials
ṛbʕa + n + tifunasin ⟶	ṛbʕa ntfunasin	four cows
ʕšṛa + n + ar:yal: ⟶	ʕšṛa w:ar:yal:	10 rials
ʕšṛa + n + tifunasin ⟶	ʕšṛa ntfunasin	10 cows

C. 11 - 19

ḥdaʕš	11
tnaʕš	12
tlṭaʕš	13
ṛbʕṭaʕš	14
xmstaʕš	15
st:aʕš	16
sbʕṭaʕš	17
tmntaʕš	18
tsʕṭaʕš	19

> <u>Num 11 - 19</u> + n + Noun (sg) c.s. (m/f)
> invariable

<u>Examples:</u>

ḥdaʕš w:ar:yal	11 rials
ḥdaʕš ntfunast	11 cows
tsʕtaʕš w:ar:yal	19 rials
tsʕtaʕš ntfunast	19 cows

D. 20 - ∞

ʕšrin	20
waḥd uʕšrin	21
tnayn uʕšrin	22
tlata wʕšrin	23
tsʕa wʕšrin	29
tlatin	30
waḥd utlatin	31
sbʕa wtlatin	37

ṛbʿin	40
xmsin	50
st:in	60
sbʿin	70
tmanin	80
tsʿin	90
my:a	100
my:a wrbʿa uxmsin	154
mitayn	200
mitayn uwaḥd utlatin	231
tlt my:a	300
ṛbʿ my:a	400
xms my:a	500
st: my:a	600
sbʿ my:a	700
tmn my:a	800
tsʿ my:a	900
tsʿmy:a wtsʿa wtsʿin	999
alf	1000
alfayn	2000
tlt alaf	3000
ṛbʿ alaf	4000
st: alaf	6000
ʿšṛ alaf	10,000
ṛbʿṭaʿšr alf	14,000

my:at alf	100,000
mitayn alf	200,000
mlyun	1,000,000
žuž mlayn	2,000,000
ṛbˁin mlyun	40,000,000
mlyar	1,000,000,000

Num 20 - ∞ + n + Noun (sg) c.s. (m/f) invariable

Examples:

st:a wˁšrin l:ˁil	26 boys
tmanya utlatin ntad:art	38 houses
tsˁ my:a uxmsa usbˁin l:ˁil	975 boys
alf ust:a ust:in ntad:art	1066 houses

Remarks:

(1) The apocopated series / tlt, ṛbˁ, xms, st:, sbˁ, tmn, tsˁ/ is used in the following constructs:

sbˁ snin	7 years
ṛbˁ my:a	400
sbˁ alaf	7,000
tlt mlayn	3,000,000

(2) The numerals 11-19 have two forms. One form ends in /___r#/ and is used before /ˁam/ "year" or /alf/ "thousand" in constructs such as 13 years (old) or 15,000. The other, without /___r#/, is used elsewhere.

11 - 19:

Forms ending in /____r#/

ḥḍaˤšr ˤam	11 years
tnaˤšr ˤam	12 years
tlṭaˤšr ˤam	13 years
ṛbˤṭaˤšr ˤam	14 years
xmsṭaˤšr yum	15 days
sṭ:aˤšr yum	16 days
sbˤṭaˤšr ˤam	17 years
tmnṭaˤšr ˤam	18 years
tsˤṭaˤšr ˤam	19 years
xmsṭaˤšr alf	15,000

Compare the above with the following:

ḥḍaˤš l:ˤil	11 boys
tlṭaˤš ntrbat:	13 girls
xmsṭaˤš l:ˤil	15 boys
tsˤṭaˤš ntad:art	19 houses

(3) my:a ~ my:at

Notice: /my:at/ is used before /alf/ or /ˤam/.
Examples:

my:a l:wašun	100 boys
ṛbˤmy:a ntfunast	400 cows
my:at alf	100,000
my:at ˤam	100 years

(4) Sometimes one gets the following answer

my:a q:l: ʕṣ̌ra	90 (rials)
my:a ɣir ʕṣ̌ra	90 (rials)
mitayn q:l: ʕšrin	180 (rials)
mitayn ɣir xmsa	195 (rials)

in response to:

šḥal aya ?	How much is this?

q:l: = minus

ɣir = except

Notice that such constructions as the above ("100 minus 10") are only used in connection with money, whereas ("5 minus 10") constructions are used in telling the time.

Examples:

lxmsa q:l: ʕṣ̌ra	4:50 (time)
s:bʕa ɣir ʕšrin	6:40 (time)
t:sʕa wxmsa	9:05 (time)
lʕṣ̌ra wʕṣ̌ra	10:10 (time)

II.2 Ordinal Numerals

amzwaru (m)	the first
tamzwarut: (f)	the first
imzwura (m.p.)	the first
timzwura (f.p.)	the first

wis:sin (m)[2]	the second
tis:snat (f)	the second
wis:šrad (m)	the third
tis:šrat: (f)	the third
wis:rbʕa (m)	the fourth
tis:rbʕa (f)	the fourth
wis:xmsa (m)	the fifth
tis:xmsa (f)	the fifth
wis:st:a (m)	the sixth
tis:st:a (f)	the sixth
wis:sbʕa (m)	the seventh
tis:sbʕa (f)	the seventh
wis:tmanya (m)	the eighth
tis:tmanya (f)	the eighth
wis:tsʕa (m)	the ninth
tis:tsʕa (f)	the ninth
wis:ʕšṛa (m)	the tenth
tis:ʕšṛa (f)	the tenth
wis:ḥdaʕš (m)	the eleventh
tis:ḥdaʕš (f)	the eleventh
wis:sṭ:aʕš (m)	the sixteenth
tis:sṭ:aʕš (f)	the sixteenth
wis:tsʕṭaʕš (m)	the nineteenth
tis:tsʕṭaʕš (f)	the nineteenth

wis:ʕšrin (m)	the twentieth
tis:ʕšrin (f)	the twentieth
wis:tsʕin (m)	the ninetieth
tis:tsʕin (f)	the ninetieth

To this we might like to add:

ang:aru (m)	the last
tang:arut: (f)	the last
ing:ura (m.p.)	the last
ting:ura (f.p.)	the last
anam:as (m)	the middle
tanam:ast (f)	the middle
inam:asn (m.p.)	the middle
tinam:asin (f.p.)	the middle

Examples:

lʕil amzwaru	the first boy
as: amzwaru	the first day
tarbat: tamzwarut:	the first girl
as: wis:ʕšra	the tenth day
tad:art tis:rbʕa	the fourth house

II.3 Fractions

amnaṣf[3]	half
t:ulut	1/3

ṛ:ubuᶜ	1/4
~ wis:ṛbᶜa	1/4
lxumıs	1/5
~ wis:xmsa	1/5
s:udus	1/6
~ wis:st:a	1/6
wis:sbᶜa	1/7
t:umın	1/8
~ wis:tmanya	1/8
wis:tsᶜa	1/9
lᶜušuṛ	1/10
~ wis:ᶜšṛa	1/10

Examples:

tsᶜud dumnaṣf	9:30 (time)
šid amnaṣfns	Give (me) half of it.
šid amnaṣf	Give me the half.
šiɣas wis:xmsa	I gave him 1/5.

Remarks:

(1) Fractions smaller than 1/10 (i.e. 1/11, 1/12, etc.) are composed of:

wis: + cardinal numeral

e.g.: wis:xmstaᶜš 1/15

(2) Fractions /t:lult/ and /t:umun/ are mainly used in connection with inheritance shares.

* * *

Notes on the Numerical System in Ayt Seghrouchen (A.S.)

1 In A.S. the only difference in the system is:

idž (m), išt (f)	one
snat (m,f)	two
tlata (m,f)	three

2 wis:snat (m,f) the second

3 amnaṣf ~ azin half

Other than these exceptions, everything else in A. A. concerning the Numerical System itself holds for A.S.

III. Pronominal Systems

This section deals with the different pronominal systems in Ayt Ayache in an exhaustive manner. It discusses Personal Pronouns, Independent Possessive Pronouns and Suffixed Possessive Pronouns used in association with objects and those used in association with kinship terms, Pronominal Affixes for verbs and prepositions, Demonstrative Pronouns, Relative Pronouns, and Indefinite Pronouns. Since this is an area where there is considerable difference between the two dialects, the student will find ample examples at the end of this section showing the differences between the two dialects under the heading Notes on the Pronominal System in Ayt Seghrouchen.

III. Pronominal Systems

III.1 Personal Pronouns

III.1.1 Independent Forms (Subject) [1]

[1] (for Comparative Notes on this Chapter see pp. 77-85)

nk: ~ nk:in	I
šg:	you (m.s.)
šm:	you (f.s.)
nt:a	he
nt:at	she
nḳ:ni	we
ḳn:i	you (m.p.)
ḳn:inti	you (f.p.)
nitni	they (m)
nitnti	they (f)

III.1.2 Emphatic Personal Pronouns (Subject)

nk: n:it	I myself
šg: n:it	you (m.s.) yourself
šm: n:it	you (f.s.) yourself
nt:a n:it	he himself
nt:at n:it	she herself
nḳ:ni n:it	we ourselves
ḳn:i n:it	you (m.p.) yourselves
ḳn:inti n:it	you (f.p.) yourselves
nitni n:it	they (m) themselves
nitnti n:it	they (f) themselves

III.2 Possessive Pronouns

III.2.1 Independent Set

III.2.1.1 Masculine (object possessed, s. or p.) [2]

winw	mine
winš	yours (m.s.)
win:m	yours (f.s.)
wins	his/hers
win:γ	ours
win:un	yours (m.p.)
win:ḳnt	yours (f.p.)
winsn	theirs (m.)
winsnt	theirs (f.)

Examples:

winmi igra ?	Whose field is this?
win ʕli (/wins/)	It's Aly's. (It's his.)
winmi iy:isin: g:mi lbab ?	Whose horse is in front of the door?
win ʕm:i (/wins/)	My uncle's. (It's his.)
win ʕt:i (/wins/)	My aunt's. (It's hers.)

III.2.1.2 Feminine (object possessed, s. or p.) [3]

tinw	mine
tinš	yours (m.s.)
tin:m	yours (f.s.)
tins	his/her

tin:γ	ours
tin:un	yours (m.p.)
tin:ḳnt	yours (f.p.)
tinsn	theirs (m)
tinsnt	theirs (f)

Examples:

tinmi tad:arta	Whose house is this?
tin ʕli (/tins/)	It's Aly's.(It's his.)
mat:a tad:artin: m:sin š:ražm izgzawn ?	Whose house is that over there with the two green windows?
tin ʕm:i (/tins/)	My uncle's. (It's his.)
tin ʕt:i (/tinɛ/)	My aunt's. (It's hers.)

III.2.2 Possessive Pronominal Suffixes

III.2.2.1 Suffixed to nouns ending in consonant [4]

axam (m.s.) tent

axam|inw	my tent
axam|nš	your (m.s.) tent
axam|n:m	your (f.s.) tent
axam|ns	his tent
axam|ns	her tent
axam|n:γ	our tent
axam|n:un	your (m.p.) tent
axam|n:ḳnt	your (f.p.) tent
axam|nsn	their (m) tent
axam|nsnt	their (f) tent

ixamn (m.p.) tents

ixamn	inw	my tents
ixamn	nš	your (m.s.) tents
ixamn	n:m	your (f.s.) tents
ixamn	ns	his tents
ixamn	ns	her tents
ixamn	n:γ	our tents
ixamn	n:un	your (m.p.) tents
ixamn	n:ḳnt	your (f.p.) tents
ixamn	nsn	their (m) tents
ixamn	nsnt	their (f) tents

tafunast (f.s.) cow

tafunast	inw	my cow
tafunast	nš	your (m.s.) cow
tafunast	n:m	your (f.s.) cow
tafunast	ns	his cow
tafunast	ns	her cow
tafunast	n:γ	our cow
tafunast	n:un	your (m.p.) cow
tafunast	n:ḳnt	your (f.p.) cow
tafunast	nsn	their (m) cow
tafunast	nsnt	their (f) cow

tifunasin (f.p.) cows

tifunasin	inw	my cows
tifunasin	nš	your (m.s.) cows

tifunasin|n:m	your (f.s.) cows
tifunasin|ns	his cows
tifunasin|ns	her cows
tifunasin|n:γ	our cows
tifunasin|n:un	your (m.p.) cows
tifunasin|n:ḳnt	your (f.p.) cows
tifunasin|nsn	their (m) cows
tifunasin|nsnt	their (f) cows

III.2.2.2 Suffixed to nouns ending in vowel

isl:i (m.s.) stone

isl:i|nw	my stone
isl:i|nš	your (m.s.) stone
isl:i|n:m	your (f.s.) stone
isl:i|ns	his stone
isl:i|ns	her stone
isl:i|n:γ	our stone
isl:i|n:un	your (m.p.) stone
isl:i|n:ḳnt	your (f.p.) stone
isl:i|nsn	their (m) stone
isl:i|nsnt	their (f) stone

amksa (m.s.) shepherd

amksa|nw	my shepherd
amksa|nš	your (m.s.) shepherd
amksa|n:m	your (f.s.) shepherd
amksa|ns	his shepherd
amksa|ns	her shepherd
amksa|n:γ	our shepherd
amksa|n:un	your (m.p.) shepherd
amksa|n:ḳnt	your (f.p.) shepherd
amksa|nsn	their (m) shepherd
amksa|nsnt	their (f) shepherd

III.2.2.3 Possessive Pronominal Suffixes Used with Kinship Terms [5]

(a) ʕm:i	my uncle "fa br"
ʕm:iš	your (m.s.) uncle
ʕm:in:m	your (f.s.) uncle
ʕm:is	his/her uncle
ʕm:in:γ	our uncle
ʕm:in:un	your (m.p.) uncle
ʕm:inḳnt	your (f.p.) uncle
ʕn:insn	their (m) uncle
ʕm:insnt	their (f) uncle

The following kinship terms follow the above paradigm: ʕm:i 'fa br', ʕt:i 'fa si', xali 'mo br', xalti 'mo si', mm:i 'son', il:i 'daughter'.

(b) b:a	my father
b:aš	your (m.s.) father
b:am	your (f.s.) father
b:as	his/her father
b:an:ɣ	our father
b:an:un	your (m.p.) father
b:an:ḳnt	your (f.p.) father
b:ansn	their (m) father
b:ansnt	their (f) father

(c) m:a	my mother
mayš	your (m.s.) mother
maym	your (f.s.) mother
mays	his/her mother
m:atnɣ	our mother
m:atun	your (m.p.) mother
m:anḳnt	your (f.p.) mother
maysn	their (m) mother
maysnt	their (f) mother

(d) nan:a	my fa mo
nan:anš	your (m.s.) fa mo
nan:an:m	your (f.s.) fa mo
nan:ans	his/her fa mo
nan:an:γ	our fa mo
nan:an:un	your (m.p.) fa mo
nan:anḳnt	your (f.p.) fa mo
nan:ansn	their (m) fa mo
nan:ansnt	their (f) fa mo

The following kinship terms follow the above paradigm:

yma 'brother', uttma 'sister'

(in 2nd person m.s. we get: ymaš and uttmaš)

(e) b:aḥl:u	my fa fa
b:aḥl:unš	your (m.s.) fa fa
b:aḥl:un:m	your (f.s.) fa fa
b:aḥl:uns	his/her fa fa
b:aḥl:un:γ	our fa fa
b:aḥl:un:un	your (m.p.) fa fa
b:aḥl:unknt	your (f.p.) fa fa
b:aḥl:unsn	their (m) fa fa
b:aḥl:usnt	their (f) fa fa

m:aḥl:u 'grandmother' (same as above paradigm)

(f)	argazinw	my husband
	argazin:m	your husband
	argazns	her husband
	argaz man	
(g)	tamḍ:uṭ:inw	my wife
	tamḍ:uṭ:nš	your wife
	tamḍ:uṭ:ns	his wife
	tamḍ:uṭ: woman	
(h)	lwašuninw	my children
	lwašunn š	your (m.s.) children
	lwašunn:m	your (f.s.) children
	lwašunn s	his/her children
	lwašunn:γ	our children
	lwašun un	your (m.p.) children
	lwašun:ḳnt	your (f.p.) children
	lwašunsn	their (m) children
	lwašunsnt	their (f) children

/aḍg:al/ 'in-law' follows the above paradigm.
/tadg̣:alt/

Notice that if the kinship term ends in a vowel, then we do not add any suffix for 1st person singular (ʕm:i, xali, b:a, m:a, b:aḥl:u ...). If the term ends in a consonant (argaz, tamḍ:uṭ: ...), then we add the suffix /-inw/ for 1st person singular.

III.3 Pronominal Affixes for Verbs and Prepositions

The Object Pronominal Affixes as well as the Orientational Affixes /d/ of proximity and /n:/ of remoteness are here referred to as movable affixes. A movable affix is one that may be either pre-verbal (i.e. prefixed to the conjugated stem) or post-verbal (i.e. suffixed to the conjugated stem).

The position of the movable affix depends on the presence or absence of:

(a) Temporal and/or Modal prefixes, i.e. prefixes deriving the different tenses and their modes: e.g., /ad-/ for future tense, /is-/ for interrogative mode and /ur-/ for negative mode

(b) One of the following prepositions and conjunctions /xf/ 'on', /qbl/ 'before', /γr/ 'to', /g/ 'until', /al:iy/ 'until', /γəs an:a/ 'when, as soon as', /l:iy/ 'when'

(c) Question words: e.g., /ma/ 'what', etc.

(d) Relative pronouns /ay/, /n:a/ 'who, which, that'

Examples (/-/ denotes morpheme boundaries)

(a) Temporal/Modal and Object Pronominal Affixes

i-sal-aγ	He asked us.
ad-aγ-i-sal	He will ask us.
da-aγ-i-t:sal	He asks us.
is-ur-aγ-i-sal	Didn't he ask us?

(b) Conjunctions and Orientational Affixes

γas an:a d-iwḍ-n iγṛ-d	As soon as they arrived (+ Prox.)
ḥusa ifaḍma	Husa called (+ Prox.) Fadma.

(c) Question words and Pronominal Affixes

ma-as tn:a faḍma iḥusa ? What did Fadma tell Husa?

(d) Relative Pronoun and Orientational Affix

argaz n:a d id:an yma ag:a The man who came is my brother.

mani luq:t ay d it:ˁayad muḥa ? When will Muha be back?

The above information may be diagrammed thus:

- [Temporal/Modal Aff. or Prep., Conjunc., Relative, Quest. word] +

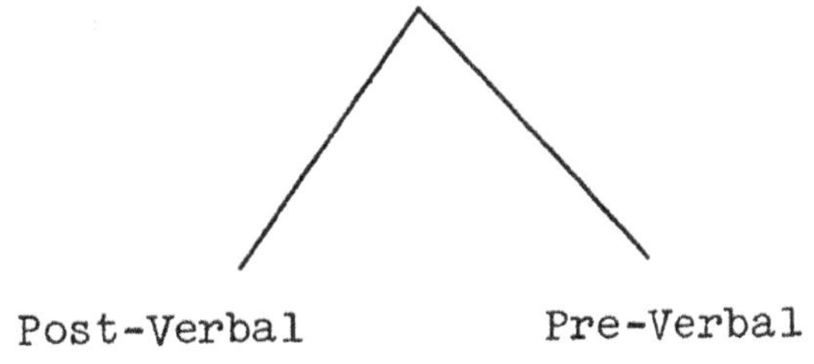

The order in which these movable affixes occur in relation to one another is as follows:

Ind. Obj. + D. Obj. + Orient. Affix

Example:

/t-saˁf-t-d. (/>tsaˁftid/) She was patient with him (+Prox.).

/i-γṛf-as-t-d/ (/>iγṛfastid/) He threw it (m) at him (+Prox.).

/ad-as-t-d-i-γṛf/ (/>adastidiγṛf/) He will throw it (m) at him(+Prox)

Notice: The anaptyctic vowel /-i-/ occurs with /t-d/⟶/tid/ in the environment of D. Obj. + Proximity Affix for persons other than first.

Compare the above with:

/t-saˤf-aɣ-d/ ⟶ /tsaˤfaɣd/ She was patient with us (+Prox.).

III.3.1 Affirmative

III.3.1.1 With Intransitive Verbs : Indirect Objects [6]

	/siwl/ (intr.)	to speak (/siwl i/'speak to')
Past:	/isiwl/	he spoke
	isiwl | i	He spoke to me.
	isiwl | aš	He spoke to you (m.s.).
	isiwl | am	He spoke to you (f.s.).
	isiwl | as	He spoke to him/her.
	isiwl | aɣ	He spoke to us.
	isiwl | awn	He spoke to you (m.p.).
	isiwl | aḳnt	He spoke to you (f.p.).
	isiwl | asn	He spoke to them (m).
	isiwl | asnt	He spoke to them (f).
Future:	/adisiwl/	he will speak
	ad | i | ysiwl	He will speak to me.
	ad | aš | isiwl	He will speak to you (m.s.).
	ad | am | isiwl	He will speak to you (f.s.).
	ad | as | isiwl	He will speak to him/her.

ad	aγ	isiwl	He will speak to us.
ad	awn	isiwl	He will speak to you (m.p.).
ad	aḳnt	isiwl	He will speak to you (f.p.).
ad	asn	isiwl	He will speak to them (m).
ad	asnt	isiwl	He will speak to them (f).

<u>Present</u>: /daysawal/ he speaks

day	isawal	He speaks to me.
daš	isawal	He speaks to you (m.s.).
dam	isawal	He speaks to you (f.s.).
das	isawal	He speaks to him/her.
daγ	isawal	He speaks to us.
dawn	isawal	He speaks to you (m.p.).
daḳnt	isawal	He speaks to you (f.p.).
dasn	isawal	He speaks to them (m).
dasnt	isawal	He speaks to them (f).

Notice:

/-a + i-/ → /-ay-/

/-a + a-/ → /-a-/

/daaš/ ⟶ /daš/

/sl:m/ 'to greet'

/sl:m/ <u>always occurs with a preposition</u>: e.g.,

sl:m xf unbyi 'greet the guest'.

The preposition /xf/ 'on' occurs before <u>nouns</u>;

it has the allomorph /γif-/ before pronouns.

Past: /isl:m/ he greeted

isl:m γif	i	He greeted me.
isl:m γif	š	He greeted you (m.s.).
isl:m γif	m	He greeted you (f.s.).
isl:m γif	s	He greeted him.
isl:m γif	s	He greeted her.
isl:m γif	nγ	He greeted us.
isl:m γif	un	He greeted you (m.p.).
isl:m γif	ḳnt	He greeted you (f.p.).
isl:m γif	sn	He greeted them (m).
isl:m γif	snt	He greeted them (f).

Notice: /-aš, -am, -as .../ have the allomorphs / -š, -m, -s .../ after prepositions.

Future: /adisl:m/ he will greet.

ad	γif	i	ysl:m	He will greet me.
ad	γif	š	isl:m	He will greet you (m.s.).
ad	γif	m	isl:m	He will greet you (f.s.).
ad	γif	s	isl:m	He will greet him.
ad	γif	s	isl:m	He will greet her.
ad	γif	nγ	isl:m	He will greet us.
ad	γif	un	isl:m	He will greet you (m.p.).
ad	γif	ḳnt	isl:m	He will greet you (f.p.).
ad	γif	sn	isl:m	He will greet them (m).
ad	γif	snt	isl:m	He will greet them (f).

Present: /dayt:sl:am/ he greets

da	γif	i	t:sl:am	He greets me.
da	γif	š	t:sl:am	He greets you (m.s.).
da	γif	m	t:sl:am	He greets you (f.s.).
da	γif	s	t:sl:am	He greets him.
da	γif	s	t:sl:am	He greets her.
da	γif	nγ	t:sl:am	He greets us.
da	γif	un	t:sl:am	He greets you (m.p.).
da	γif	ḳnt	t:sl:am	He greets you (f.p.).
da	γif	sn	t:sl:am	He greets them (m).
da	γif	snt	t:sl:am	He greets them (f).

III.3.1.2 With Transitive Verbs: Direct Objects

/sal/ (trans.) to ask

Past: isal he asked

isal	i	He asked me.
isal	š	He asked you (m.s.).
isal	šm	He asked you (f.s.).
isal	t	He asked him.
isal	t:	He asked her.
isal	aγ	He asked us.
isal	ḳn	He asked you (m.p.).
isal	ḳnt	He asked you (f.p.).
isal	tn	He asked them (m).
isal	tnt	He asked them (f).

<u>Future</u>: /adisal/ — he will ask

adi	ysal	He will ask me.
ak:	isal	He will ask you (m.s.).
ak:m	isal	He will ask you (f.s.).
at:	isal	He will ask him.
at:	isal	He will ask her.
adaγ	isal	He will ask us.
aḳ:n	isal	He will ask you (m.p.).
aḳ:nt	isal	He will ask you (f.p.).
at:n	isal	He will ask them (m).
at:nt	isal	He will ask them (f).

Notice:

/-d + š-/ ⟶ /k:/

/-d + t-/ ⟶ /t:/

/-d + t:-/ ⟶ /t:/

/-d + ḳ-/ ⟶ /ḳ:/

<u>Present</u>: /dayt:sal/ — he asks

day	it:sal	He asks me.
daš	it:sal	He asks you (m.s.).
dašm	it:sal	He asks you (f.s.).
dat	it:sal	He asks him.
dat:	it:sal	He asks her.
daγ	it:sal	He asks us.
daḳn	it:sal	He asks you (m.p.).

daḳnt | it:sal	He asks you (f.p.).
datn | it:sal	He asks them (m).
datnt | it:sal	He asks them (f).

/nɣ/	to kill
/inɣa/	he killed
inɣa y | i	He killed me.
inɣa | š	He killed you (m.s.).
inɣa | šm	He killed you (f.s.).
inɣa | t	He killed him.
inɣa | t:	He killed her.
inɣa y | aɣ	He killed us.
inɣa | ḳn	He killed you (m.p.).
inɣa | ḳnt	He killed you (f.p.).
inɣa | tn	He killed them (m).
inɣa | tnt	He killed them (f).

Notice: /-a + i-/ ⟶ /ay/

/adinɣ/	he will kill 6
adi | ynɣ	He will kill me.
ak: | inɣ	He will kill you (m.s.).
ak:m | inɣ	He will kill you (f.s.).
at: | inɣ	He will kill him.
at: | inɣ	He will kill her.
adaɣ | inɣ	He will kill us.
aḳ:n | inɣ	He will kill you (m.p.).

ak̦:nt	inγ	He will kill you (f.p.).
at:n	inγ	He will kill them (m).
at:nt	inγ	He will kill them (f).

Present: /daynq:a/ he kills

day	inq:a	He kills me.
daš	inq:a	He kills you (m.s.).
dašm	inq:a	He kills you (f.s.).
dat	inq:a	He kills him.
dat:	inq:a	He kills her.
daγ	inq:a	He kills us.
dak̦n	inq:a	He kills you (m.p.).
dak̦nt	inq:a	He kills you (f.p.).
datn	inq:a	He kills them (m).
datnt	inq:a	He kills them (m).

III. 3.2 Negative

III. 3.2.1 With Intransitive Verbs: Indirect Objects

/siwl/ to speak

Past: /urisiwl/ he did not speak

uri	ysiwl	He did not speak to me.
uraš	isiwl	He did not speak to you (m.s.).
uram	isiwl	He did not speak to you (f.s.).
uras	isiwl	He did not speak to him/her.

uraγ	isiwl	He did not speak to us.
urawn	isiwl	He did not speak to you (m.p.).
uraḳnt	isiwl	He did not speak to you (f.p.).
urasn	isiwl	He did not speak to them (m).
urasnt	isiwl	He did not speak to them (f).

Future: /ur in:i adisiwl/* he will not speak

ur	in:i	adi	ysiwl	He will not speak to me.
ur	in:i	adaš	isiwl	He will not speak to you (m.s.).
ur	in:i	adam	isiwl	He will not speak to you (f.s.).
ur	in:i	adas	isiwl	He will not speak to him/her.
ur	in:i	adaγ	isiwl	He will not speak to us.
ur	in:i	adawn	isiwl	He will not speak to you (m.p.).
ur	in:i	adaḳnt	isiwl	He will not speak to you (f.p.).
ur	in:i	adasn	isiwl	He will not speak to them (m).
ur	in:i	adasnt	isiwl	He will not speak to them (f).

Present: /urdaysawl/ he does not speak

urday	isawal	He does not speak to me.
urdaš	isawal	He does not speak to you (m.s.).
urdam	isawal	He does not speak to you (f.s.).

---

*/in:i/ comes from verb /ini/ 'to say'; /urin:i/ 'he did not say' + /adisiwl/ 'he will speak'. This is the regular way of expressing future construction in the negative. Thus we get /urn:iγ ad:d:uγ/ 'I will not come'; /ur tn:i at:š/ 'she will not eat'; /ur n:in adsiwl:/ 'they will not speak'; etc.

urdas	isawal	He does not speak to him/her.
urdaγ	isawal	He does not speak to us.
urdawn	isawal	He does not speak to you (m.p.).
urdaḳnt	isawal	He does not speak to you (f.p.).
urdasn	isawal	He does not speak to them (m).
urdasnt	isawal	He does not speak to them (f).

/sl:m/ to greet

Past: /urisl:im/ he did not greet

ur	γif	i	ysl:im	He did not greet me.
ur	γif	š	isl:im	He did not greet you (m.s.).
ur	γif	m	isl:im	He did not greet you (f.s.).
ur	γif	s	isl:im	He did not greet him/her.
ur	γif	nγ	isl:im	He did not greet us.
ur	γif	un	isl:im	He did not greet you (m.p.).
ur	γif	ḳnt	isl:im	He did not greet you (f.p.).
ur	γif	sn	isl:im	He did not greet them (m).
ur	γif	snt	isl:im	He did not greet them (f).

Future: /ur in:i adisl:m/ he will not greet

ur	in:i	ad γif	i	ysl:m	He will not greet me.
ur	in:i	ad γif	š	isl:m	He will not greet you (m.s.).
ur	in:i	ad γif	m	isl:m	He will not greet you (f.s.).
ur	in:i	ad γif	s	isl:m	He will not greet him/her.

ur	in:i	ad ɣif	nɣ	isl:m	He will not greet us.
ur	in:i	ad ɣif	un	isl:m	He will not greet you (m.p.).
ur	in:i	ad ɣif	ḳnt	isl:m	He will not greet you (f.p.).
ur	in:i	ad ɣif	sn	isl:m	He will not greet them (m).
ur	in:i	ad ɣif	snt	isl:m	He will not greet them (f).

<u>Present:</u> /urdayt:sl:am/ he does not greet

ur	daɣif	i	yt:sl:am	He does not greet me.
ur	daɣif	š	it:sl:am	He does not greet you (m.s.).
ur	daɣif	m	it:sl:am	He does not greet you (f.s.).
ur	daɣif	s	it:sl:am	He does not greet him/her.
ur	daɣif	nɣ	it:sl:am	He does not greet us.
ur	daɣif	un	it:sl:am	He does not greet you (m.p.).
ur	daɣif	ḳnt	it:sl:am	He does not greet you (f.p.).
ur	daɣif	sn	it:sl:am	He does not greet them (m).
ur	daɣif	snt	it:sl:am	He does not greet them (f).

III. 3.2.2 <u>With Transitive Verbs:</u> <u>Direct Objects</u>

/sal/ to ask

<u>Past:</u> /urisal/ he did not ask

ur	i	ysal	He did not ask me.
ur	š	isal	He did not ask you (m.s.).
ur	šm	isal	He did not ask you (f.s.).
ur	t	isal	He did not ask him.
ur	t:	isal	He did not ask her.

ur	aγ	isal	He did not ask us.
ur	ḳn	isal	He did not ask you (m.p.).
ur	ḳnt	isal	He did not ask you (f.p.).
ur	tn	isal	He did not ask them (m).
ur	tnt	isal	He did not ask them (f).

<u>Future</u>: /ur in:i adisal/ he will not ask

ur	in:i	adi	ysal	He will not ask me.
ur	in:i	ak:	isal	He will not ask you (m.s.).
ur	in:i	ak:m	isal	He will not ask you (f.s.).
ur	in:i	at:	isal	He will not ask him.
ur	in:i	at:	isal	He will not ask her.
ur	in:i	adaγ	isal	He will not ask us.
ur	in:i	aḳ:n	isal	He will not ask you (m.p.).
ur	in:i	aḳ:nt	isal	He will not ask you (f.p.)
ur	in:i	at:n	isal	He will not ask them (m).
ur	in:i	at:nt	isal	He will not ask them (f).

<u>Present</u>: /urdayt:sal/ he does not ask

ur	day	it:sal	He does not ask me.
ur	daš	it:sal	He does not ask you (m.s.).
ur	dašm	it:sal	He does not ask you (f.s.).
ur	dat	it:sal	He does not ask him.
ur	dat:	it:sal	He does not ask her.

ur	daγ	it:sal	He does not ask us.
ur	daḳn	it:sal	He does not ask you (m.p.).
ur	daḳnt	it:sal	He does not ask you (f.p.).
ur	datn	it:sal	He does not ask them (m).
ur	datnt	it:sal	He does not ask them (f).

/nγ/ to kill

<u>Past:</u> /urinγi/ he did not kill

uri	ynγi	He did not kill me.
urš	inγi	He did not kill you (m.s.).
uršm	inγi	He did not kill you (f.s.).
urt	inγi	He did not kill him.
urt:	inγi	He did not kill her.
uraγ	inγi	He did not kill us.
urḳn	inγi	He did not kill you (m.p.).
urḳnt	inγi	He did not kill you (f.p.).
urtn	inγi	He did not kill them (m).
urtnt	inγi	He did not kill them (f).

/-i + i-/ ⟶ /-iy-/

<u>Future:</u> /ur in:i adinγ/ he will not kill

ur	in:i	adi	ynγ	He will not kill me.
ur	in:i	ak:	inγ	He will not kill you (m.s.).
ur	in:i	ak:m	inγ	He will not kill you (f.s.).

ur	in:i	at	inγ	He will not kill him.
ur	in:i	at:	inγ	He will not kill her.
ur	in:i	adaγ	inγ	He will not kill us.
ur	in:i	aḳ:n	inγ	He will not kill you (m.p.).
ur	in:i	aḳ:nt	inγ	He will not kill you (f.p.).
ur	in:i	at:n	inγ	He will not kill them (m).
ur	in:i	at:nt	inγ	He will not kill them (f).

Present: /urdaynq:a/ he does not kill

ur	day	inq:a	He does not kill me.
ur	daš	inq:a	He does not kill you (m.s.).
ur	dašm	inq:a	He does not kill you (f.s.).
ur	dat	inq:a	He does not kill him.
ur	dat:	inq:a	He does not kill her.
ur	daγ	inq:a	He does not kill us.
ur	daḳn	inq:a	He does not kill you (m.p.).
ur	daḳnt	inq:a	He does not kill you (f.p.).
ur	datn	inq:a	He does not kill them (m).
ur	datnt	inq:a	He does not kill them (f).

III. 3.3 Interrogative

III.3.3.1 With Intransitive Verbs: Indirect Objects

/siwl/ to speak

Past:	/is isiwl/				did he speak?
	is	i	ysiwl		Did he speak to me?
	is	aš	isiwl		Did he speak to you (m.s.)?
	is	am	isiwl		Did he speak to you (f.s.)?
	is	as	isiwl		Did he speak to him/her?
	is	aγ	isiwl		Did he speak to us?
	is	awn	isiwl		Did he speak to you (m.p.)?
	is	aḳnt	isiwl		Did he speak to you (f.p.)?
	is	asn	isiwl		Did he speak to them (m)?
	is	asnt	isiwl		Did he speak to them (f)?

Future:	/id: adisiwl/				will he speak?
	id:	ad	i	ysiwl	Will he speak to me?
	id:	ad	aš	isiwl	Will he speak to you (m.s.)?
	id:	ad	am	isiwl	Will he speak to you (f.s.)?
	id:	ad	as	isiwl	Will he speak to him/her?
	id:	ad	aγ	isiwl	Will he speak to us?
	id:	ad	awn	isiwl	Will he speak to you (m.p.)?
	id:	ad	aḳnt	isiwl	Will he speak to you (f.p.)?
	id:	ad	asn	isiwl	Will he speak to them (m)?
	id:	ad	asnt	isiwl	Will he speak to them (f)?

/sl:m/ — to greet

Past: /is isl:m/ — did he greet?

is	γif	i	ysl:m	Did he greet me?
is	γif	š	isl:m	Did he greet you (m.s.)?
is	γif	m	isl:m	Did he greet you (f.s.)?
is	γif	s	isl:m	Did he greet him/her?
is	γif	nγ	isl:m	Did he greet us?
is	γif	un	isl:m	Did he greet you (m.p.)?
is	γif	ḳnt	isl:m	Did he greet you (f.p.)?
is	γif	sn	isl:m	Did he greet them (m)?
is	γif	snt	isl:m	Did he greet them (f)?

Future: /id: ad isl:m/ — will he greet?

id:	ad	γif	i	ysl:m	Will he greet me?
id:	ad	γif	š	isl:m	Will he greet you (m.s.)?
id:	ad	γif	m	isl:m	Will he greet you (f.s.)?
id:	ad	γif	s	isl:m	Will he greet him/her?
id:	ad	γif	nγ	isl:m	Will he greet us?
id:	ad	γif	un	isl:m	Will he greet you (m.p.)?
id:	ad	γif	ḳnt	isl:m	Will he greet you (f.p.)?
id:	ad	γif	sn	isl:m	Will he greet them (m)?
id:	ad	γif	snt	isl:m	Will he greet them (f)?

Present: /is dayt:sl:am/	does he greet?
is | da | γif | i | yt:sl:am	Does he greet me?
is | da | γif | š | it:sl:am	Does he greet you (m.s.)?
is | da | γif | m | it:sl:am	Does he greet you (f.s.)?
is | da | γif | s | it:sl:am	Does he greet him/her?
is | da | γif | nγ | it:sl:am	Does he greet us?
is | da | γif | un | it:sl:am	Does he greet you (m.p.)?
is | da | γif | ḳnt | it:sl:am	Does he greet you (f.p.)?
is | da | γif | sn | it:sl:am	Does he greet them (m)?
is | da | γif | snt | it:sl:am	Does he greet them (f)?

III. 3.3.2 With Transitive Verbs: Direct Objects

/sal/	to ask
Past: /is isal/	did he ask?
is | i | ysal	Did he ask me?
is | aγ | isal	Did he ask us?
is | tnt | isal	Did he ask them (f)?
Future: /id: adisal/	will he ask?
id: | ak: | isal	Will he ask you (m.s.)?
id: | at: | isal	Will he ask him?
id: | aḳ:n | isal	Will he ask you (m.p.)?
id: | at:nt | isal	Will he ask them (f)?
Present: /is dayt:sal/	does he ask?
is | day | it:sal	Does he ask me?
is | dašm | it:sal	Does he ask you (f.s.)?

is	dat:	it:sal	Does he ask her?
is	daḳn	it:sal	Does he ask you (m.p.)?
is	datn	it:sal	Does he ask them (m)?

/nγ/ to kill

Past: /is inγa/ did he kill?

is	i	ynγa	Did he kill me?
is	t:	inγa	Did he kill her?
is	aγ	inγa	Did he kill us?
is	tn	inγa	Did he kill them (m)?

Future: /id: adinγ/ will he kill?

id:	adi	ynγ	Will he kill me
id:	ak:m	inγ	Will he kill you (f.s.)?
id:	at:	inγ	Will he kill him?
id:	adaγ	inγ	Will he kill us?
id:	aḳ:nt	inγ	Will he kill you (f.p.)?
id:	at:nt	inγ	Will he kill them (f)?

Present: /is daynq:a/ does he kill?

is	day	inq:a	Does he kill me?
is	dašm	inq:a	Does he kill you (f.s.)?
is	dat	inq:a	Does he kill him?
is	daγ	inq:a	Does he kill us?
is	daḳnt	inq:a	Does he kill you (f.p.)?
is	datnt	inq:a	Does he kill them (f)?

III. 3 .4 Negative Interrogative

III.3.4.1 With Intransitive Verbs: Indirect Objects

/siwl/			to speak
/isur isiwl/			didn't he speak?
isur	i	ysiwl	Didn't he speak to me?
isur	aš	isiwl	Didn't he speak to you (m.s.)?
isur	am	isiwl	Didn't he speak to you (f.s.)?
isur	as	isiwl	Didn't he speak to him/her?
isur	aγ	isiwl	Didn't he speak to us?
isur	awn	iniwl	Didn't he speak to you (m.p.)?
isur	aḳnt	isiwl	Didn't he speak to you (f.p.)?
isur	asn	isiwl	Didn't he speak to them (m)?
isur	asnt	isiwl	Didn't he speak to them (f)?

Future: /isur isawal/ won't he speak?

Notice that in this particular construction, the future is formed from the conjugated Habitual Verb Stem.

isur	i	ysawal	Won't he speak to me?
isur	aš	isawal	Won't he speak to you (m.s.)?
isur	am	isawal	Won't he speak to you (f.s.)?
isur	as	isawal	Won't he speak to him/her?
isur	aγ	isawal	Won't he speak to us?
isur	awn	isawal	Won't he speak to you (m.p.)?
isur	aḳnt	isawal	Won't he speak to you (f.p.)?

isur	asn	isawal	Won't he speak to them (m)?
isur	asnt	isawal	Won't he speak to them (f)?

Present: /isur daysawal/ doesn't he speak?

isur	day	isawal	Doesn't he speak to me?
isur	daš	isawal	Doesn't he speak to you (m.s.)?
isur	dam	isawal	Doesn't he speak to you (f.s.)?
isur	das	isawal	Doesn't he speak to him/her?
isur	daγ	isawal	Doesn't he speak to us?
isur	dawn	isawal	Doesn't he speak to you (m.p.)?
isur	dakٜnt	isawal	Doesn't he speak to you (f.p.)?
isur	dasn	isawal	Doesn't he speak to them (m)?
isur	dasnt	isawal	Doesn't he speak to them (f)?

/sl:m/ to greet

Past: /isur isl:im/ didn't he greet?

isur	γif	i	ysl:im	Didn't he greet me?
isur	γif	š	isl:im	Didn't he greet you (m.s.)?
isur	γif	m	isl:im	Didn't he greet you (f.s.)?
is	γif	s	isl:im	Didn't he greet him/her?
isur	γif	nγ	isl:im	Didn't he greet us?
isur	γif	un	isl:im	Didn't he greet you (m.p.)?
isur	γif	ḳnt	isl:im	Didn't he greet you (f.p.)?
isur	γif	sn	isl:im	Didn't he greet them (m)
isur	γif	snt	isl:im	Didn't he greet them (f)?

Future: /isur it:sl:am/ won't he greet?

isur	γif	i	yt:sl:am	Won't he greet me?
isur	γif	š	it:sl:am	Won't he greet you (m.s.)?
isur	γif	m	it:sl:am	Won't he greet you (f.s.)?
isur	γif	s	it:sl:am	Won't he greet him/her?
isur	γif	nγ	it:sl:am	Won't he greet us?
isur	γif	un	it:sl:am	Won't he greet you (m.p.)?
isur	γif	ḳnt	it:sl:am	Won't he greet you (f.p.)?
isur	γif	sn	it:sl:am	Won't he greet them (m)?
isur	γif	snt	it:sl:am	Won't he greet them (f)?

Present: /isur dayt:sl:am/ doesn't he greet?

isur	da	γif	i	yt:sl:am	Doesn't he greet me?
isur	da	γif	š	it:sl:am	Doesn't he greet you (m.s.)?
isur	da	γif	m	it:sl:am	Doesn't he greet you (f.s.)?
isur	da	γif	s	it:sl:am	Doesn't he greet him/her?
isur	da	γif	nγ	it:sl:am	Doesn't he greet us?
isur	da	γif	un	it:sl:am	Doesn't he greet you (m.p.)?
isur	da	γif	ḳnt	it:sl:am	Doesn't he greet you (f.p.)?
isur	da	γif	sn	it:sl:am	Doesn't he greet them (m)?
isur	da	γif	snt	it:sl:am	Doesn't he greet them (f)?

III.3.4.2 With Transitive Verbs: Direct Objects

/sal/ to ask

Past: /isur isal/ didn't he ask?

isur	i	ysal	Didn't he ask me?
isur	š	isal	Didn't he ask you (m.s.)?
isur	šm	isal	Didn't he ask you (f.s.)?
isur	t	isal	Didn't he ask him?
isur	t:	isal	Didn't he ask her?
isur	aγ	isal	Didn't he ask us?
isur	ḳn	isal	Didn't he ask you (m.p.)?
isur	ḳnt	isal	Didn't he ask you (f.p.)?
isur	tn	isal	Didn't he ask them (m)?
isur	tnt	isal	Didn't he ask them (f)?

Future: /isur it:sal/ won't he ask?

isur	i	yt:sal	Won't he ask me?
isur	š	it:sal	Won't he ask you (m.s.)?
isur	šm	it:sal	Won't he ask you (f.s.)?
isur	t	it:sal	Won't he ask him?
isur	t:	it:sal	Won't he ask her?
isur	aγ	it:sal	Won't he ask us?
isur	ḳn	it:sal	Won't he ask you (m.p.)?
isur	ḳnt	it:sal	Won't he ask you (f.p.)?
isur	tn	it:sal	Won't he ask them (m)?
isur	tnt	it:sal	Won't he ask them (f)?

/nγ/ to kill

Past: /isur inγi/ didn't he kill?

isur	i	ynγi	Didn't he kill me?
isur	š	inγi	Didn't he kill you (m.s.)?
isur	šm	inγi	Didn't he kill you (f.s.)?
isur	t	inγi	Didn't he kill him?
isur	t:	inγi	Didn't he kill her?
isur	aγ	inγi	Didn't he kill us?
isur	ḳn	inγi	Didn't he kill you (m.p.)?
isur	ḳnt	inγi	Didn't he kill you (f.p.)?
isur	tn	inγi	Didn't he kill them (m)?
isur	tnt	inγi	Didn't he kill them (f)?

Future: /isur inq:a/ won't he kill?

isur	i	ynq:a	Won't he kill me?
isur	š	inq:a	Won't he kill you (m.s.)?
isur	šm	inq:a	Won t he kill you (f.s.)?
isur	t	inq:a	Won't he kill him?
isur	t:	inq:a	Won't he kill her?
isur	aγ	inq:a	Won't he kill us?
isur	ḳn	inq:a	Won't he kill you (m.p.)?
isur	ḳnt	inq:a	Won't he kill you (f.p.)?
isur	tn	inq:a	Won't he kill them (m)?
isur	tnt	inq:a	Won't he kill them (f)?

Present: /isur daynq:a/ doesn't he kill?

isur	day	inq:a	Doesn't he kill me?
isur	daš	inq:a	Doesn't he kill you (m.s.)?
isur	dašm	inq:a	Doesn't he kill you (f.s.)?
isur	dat	inq:a	Doesn't he kill him?
isur	dat:	inq:a	Doesn't he kill her?
isur	daγ	inq:a	Doesn't he kill us?
isur	daḳn	inq:a	Doesn't he kill you (m.p.)?
isur	daḳnt	inq:a	Doesn't he kill you (f.p.)?
isur	datn	inq:a	Doesn't he kill them (m)?
isur	datnt	inq:a	Doesn't he kill them (f)?

III.4 Demonstrative Pronouns (Independent Set)[7]

III.4.1 Singular

	Proximate	Remote
m.	wa	wan:
f.	ta	tan:

III.4.2 Plural

	Proximate	Remote
m.	wi	win:
f.	ti	tin:

III.4.3 Demonstrative Pronominal Suffixes[8]

III.4.3.1 /-a#/ / -in:#/

/-a#/	/ -in:#/
this	that
(m,f,s,p)	(m,f,s,p)

Suffixed to nouns ending in {-a#, -u#} ⟶ {-ya# this, -yu#, -yin:# that}

i.e. /-a# + -a#/ ⟶ /-aya#/
/-u# + -u#/ ⟶ /-uyu#/
/-a# + -in:#/ ⟶ /-ayin:#/
/-u# + -in:#/ ⟶ /-uyin:#/

Examples:

tad:arta	this house
ṣ:baḥa	this morning
tad:artin:	that house
tad:rwinin:	those houses
tabardaya (<tabrda)	this pack-saddle
tabardayin:	that pack-saddle
ag:uya (<ag:u)	this smoke

III.4.3.2 /-d:ɣ/ this

tad:artd:ɣ	this house
ṣ:baḥd:ɣ	this morning
tad:rwind:ɣ	these houses
tabardad:ɣ	this pack-saddle

III.4.3.3 /-n:a/ that

For things which you do not see.

tad:artn:a	that house
tad:rwinn:a	those houses
tabardan:a	that pack-saddle
argazn:a	that man
irgznn:a	those men

III.4.4 The Demonstrative ha, han

(Must be followed by Noun or Pronoun)

ha	here, there
ha muḥa id:ad	Here comes Muha.
ha faḍma td:ad	Here comes Fadma.
ha lwašun d:and	Here come the kids.
han	here, there
han muḥa id:ad	Here comes Muha.
han lwašun d:and	Here come the kids.

III.4.4.1 ha + Personal Pronouns

hank:	Here I am.
həšg:	Here you are (m.s.).
hašm:	Here you are (f.s.).
hant:a	Here he is.
hant:at	Here she is.
hanḳ:ni	Here we are.
hanḳn:i	Here you are (m.p.).
hanḳn:inti	Here you are (f.p.).
hanitni	Here they are (m).
hanitnti	Here they are (f).

Examples:

hant:a uriri adid:u	(here) He doesn't want to go.
hanḳ:ni urnri and:u	(here) We don't want to go.

III.4.4.2 hat here, there

In III.4.4 above, /ha/ or /han/ 'here, there' must be followed by a Noun or a Pronoun. In this section we will see that /hat/ 'here, there' must be followed by a verb.

hat id:ad	There he comes.
hat td:ad	There she comes.
hat d:and	There they come (m).
hat d:and	There they come (f).

In the case of third person singular and plural, we can get pronominal suffixes following ha:

hat	There he is.
hat:	There she is.
hatn	There they are (m).
hatnt	There they are (f).
hat id:ad	Here he comes.
hatnt d:and	Here they (f) come.

III.5 Relative Pronouns [9]

III.5.1 Subject

(a) n:a	who (invariable)
	which
a gaz n:a did:an yma ag:a.	The man who came is my brother.
(b) ay	who
nitni ag: d:an γr s:uq:	It is them who went to the market.

ay + id:an ⟶ ag: d:an

N.B.: /id:an/ is past participle of /d:u/, which is used only with the Subject Relative Pronouns. It has the invariable form /id:an/ with m,f,s, or p. Final /-y#/ of /ay/ plus initial /i-/ of the past participle always ⟶ /g:/. The Past Participle is formed by suffixing /-n#/ to verb inflected for $P_3N_sG_m$ in the past tense. The Present Participle is formed by suffixing /-n#/ to verb VH form inflected for $P_3N_sG_m$. (See Grammar of the Verb.)

(c) a	who
nk: a s in:an d:u	It was me who told him to go.
(d) un:a	he who
un:a uririn adid:u ,	He who does not want to go,
iq:im	let him stay.
un:a yran adid:u id:u	He who wants to go, let him go.
(e) tn:a	she who
tn:a uririn at:d:u ,	She who does not want to go,
tq:im	let her stay.
(f) win:a	those (m) who
win:a uririn add:un, q:imn	Those who do not want to go,
	let them stay.

(g) tin:a	those (f) who
tin:a uririn add:unt ,	Those who do not want to go,
q:imnt	let them stay.
(h) l:i	who, which
argaz l:i did:an yma ag:a	The man who came is my brother.

III.5.2 Object [10]

(a) n:a	whom, which
tamḍ:uṭ: n:a tan:ayd ,	The woman whom you saw is
ut:ma ay tga	my sister.
(b) l:i	whom, which
tamḍ:uṭ: l:i tan:ayd ,	The woman whom you saw is
ut:ma ay tga	my sister.
(c) ay	whom, which
irdn ay nz:nza	It is the wheat which we sold.

III.6 Indefinite Pronouns [11]

'this other one', 'that other one','these other ones'

'those other ones'

III.6.1 Proximate Indefinite Pronouns [12]

	m.	f.
sg.	wayaḍn ~ wayaḍnin	tayaḍn ~ tayaḍnin
pl.	widyaḍn ~ widyaḍnin	tidyaḍn ~ tidyaḍnin

- id: argaza ag:d:an γr s:uq: ?	Is it this man who went to the market?
= la wayaḍn	No, it is this other one.
- id : md:na ag:d:an γr s:uq: ?	Is it these people who went to the market?
= la widyaḍnin	No, it is those others.
- id: tamḍ:uṭ:a ag:d:an γr s:uq: ?	Is it this woman who went to the market?
= la tayaḍn	No, it is this other one.
- id: tiwtmina ag:d:an γr s:uq: ?	Is it these women who went to the market?
= la tidyaḍnin	No, it is those others.

III.6.2 Remote Indefinite Pronouns

	m.	f.
sg.	wan:yaḍn ~ wan:yaḍnin	tan:yaḍn ~ tan:yaḍnin
pl.	win:yaḍn ~ win:yaḍnin	tin:yaḍn ~ tin:yaḍnin

N.B.: yaḍn ~ yaḍnin = other or others

-id: s:rwala ay trid ?	Do you want this pair of trousers?
= la wan:yaḍn	No, (I want) that other one.
- id: s:rawla ay trid ?	Do you want these trousers?
= la win:yaḍn	No, (I want) those other ones.

- id: lq:amiža ay trid ?	Do you want this shirt?
= la tan:yaḍn	No, I want that other one.
- id: lq:mayza ay trid ?	Do you want these shirts?
= la tin:yaḍnin	No, I want those others.

III.6.3 Every, Each

k:u	every
k:uša	everyone
k:uyun	each one (m)
k:uyut	each one (f)

k:u argaz ɣuṛs iy:is	Every man has a horse.
k:u tamd:ut: ɣuṛs taq:b:ut:	Every woman has a djellaba.
k:uša id:a ibrdan:s	Everyone went his way.
k:uyun ɣuṛs iy:is	Each one (m) has a horse.
k:uyut ɣuṛs taq:b:ut:	Each one (f) has a djellaba.

* * *

Notes on the Pronominal System in Ayt Seghrouchen (A.S.)

1 In Ayt Seghrouchen this appears as:

ntš ~ ntšint	I
šk: ~ šk:int	you (ms)
šm: ~ šm:int	you (fs)
nt:a ~ nt:an	he
nt:at	she
ntšni	we (m)
ntšninti	we (f)
šn:i	you (mp)
šn:inti	you (fp)
nitni	they (m)
nitnti	they (f)

2 The Ayt Seghrouchen paradigm is:

/winw, win:š, win:m, win:s,
win:x, win:un, win:šnt,
win:sn, win:snt/ 'mine' (m), 'yours' (ms) etc.

3 The Ayt Seghrouchen paradigm is:

/tinw, tin:š, tin:m,
tin:s, tin:x, tin:um,
tin:šnt, tin:sn, tin:snt/ 'mine' (f),'yours' (fs), etc.

4 The Ayt Seghrouchen paradigm is:

axam	inw	my tent
axam	n:s	your (ms) tent
axam	n:m	your (fs) tent
axam	n:s	his tent
axam	n:s	her tent
axam	n:x	our tent
axam	n:un	your (mp) tent
axam	n:šnt	your (fp) tent
axam	n:sn	their (m) tent
axam	n:snt	their (f) tent

5 The kinship terms pronominal suffixes in Ayt Seghrouchen are for:

(a) ʕm:i my uncle "Frabr"

ʕm:i, ʕm:iš, ʕm:im, ʕm:is,
ʕm:itnx, ʕm:itun, ʕm:išnt,
ʕm:itsn, ʕm:itsnt

(b) ib:a my father

im:a my mother

nan:a my fa mo

dad:a my fa fa

ib:a, ib:aš, ib:am, ib:as,
ib:atnx, ib:atun, ib:ašnt,
ib:asn, ib:atsnt

(c) lawšun   child

aryaz   man

tamṭ:uṭ: woman

lwašuninw, lwašunn:s, lwašunn:m,
lwašunn:s, lwašunn:x, lwašunn:un,
lwašunn:šnt, lwašunn:sn, lwašunn:snt

6 The Ayt Seghrouchen paradigms are:

(a) for Indirect Objects (i.e. with intransitive verbs, e.g., /s:iwl/ 'to speak')

is:iwl	i	he spoke to me
is:iwl	aš	he spoke to you (ms)
is:iwl	am	he spoke to you (fs)
is:iwl	as	he spoke to him
is:iwl	ax	he spoke to us
is:iwl	awn	he spoke to you (mp)
is:iwl	awnt ~ ašnt	he spoke to you (fp)
is:iwl	asn	he spoke to them (m)
is:iwl	asnt	he spoke to them (f)

(b) for Direct Objects (i.e. with transitive verbs, e.g., /sal/ 'to ask')

isal	i	he asked me
isal	š	he asked you (ms)
isal	šm	he asked you (fs)
isal	t	he asked him
isal	t:	he asked her
isal	ax	he asked us

isal	šun	he asked you (mp)
isal	šunt	he asked you (fp)
isal	tn	he asked them (m)
isal	tnt	he asked them (f)

Notice:

With the Habitual stem prefix /l:a-/ in Ayt Seghrouchen, the pronominal affix can be either pre-verbal or post-verbal: e.g.,

damisawal	(A.A.)	he speaks to you **(fs)**
dašmit:sal	(A.A.)	he asked you **(fs)**

Compare

l:ayamis:awal ~ l:ays:awalam (A.S.)
l:ašmit:sal ≈ l:ayt:salšm (A.S.)

7 The Ayt Seghrouchen pronominal suffixed set associated with a transitive verb in the future is:

adi	ynγ	he will kill me
aš:	inγ	he will kill you (ms)
as:m	inγ	he will kill you (fs)
at:	inγ	he will kill him
adt:	inγ	he will kill her
adax	inγ	he will kill us
aš:un	inγ	he will kill you (mp)
at:n	inγ	he will kill them (m)
at:nt	inγ	he will kill them (f)

8 The Ayt Seghrouchen Demonstrative Pronouns are:

1. **Singular**
   wu, win:
   tu, tin:

2. **Plural**
   inu, inin:
   tinu, tinin:

9 Demonstrative Suffixes in Ayt Seghrouchen:

/-u#/ , /-in:#/

10 Relative Pronouns, Subject in Ayt Seghrouchen:

(a) din — who, which

aryaz din d:iraḥn una ag:žu
The man who came is my brother

(b) ay — who

muḥnd ag:usin z:it
It's Muha who took (carried) the oil.

(c) a — who

ntš ayas (~ as) in:an adiraḥ
It's me who told him to go.

(d) udin — he who

udin uribγin adiraḥ iq:im
He who does not want to go, let him stay.

(e) td:in td:in — she who

td:in uribɣin ad:ṛaḥ tq:im
She who does not want to ge, let her stay.

(f) idin — those (m) who

idin uribɣin adṛaḥn q:imn
Those (m) who do not want to go, let them stay.

(g) tidin — those (f) who

tidin uribɣin adṛahnt q:imnt
Those (f) who do not want to go, let them stay.

(h) din — who, which

aryaz din d:iraḥn, uma ag:žu
The man who came is my brother.

11 <u>Object</u>

(a) & (b) din — whom, which

tamṭ:uṭ: din tẓriṭ ultma ay tžu
The woman whom you saw is my sister.

(c) same

12 (a) Proximate Indefinite Pronouns

	m	f
s	wuyḍnin ~ wuḍnin	tuyḍnin ~ tuḍnin
pl	inuyḍnin ~ inuḍnin	tinuyḍnin ~ tinuḍnin

Examples:

__isd aryazu ag:ṛaḥn ɣr s:uq: ?

= la wuḍnin

- Is it this man who went to the market?
- No, it is this other one.

__isd mid:nu ag:raḥn ɣr s:uq: ?

= ihi, inuḍnin

- Is it these people who went to the market?
- No, it is those others.

__isd tamṭ:ut:u ag:ṛaḥn ɣr s:uq: ?

= ihi, tnḍnin.

- Is it this woman who went to the market?
- No, it is this other one.

__isd tiʕy:alinu ag:ṛaḥn ɣr s:uq: ?

= ihi, tinuyḍnin .

- Is it these women who went to the market?
- No, it is those others.

(b) Remote Indefinite Pronouns

	m	f
s	udinḍnin	td:inḍnin
pl	idinḍnin	tidinḍnin

N.B. :ḍnin = other, others; iḍnin = others

Examples:

__isd s:rawlu ay tbγit ?
__la, udinḍnin

- Do you want this pair of trousers?
- No, (I want) that other one.

__isd s:rawlu ay tbγit ?
__la, idinḍnin

- Do you want these trousers ?
- No, (I want) those other ones.

__isd lq:amižayu ay tbγit ?
__ihi, td:inḍnin .

- Do you want this shirt ?
- No, I want that other one.

__isd lq:mayžu ay tbγit ?
__la, tidinḍnin .

- Do you want these shirts?
- No, I want those others.

(c) Every, each

kul:	every
kul:ša, kul:	everyone
kul:idž	each one (m)
kul:išt	each one (f)

- kul: aryaz γrs yis .
  Every man has a horse.

- kul: tamṭ:ut γrs taqb:ut: .
  Every woman has a djellaba .

- kul:ša iraḥ ibrdann:s .
  Everyone went his way.

- kul:idž γrs yis ,
  Each one (m) has a horse.

- kul:išt γrs taq:b:ut: .
  Each one (f) has a djellaba.

IV. Grammar of the Noun

This section on the grammar of the noun is concerned mainly with Ayt Ayache. In general, the basic concepts of the system apply to Ayt Seghrouchen as well. Derivations (Noun stems from verb stems, those of number and gender, Augmentatives, Diminutives, etc.) are similar in both dialects. Construct State of the Noun is also more or less alike in both dialects. In other words, the differences between the two dialects as far as the grammar of the noun is concerned are phonological and lexical rather than morphological. Notes showing such differences appear at the end of this section.

IV. The Noun

IV.1 Introduction

Morphemes in Tamazight may be divided into three major classes: particles, stems and affixes, or if considered in terms of more general terminology, into two classes, namely Major and Minor classes of morphemes. The major classes are stems; the minor classes are particles and affixes. This classification into stems, particles and affixes is based on the two morphological features shown in this figure:

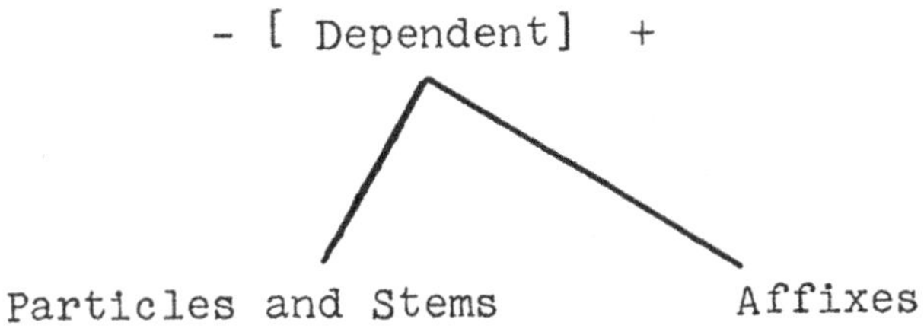

Stems are either Verb Stems or Noun Stems. This distinction is based on the kind of affix with which they occur. For a complete discussion of the Verb Stems see Grammar of the Verb. Any stem in Tamazight is either Basic or Derived.

Affixes are either verb or noun affixes. Verb affixes are either movable or fixed affixes. (See Grammar of the Verb.) All noun affixes are fixed affixes.

IV.2 Basic and Derived Noun Stems and Nouns

A Basic Noun Stem is one which has no relation to any verb stem from which it could be derived. Examples of a Derived Noun Stem are the stems of Nouns of Action (N-act), Agent (N-agt), Instrument (N-instr), Place (N-loc), and Occupation (N-occup). This means that the stems of such nouns are derived from verbs that exist in the language and that the different numbers and genders of the nouns are derived by the noun affixes discussed in IV.2-1 below.

IV.2.1 Basic Noun Stems and Nouns

A Basic Noun occurs with the same affixes as a derived noun. In most cases whether the noun is basic or derived, its number and gender are distinguished thus: (a) a plural noun has the suffix /-n/; (b) a singular noun does not have this suffix, but has the prefix /#a-/ whereas the plural has prefix /#i-/; (c) a feminine noun has the prefix and/or the suffix /t-/:

$$\left\{\begin{array}{ll} \left\{\begin{array}{l} /t\_\_/ \sim /t\_\_t/ \sim /t\_\_t{:}/ \sim /\_\_t/ \sim \\ /ta\_\_/ \sim /ta\_\_t/ \sim /ta\_\_t{:}/ \end{array}\right\} & \text{for f.s.} \\ /ti\_\_/ \sim /ti\_\_in/ \sim /t\_\_/ \sim /\_\_t/ & \text{for f.p.} \end{array}\right\}$$ [1]

This information concerning gender and number for nouns, both basic and derived, may be diagrammed thus:

(a) for Number

- [/-n#/] +

Singular Plural

(b) for Gender

- [{ /___t#/ , /#t___/ , /#t___t#/ , /#t___t:#/ }] +

Masculine Feminine

Many basic nouns in Tamazight are borrowed from Arabic. Some of the Arabic loan nouns were borrowed with the Arabic definite article /ʔal-/ 'the' (→/l-/ in Moroccan-Arabic and Tamazight), which loses its syntactic function in Tamazight and comes to be an inseparable part of the noun since the opposition Definite/Indefinite is NOT operable through the article:

e.g., Arabic loan basic nouns /lk:as/ 'a glass' or 'the glass', /lbab/ 'a door' or 'the door', /ṣ:aliḥ/* 'a saint' or 'the

---

* Rules concerning the assimilation of /l-/ of the Arabic definite article to a following dental operate in Tamazight as well. Also note that the formation of the plurals of such loan nouns in most cases follows the Arabic pattern whether Classical or Colloquial: e.g., /lk:as/ has plural /lk:isan/, /lbab/ has plural /lbiban/ and /ṣ:aliḥ/ has plural /ṣ:aliḥin/.

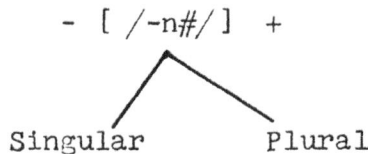

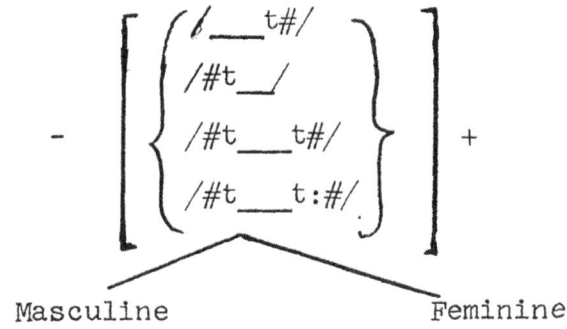

saint' as well as native basic nouns: /argaz/ 'a man' or 'the man', /aḍaḍ/ 'a finger' or 'the finger', /agl:id/ 'a king' or 'the king'.

Another set of basic nouns (also Arabic loans) has undergone accomodation to the native pattern: e.g., Moroccan-Arabic (M.A.) /xb:az/ 'baker' and its plural /xb:aza/ are derived from the M. A. verb /xbz/ 'to bake', whereas Tamazight has /a-xb:az/ 'baker', /i-xb:az-n/ 'bakers' but not the basic verb stem /xbz/ from which the nouns referred to above are derived. However, a look at Tamazight derived nouns explains the above pattern of derivation. There is a native pattern that derives the following nouns from the basic verb **V**: /zdm/ 'to collect wood', /azd:am/ 'one who collects wood (m.s.)', /izd:amn/ (m.p.); /xdm/ 'to work', /axd:am/ 'worker (m.s.)', /ixd:amn/ (m.p.). Notice that the same derivational pattern applies to /zdm/, a native stem, as well as to the Arabic loan stem /xdm/. The difference between /azd:am/, /izd:amn/, /axd:am/, /ixd:amn/ on one hand and /axb:az/, /ixb:azn/ on the other hand is that the first set shows derived nouns whereas members of the latter do not. In almost all the cases the gender of the loan word is preserved: e.g., Berber /tawriq:t:/'a piece of paper' (<classical Arabic /waraqat-/'a piece of paper' f.s.) has the Berber affix /ta___t:/ denoting f.s. noun. Compare this to the derived noun stem /tararit:/ 'vomiting/ (</rar/ 'to give back'). In Arabic, as well as Berber, all nouns ending in /-t/ are

feminine. Very few Arabic exceptions have been observed: e.g., /ʔalxalifat-/ 'Caliph' is a masculine noun in classical Arabic. This Arabic loan appears in Berber as /lxlift/ 'administrative job' which is, among the very few Berber exceptions, a masculine noun. In Moroccan Arabic /lxlift/ is also masculine.

A third set of basic nouns (i.e. not derived from verb stems) borrowed the singular noun only but formed their plurals according to native patterns: e.g., Berber /lfqih/ ' learned man, a teacher' is borrowed from classical Arabic /ʔalfaqīh/ 'legist, jurisprudent' which in turn is derived from the Arabic verb /faqiha/ 'to understand, comprehend'. The plural of the Arabic noun /ʔalfaqīh/ is /ʔalfuqahaʔ/ whereas the plural of the Berber /lfqih/ is /idlfqih/. Here, /lfqih/ is a basic noun (no Berber verb /fqh/) and /idlfqih/ is derived from the basic noun, by the Berber plural prefix /id-/. Compare this to /butarda/ 'washer (m.s.)' /idbutarda/ 'washers (m.p.)' derived from the native verb stem /arid/ 'to be washed'.

Another set of basic nouns are the numerals 4 - ∞ which are borrowed from Arabic. Together with the Arabic cardinal numerals 1-3 there is a native set (for more information on the numerals see Numerical System, pp. 22-29).

Another set of basic nouns shows borrowing from French: e.g., Berber /lag:ar/ 'station', /lik:ul/ 'school', /lbiru/ 'office', /lk:riyu/ 'pencil', /t:rik:u/ 'sweater', /ṭ:umubil/ 'motor-car', /ž:rda/ 'garden' for French "la gare, l'école, le bureau, le crayon, le tricot, l'automobile, le jardin" respectively. It is interesting to notice the assimilation of /l-/ to a following dental in the last three examples.

IV.2.2 Derived Noun Stems and Nouns

As stated in IV.1 above, a derived noun is one that is related (by derivation) to a noun stem, which in turn is derived from a verb stem in the language by one of the derivational affixes shown in IV.2.1 above: e.g., (Noun stems are underlined.)

Verb		N-m.s.	N-m.p.	N-f.s.	N-f.p.
xdm	to work	a-xd:am	i-xd:am-n	ta-xd:am-t	ti-xd:am-in 'worker'
zdm	to collect wood	a-zd:am	i-zd:am-n	ta-zd:am-t	ti-zd:am-in 'wood collector'

IV.3 Definiteness, Gender and Number

IV.3.1 Definite/Indefinite

The definite article does not exist in Berber. Thus the word /argaz/ can mean either 'a man' or 'the man'. Nouns borrowed from Arabic appear in Berber with the definite article if they happen to be borrowed with the Arabic definite article / al-/ (which is also /l-/ in Berber). Assimilation rules observed in Arabic for the /-l-/ of the definite article before a dental are also applicable to Arabic loan words in Berber if they happen to be borrowed with the definite article:

e.g., /s:ḳ:r/ 'sugar', /ṣ:aliḥ/ 'saint', /z:bib/ 'raisins', /ṭ:alab/ 'request', /d:unit/ 'the world', /ḍ:ra/ 'corn' (</lsḳ:r/, /lṣaliḥ/, /lzbib/, /lṭalab/, /ldunit/, /lḍra/). All the above nouns, borrowed with the definite article from Arabic can be translated as either definite or indefinite in Berber.

IV.3.2 Gender and Number

Nouns in Berber are either masculine or feminine in gender and singular or plural in number. In most cases the gender and number of a noun could be distinguished by its affix.

IV.3.2.1 Noun Affixes

IV.3.2.1-a Masculine Singular Prefixes

{ /a-/
/am-/
/u-/
/i-/
/l-/
/X:-/ }

Note: 1) /u-/ and /i-/ are not common prefixes for m.s. nouns.

2) /l-/ occurs mainly in Arabic borrowings

3) /X:-/ refers to a tense segment that results from assimilation of /l-/ referred to above to a following dental.

Examples:

kašf	to foretell	akašf	foretelling
rdm	to demolish	ard:am	demolisher
ʕawn	to help	amʕawn	helper
f:γ	to go out	ufuγ	going out
arid	to be washed	butarda	washer
bd:	to stand up	ibd:i	standing up
hbl	to become silly	lhbal	silliness
ṭṛẓ	to embroider	ṭ:ṛẓ	embroidering
		azg̣u	wind
		anu	well
		isl:i	stone
		urti	garden
		amḥḍar	pupil
		lγul	ogre
		ṣ:nduq:	box

IV.3.2.1-b Masculine Plural Affixes

{ /i___n/
/im___n/
/i___tn/
/i___/ }

Note: /i-/ is prefixed to nouns that are referred to as "Broken Plurals" as opposed to /i___n/ that is affixed to nouns referred to as "Sound Plurals".

Examples:

rgm	to insult	argam	insulting	irgamn	insults
kašf	to foretell	amkašf	foreteller	imkašfn	foretellers
dawa	to cure	adawa	cure	idawatn	cures
d:uk:l	make friends	amd:aḳ:l	friend	imd:uk:al	friends
		adašu	sandal	iduša	sandals
		ag̣lmam	lake	ig̣ulmamn	lakes
		abluḥ	date(fruit)	ibluḥn	dates

IV.3.2.1-c Feminine Singular Affixes

/t(a)___t(:)/
/ti___(t)/
/tu___(t)/
/m___t/
/l___t/
/X:___t/

Note: (1) /l___t/ occurs in Arabic loans

(2) /X:___/ of the affix /X:___t/ represents an /l-/ that assimilates to a following dental: e.g., /l-d-/ → /d:-/ as in /d:ˤut/ 'a case' (</ldˤut/).

Examples:

kašf to foretell amkašf foreteller (m.s.) tamkašft (f.s.)

lum	to blame	talumt	blame
ẓ:aḷ	to pray	taẓal:it:	praying
k:	to pass	tik:it	passing
f:r	to hide	tufra	hiding
ls	to dress	mlsiwt	dressing
xdm	to work	lxdmt	work
dʕu	to sue	ḍ:ʕut	case

IV.3.2.1-d Feminine Plural Affixes

/ti(m)____in/
/ti___/
/tu____n/
/ist-/
/ta____in/

Note: (1) /ti___/ derives a "Broken" feminine plural noun whereas /ti____n/ derives a "Sound" feminine plural noun.

(2) /ta____in/ is a rare femine plural affix.

Examples:

rḥl	to move	tarḥ:alt	nomad (f.s.)	tirḥ:alin (f.p.)
safr	to travel	tamsafrt	traveller (f.s.)	timsafrin (f.p.)
zuz:r	to winnow	tazrt	pitchfork (f.s.)	tizar (f.p.)
ḥm:m	to bathe	m:lḥm:am	public bath attendant (f.s.)	istm:lḥm:am (f.p.)

tudayt	Jew (f.s.)	tudayin (f.p.)
tuš:nt	jackal (f.s.)	tuš:an (f.p.)
taxamt	tent (f.s.)	tixamin (f.p.)
tal:unt	drum (f.s.)	tal:unin (f.p.)
taq:ayt	head (f.s.)	taq:ayin (f.p.)

IV.4 Plural Nouns

Plural Nouns besides being masculine or feminine are divided into

(a) External Plurals or Sound Plurals

(b) Internal or Broken Plurals

(c) Mixed Plurals

IV.4.1 Masculine Plurals

IV.4.1.1 External Plurals (or Sound Plurals)

Sing: /#a_____#/ ⟶ Pl. /#i_____n#/

Examples:

Singular	Plural	
axd:am	ixd:amn	laborer
axam	ixamn	big tent
amaziγ	imaziγn	Berber
aγanim	iγanimn[2]	reed
aγ̣lyas	iγ̣lyasn	panther
aslix	islixn	animal skin

asg̣:as	isg̣:asn	year
akš:iḍ	ikš:iḍn	a piece of wood
ag̣lmam	ig̣lmamn	lake
aγ̣r:am	iγ̣r:amn	saint, Sharif (of the Prophet's family)
aful:us	iful:usn	rooster
afl:aḥ	ifl:aḥn	farmer
aḥž:am	iḥž:amn	barber
abn:ay	ibn:ayn	mason
axr:az	ixr:azn	shoe-maker
axb:az	ixb:azn	baker
afray	ifrayn	fence
abr:aḥ	ibr:aḥn	town crier
aburks	iburksn	shoe
alus	ilusn	brother-in-law
aγ̣r:af	iγ̣r:afn	pitcher
aγmaz	iγmazn	wink
amrwas	imrwasn	debt
aγris	iγrisn	wool thread
aγw:aγ	iγw:aγn	rebel
aḥb:as	iḥb:asn	prisoner
aḥšlaf	iḥšlafn	dry grass or bush
aḥbib	iḥbibn	dear friend
aḥd:ad	iḥd:adn	blacksmith
aḥdž:am	iḥdž:amn	tatoo

aḥl:uf	iḥl:ufn	pig
aḥm:am	iḥm:amn	pigeon
aḥlaf	iḥlafn	woman's overdress
axd:aʕ	ixd:aʕn	deceiver, traitor
abariq:	ibariq:n	slap
abaw	ibawn	fava bean
abṛ:iḍ	ibṛ:iḍn	male goat
abr:ad	ibr:adn	tea-pot
abẓ:iḍ	ibẓ:iḍn	urine
abluḥ	ibluḥn	unripe date
adb:aγ	idb:aγn	tanner, dyer
aḍbib	iḍbibn	physician
aflidž	iflidžn	strip of tent
axm:už	ixm:užn	bad smell
axy:aḍ	ixy:aḍn	tailor
axlidž	ixlidžn	tree
axmim	ixmimn	lip
ayd:id	iyd:idn	leather bag for carrying water
ažm:uʕ	ižm:uʕn	gathering
aḳnn:ay	iḳnn:ayn	rock
aḳẓaẓ	iḳẓaẓn	gravel
aydžiy	iydžiyn	flower
aγ̣š:aš	iγ̣š:ašn	cheat
amaḥsad	imaḥsadn	jealous

amdyaz	imdyazn	singer
amd:aḥ	imd:aḥn	religious singer

Notice:

(1) Nouns having the following changes are also Sound Plurals.[3]

/-r# + -n#/ ⟶ /-r:#/

/-l# + -n#/ ⟶ /-l:#/

/-n# + -n#/ ⟶ /-n:#/

Singular	Plural	
agrur	igrur: (<igrurn)	pile of stones
aγḍ:ar	iγḍ:ar:	traitor
ahaq:ar	ihaq:ar:	crow
aḥam:ar	iḥam:ar:	main pole of the tent
aḥndir	iḥndir:	blanket
aḥrir	iḥrir:	soup
ayḍrur	iyḍrur:	dust
abaq:ar	ibaq:ar:	catastrophe (used in swearing)
abḥ:ar	ibḥ:ar:	garden
abulxir	ibulxir:	pig
aḍγar	iḍγar:	place, spot
aḍṛḍur	iḍṛḍur:	deaf

afq:ir	ifq:ir:	old man
ašabar	išabar:	caravan
almsir	ilmsir:	sheep skin
amazdar	imazdar:	inferior
amḥḍar	imḥḍar:	student
ams:utr	ims:utr:	beggar
amγar	imγar:	old man
amxiḍar	imxiḍar:	bet
anž:ar	inž:ar:	carpenter
aḍar	iḍar:	foot
agz:ar	igz:ar:	butcher
ašiḍar	išiḍar:	draft horse
ašf:ar	išf:ar:	thief
aγz:al	iγz:al: (<iγz:aln)	plate, stick
ag̣dal	ig̣dal:	pasture
aḥl:al	iḥl:al:	liar
axlxal	ixlxal:	ring, link (in a chain)
abuγlal	ibuγlal:	snail
aḍrγal	iḍrγal:	blind
adrbal	idrbal:	rag
adl:al	idl:al:	wandering salesman
ažmil	ižmil:	favor
ašw:al	išw:al:	harvester (person)
amaž:yal	imaž:yal:	superior
aγ̣užil	iγ̣užil:	orphan

amḥawal	imḥawal:	reconciliation
abḍ:an	ibḍ:an: (<ibḍ:ann)	skin
afṛ:an	ifṛ:an:	oven
axw:an	ixw:an:	thief
alg̣un	ilg̣un:	pick axe
amt:in	imt:in:	corpse
aˤban	iˤban:	a piece of cloth

(2) Nouns ending in vowels have the suffix $\left\{\begin{array}{l}\text{-tn\#}\\ \text{-wn\#}\\ \text{-yn\#}\end{array}\right\}$ rather than /-n#/ in their plurals and they too are here treated as sound plurals.

Singular	Plural	
amksa	imksawn	shepherd
aškša	iškšawn	chick
amtna	imtnawn	bad winter (snow fall)
amẓḍa	imẓḍawn	weaver
adu	aḍutn	wind
aγrda	iγrdayn	rat
abiba	ibibatn	mosquito
adida	ididatn	talk
amžuṛ:u	imžuṛ:utn	waterfall
ag:u	ag:utn	smoke
arwa	irwatn	threshing
asaka	isakatn	shallow passage in a river
aʕsk:ri	iʕsk:riyn	soldier
abulisi	ibulisiyn	policeman
aḥmami	iḥmamiyn	black horse
aḥuli	iḥuliyn	ram
abali	ibaliyn	old
abr:ani	ibr:aniyn	foreigner, stranger
afasi	ifasiyn	right-handed
afrḍi	ifrḍiyn	unique
afḍuli	ifḍuliyn	curious

ažnwi	ižnwiyn	knife
akurbi	ikurbiyn	shoe
amxzni	imxzniyn	soldier of the makhzen or the government
aḥrami	iḥramitn	clever
aḥili	iḥilitn	clever
ažur:u	ižur:utn	waterfall
azg̣u	izg̣utn	wind
akurdu	ikurdutn	flea

IV.4.1.2 Internal (or Broken) Plurals

a) change of /#a-/ of the singular to /#i-/ in plural

b) no suffix /-n#/

c) internal (medial and/or final) change

Examples:

Singular	Plural	
adašu	iduša	sandal
asklu	isḳla	tree
axbu	ix̣ba	hole
ayḍiḍ	iyḍaḍ	bird
agrtil	igrtal	mat
aḥanu	iḥuna	stable
aγyul	iγ̣yal	donkey

abaγ:us	ibuγ:as	monkey
amd:aḳ:l	imd:uk:al	friend
aqmu	iq̣ma	mouth
ašniḍ	išnaḍ	ass
awtul	iwtal	rabbit
anždi	inžda	traveller
asrdun	isrdan	mule
amẓluḍ	imẓlad	poor, broke
amnzu	imnza	early plowing
amaẓuẓ	imuẓaẓ	late plowing
aḥidus	iḥidas	dance
aḥyuḍ	iḥyaḍ	crazy
aknbuš	iḳnbaš	scarf
axnšuš	ixnšaš	face
aḥizun	iḥizan	lame
abux:u	ibux:a	worm
abadu	ibuda	edge of a field
abrḍud	ibrḍad	tail
afrši	ifrša	bark, peel
abrduz	ibrdaz	rag
aglmus	iγ̣lmas	hood
agru	iγ̣ra	frog
aγbalu	iγbula	spring
ahitur	ihitar	sheep skin

amadl	imudal	cheek
amalu	imula	shadow
amazir	imizar	country, campsite
agadir	iγ̣udar	wall
amḥruš	imḥraš	active, intelligent
amd:al:u	imd:ul:a	coward
agatu	iγ̣uta	rope

Notice the following broken plurals having the Arabic definite article:

lxlift	lxlayf	administrative job
lmus:	lamwas:	knife
lʕib	lʕyub	shame
lq:hwa	lq:hawi	coffee
lγul	laγwal	ogre
lštab	lštub	book
š:iḍ:an	š:waḍ:n	devil
s:uq:	laswaq:	market
ṣ:nduq:	laṣnadq:	box
ṛ:bḥ	larbaḥ	profit

IV.4.1.3 Mixed Plurals

(Internal plurals with External suffixes)

Singular	Plural	
afus	ifas:n	hand
argaz	irgzn	man
asif	isaf:n	river
afud	ifad:n	knee
abrid	ibrdan	road
aḍaḍ	iḍuḍan	finger
adis	idusan	belly
agl:id	igldan	king
alγ̣m	ilγ̣man	camel
axdul	ixdlan	round loaf of bread
ayrḍ	iyrḍan	neck
aγtir	iγtran	thorn
aγuṛ	iγ̣ran	honey comb
axdil	ixdlan	belly

Remarks on the Pluralization of Masculine Nouns

Sometimes the /#a-/ of the singular does not change in the plural. Singular nouns that have /#i-/ or /#u-/ show the same prefix in their plural forms. Sometimes prefix /#a-/ of the singular noun changes to /#u-/.

axbaš	axbašn	claw
aluq:id	aluq:idn	match
ad:bliž	ad:bližn	bracelet
ašbab	ašbabn	eye lash
anšuš	anšušn	lip
ag̣:a	ag̣:atn	burden
ad:žar	ad:žar:	neighbor
anu	anutn	well
imšli	imšliwn	lunch
ilis	ilisn	raw wool
imnsi	imnsitn	supper
izikr	izakar:	cord
ifd:iwž	ifd:iwžn	spark[4]
iγil	iγal:n	arm
iḥnbl	iḥnbl:	blanket
iγzdis	iγzdisan	rib
ilγ	ilγan	leg
itri	itran	star
iḍ	iḍan	night
izli	izlan	song
isli	islan	bridegroom
isl:i	isl:iwn	stone
ixf	ixfawn	head
urti	urtan	garden

uš:n	uš:an:	jackal
anu	una	well
as:	us:an	day
iš:	aš:iwn	horn (of an animal)

IV.5 Feminine Plurals

IV.5.1. External Plurals (or Sound Plurals)

(a) Sing: /#ta-/ ⟶ Pl: /#ti-/

(b) delete /____t#/ of the singular

(c) add suffix /-in#/ for plural

Singular	Plural	
taxamt	tixamin	tent
tafunast	tifunasin	cow
taful:ust	tiful:usin	hen
taq:bilt	tiq:bilin	tribe
tazlaft	tizlafin	platter
tamɣart	timɣarin	old woman
tabḥirt	tibḥarin	garden
tawrirt	tiwririn	hill
tanslmt	tinslmin	Moslem
tamsafrt	timsafrin	traveller
tamq:ablt	timq:ablin	caretaker
tamzawg:t	timzawg:in	one who asks protection
tamzayt: (<tmzaydt)	timzaydin	one who adds

tamˁawnt	timˁawnin	helper
taγ̣š:ašt	tiγ̣š:ašin	cheater
tamk:ust	timk:usin	heiress
tams:ufst	tims:ufsin	one who spits
tamẓurt	timẓurin	pilgrim
taˁw:amt	tiˁw:amin	swimmer
tamksawt	timksawin	shepherdess
tamẓḍawt	timẓḍawin	weaver
tams:utrt	tims:utrin	beggar
taḥb:ast	tiḥb:asin	prisoner
tamr:ayt	timr:ayin	masseuse
tarḥ:alt	tirḥ:alin	nomad
tast:ayt	tist:ayin	filter
tašṭ:aḥt	tišṭ:aḥin	dancer
tazd:amt	tizd:amin	wood collector
taˁšaqt	tiˁšaqin	sweetheart, beloved
taxd:amt	tixd:amin	worker
taxd:aˁt	tixd:aˁin	deceiver
tabš:art	tibš:arin	bearer of good tidings
tamḍl:ˁt	timḍl:ˁin	loaf of bread
taḥal:ast	tiḥal:asin	saddle
taḥr:aft	tiḥr:afin	a piece of cloth for carrying a baby on the back
tasḥ:art	tisḥ:arin	magician
taṣm:art	tiṣm:arin	hammer

tašṭ:abt	tišṭ:abin	broom
tašk:amt	tišk:amin	denouncer
tašf:art	tišf:arin	thief
taʕs:ast	tiʕs:asin	guard
taxw:ant	tixw:anin	thief
tamašart	timašarin	thief
tamazant	timazanin	sender
tašr:ayt	tišr:ayin	lessee

Notice: Nouns ending in vowels may have the suffix /-iwin#/

Singular	Plural	
tamγra	timγriwin	wedding
tabarda	tibardiwin	saddle

IV.5.2. Internal Plurals(or Broken Plurals)

(a) /#ta-/ of Sing. ⟶ /#ti-/ in pl.

(b) Internal change

(c) deletion of final /-t#/

(d) no suffix

Singular	Plural	
tisirt	tisar	mill
tal:st	til:as	darkness, dusk
taγγult	tiγγal	female donkey
tamd:aḳ:lt	timd:uk:al	girl friend
tiym:i	tiym:a	community of nomads

tazrt	tizar	pitchfork
tagrtilt	tigrtal	mat
tamazirt	timizar	property
tuš:nt	tuš:an	jackal
taq:b:ut	tiq̣:b:a	djellaba
tamγṛuṣt	timγṛas	sacrifice
tagal:it	tig̣ul:a	swearing
taqdurt	tiq̣dar	pot
talxatmt	tilxutam	ring
r:iḥt	r:wayḥ	odor
lḥašt	lḥwayž	thing
lxuḍrt	lxuḍrat	vegetable
lγabt	lγwabi	forest

IV.5.3 <u>Mixed Plurals</u>

(Internal Plurals with External Suffixes)

tadist	tidusin	belly
tafust	tifusin	hand
tawariyt	tiwaryiwin	dream
tad:art	tad:rwin	house

<u>Notes on Some Feminine Nouns</u>

(1) Some feminine Arabic nouns were borrowed into Berber with the Arabic feminine marker /-a#/ in dialectical Arabic (/-t-/ in classical Arabic), e.g.:

Dialectical Arabic	Berber	
r:iḥa	r:iḥt	odor
ʔlḥaža	lḥašt	thing
lγaba	lγabt	forest
lqaʕida	lq:aʕida	tradition
ṣ:ulṭa	ṣ:ulṭa	authority
lḥkuma	lḥk:uma	government
lžamaʕa	lžamaʕa	council

(2) Some singular feminine nouns (native or loan) do not change their /#ta-/ to /#ti-/ in the plural, e.g.:

Singular	Plural	
tal:unt	tal:unin	drum
tad:art	tad:rwin	house
tadžart	tadžarin	neighbor
taq:ayt	taq:ayin	head
taγma	taγmiwin	thigh
tašna	tanšnwin	term of reference for co-wife

(3) Some feminine singular nouns ending in /-t:#/ show the following change in plural: /-t:#/ ⟶ /-t-/

Singular	Plural	
talat:	talatin	ditch
tislit:	tislatin	bride
tizit:	tizatin	fly
tifrit:	tifratin	cave

IV.6 Miscellaneous

IV. 6.1 Plurals with /id-/ (m,f) and /ist:/ (f) [5]

Singular	Plural	
lfq:ih	idlfq:ih	learned person
bab	idbab	owner
bibi	idbibi	turkey
ʕm:i	idʕm:i	my paternal uncle
xali	idxali	my maternal uncle
ʕt:i	ist:ʕt:i ~ idʕt:i	my maternal aunt
xalti	ist:xalti ~ idxalti	my maternal aunt
ut:ma	ist:ut:ma	my sister
lxzin	idlxzin	storing place
lmizan	idlmizan	balance, set of scales
lḥm:mam	idlḥm:am	bathroom
lḥzam	idlḥzam	belt

butarda	idbutarda	washer (m)
m:tarda	idm:tarda	washer (f)
d:unit	idd:unit	world
s:rir	ids:rir	bed
t:aman	idt:aman	price

IV. 6.2 <u>Plurals with/ayt-/</u> (m)

unḍir	aytunḍir	a man from the tribe of Ayt Oundir
wiγrm	aytiγrm	a man from one's village

IV. 6.3 <u>Plurals of Different Roots</u>[6]

Singular	Plural	
lˤil	lwašun	boy
tarbat:	tišir:atin	girl
tamḍuṭ:	tiwtmin	woman
tagmart	tiγal:in	mare
tixsi	ul:i	sheep
tiḍ:	al:n	eye

IV.6.4 <u>Diminutives</u>[7]

Certain masculine nouns give a diminutive noun by prefixation of /#t-/ and suffixation of /-t:#/ (or /-t#/).

Masculine Noun	Diminutive	Meaning
afus	tafust:	small hand
aḍar	taḍart:	small foot
aγbalu	taγbalut:	small spring
agrtil	tagrtilt	small mat

IV.6.5 Augmentative [8]

Certain feminine nouns give Augmentatives by a process that is the reverse of Diminutive Formation mentioned in IV.6.4 above

Feminine Noun	Augmentative	Meaning
taxamt	axam	big tent
tašṭ:abt	ašṭ:ab	big broom
tamart	amar	big beard
tabḥirt	abḥir	big garden

IV.6.6 Collective Nouns [9]

IV.6.6.1 Singular Collective Nouns

udi	butter
uz:al	iron
az:ar	hair
imndi	grain
ḍ:ṛa	corn
aγṛum	bread
aγ:u	milk
tadunt	grease , shortening, cooking fat

tduṭ:	wool
tisnt	salt
tuya	grass
iγd	ashes

IV.6.6.2 Plural Collective Nouns [10]

aman	water
idam:n	blood
ilam:n	bran
lflus	money
md:n	people
irdn	wheat
tarwa	offspring, progeny
tiγrad	salary
imas:n	plough
tir:a	writing
timẓin	barley
tuzlin	scissors
imrγan	sauce
iršan	dirt
ifsan	seeds

IV.6.7 Noun of Unity [11]

The noun of unity is formed from a collective noun by the same process used in IV.6.4 above for the formation of Diminutives.

aẓaḷim	onions	taẓaḷimt	an onion
z:nbuˁ	oranges	taz:nbuˁt	an orange
lmšmaš	apricots	talmšmašt	an apricot
lxux	peaches	talxuxt	a peach
xiz:u	carrots	taxiz:ut	a carrot

In some cases the noun of unity is achieved by the use of /aḥbub/ "grain" before the collective noun, e.g.:

aḥbub nṛ:uz	a grain of rice
aḥbub nḍ:ṛa	a kernel of corn
aḥbub w:aḍil	a grape

IV.6.8 Composed Nouns[12]

(1) u = (son of)	of (m.s.)
(2) ut = (daughter of)	of (f.s.)
utmazirt	country man
ut:mazirt (<uttmazirt)	country woman
(3) ayt-	(m.p.)
(4) ist:-	(f.p.)
ayt:mazirt	country men
ist:mazirt	country women
(5) bu- (father of)	of (m.s.)
(6) idbu-	of (pl.)
buyḥl:al	liar (m)
idbuyḥl:al	liars (m)

(7) m: (mother of) — of (f.s.)

(8) idm:- — of (f.p.)

m:iḥl:al — liar (f)

idm:iḥl:al — liars (f)

(9) bab (owner) — master of, owner

bab ntad:art — master of the house

(10) lal: — (fem.)

lal: ntad:art — mistress of the house

(11) /bu-/ and /m:/ can denote a 'trade' or 'occupation'

buʕari — one in charge of a forest

buwɣanim * — one who plays the flute

bulḥm:am — public bath attendant (m)

m:lḥm:am — public bath attendant (f)

* (aɣanim 'reed'; for change of a to w see IV. below)

IV.7 Construct State of the Noun[13]

A noun in the construct state (c.s.) changes its shape.

(/tafunast/ ⟶ /tfunast/ 'cow'; /argaz/ ⟶ /urgaz/ 'man' ...etc.)

IV.7.1 Changes occuring in masculine nouns

/#a-/ ⟶ {-u- / -w:- / -wa-}

/#i-/ ⟶ {-i- / -y- / -yi-}

/#u-/ ⟶ /-wu-/

babuxam (<axam)	head of the house
lk:as w:atay (<atay)	a glass of tea
axam isli (<isli)	the tent of the fiance
aġ:r: yirdn (<irdn)	wheat flour
taql:alt w:udi (<udi)	the butter jar
iˁd:a utfl (<atfl)	plenty of snow
tad:art uryaz (<aryaz)	the house of the man
aɣṛum yirdn (<irdn)	wheat bread
inɣayi wuxs (<uxs)	tooth ache (it killed me of the teeth)
lbab w:urti (<urti)	the door of the garden
taḍuṭ: w:ul:i (<ul:i)	wool of the sheep
šrad w:us:an (<us:an)	three days

IV.7.2 <u>Changes occuring in feminine nouns</u>

/#ta-/ ⟶ { -t- ; -ta- rarely }

/#ti-/ ⟶ { -t- ; -ti- rarely }

/#tu-/ ⟶ /-tu-/

argaz ntmḍ:ut: (<tamd:ut:)	husband
ṣ:aliḥin ntmizar (<timizar)	local saints
ixf ntuš:nt (<tuš:nt)	head of a jackal
utmazirt (<tamazirt)	someone from your country
iš: ntfunast (<tafunast)	the horn of the cow
taqb:ut ntaḍuṭ (<taḍuṭ)	a woolen garment

iy:is ntslit (<tislit)	the horse of the bride
amksa ntγḍ:n (<tiγḍ:n)	the shepherd of goats
aman ntisirt (<tisirt)	the water of the mill
šrat: ntuzlin (<tuzlin)	three scissors
bu tuzlin (<tuzlin)	the owner of the scissors
lbab ntad:art (<tad:art)	the door of the house

IV.6.3 <u>The noun is in the construct state if:</u>

(a) <u>the noun is in genitive construct</u> N_1 of N_2 (N_2 changes)

tad:art urgaz	the house of the man
(urgaz c.s. of argaz)	
lk:as w:atay	a cup of tea
(watay c.s. of atay)	
argaz ntmḍ:uṭ:	husband (man of the woman)
(tmḍ:uṭ: c.s. of tamḍ:uṭ:)	
iš: ntfunast	the horn of the cow
(tfunast c.s. of tafunast)	

(b) <u>the noun is the subject of a verb and it follows the verb</u>

if:γ umaziγ	The Berber went out.
(umaziγ c.s. of amaziγ)	

iswa urgaz atay The man drank tea.

(urgaz c.s. of argaz)

Compare the above two examples with the following where the noun is also the subject of the verb but precedes it:

amaziγ if:γ The Berber went out.

argaz iswa atay The man drank tea.

However, we have to state that the native speaker of Berber prefers the order vb. + subj. rather than subj. + vb.

(c) the noun follows a numeral, e.g.:

(yun [m] , yut [f] 'one' , xmsṭaʕš 'fifteen' , sṭ:aʕš 'sixteen')

yun was: a day (one day)

(was: c.s. of as:)

yut tmḍ:ut: a lady (one lady)

(tmḍ:ut: c.s. of tamḍ:ut:)

xmsṭaʕš ntfunast 15 cows

(tfunast c.s. of tafunast)

sṭ:aʕš war:yal 16 rials

(war:yal c.s. ar:yal)

(d) the noun follows a certain preposition:

γ txamt in the tent

(txamt c.s. of taxamt)

xf tfunast on the cow

(tfunast c.s. of tafunast)

γr txamt (f) (<taxamt)	to the tent
γr argaz (m) (<argaz)	to the man

(only fem. nouns following /γr/ are in the c.s.)

iurgaz (<argaz)	to the man
itfunast (<tafunast)	to the cow
sufus (<afus)	by/with the hand
zy tmazirt (<tamzirt)	from the country

(i) **Preposition after which only feminine nouns are in the construct state:**

γr	to

(ii) Prepositions after which the nouns are in the construct state:

i	to
y	in
s	with (instrumental)
am:	like
xf	on
zy	from
d	with
n	of
d:aw	under
ingr ~ ngr	between

(iii) Prepositions after which nouns are NOT in the construct state:

s	to (directional)

qbl	before
bʕd	after
bla	without
ar	until (to)
al:	until (to)

<u>Notes on the preposition "n" (of)</u>

(i) n → -l before a noun with initial /#l-/

n → -w before a noun with initial /#a-/

n → -y before a noun with initial /#i-/

n → -n elsewhere

(ii) Nouns with initial /#a-/ drop their /#a-/ in the construct: 'some of' + Noun with /#a-/ i.e. (šan + N)

ša n lḥlib →	ša l lḥlib →	ša l:ḥlib	some milk
ša n aksum	ša w ksum	ša wksum	some meat
ša n lg:ayz	ša l lg:ayz	ša l:g:ayz	some kerosene
ša n lbitrun	ša l lbitrun	ša l:bitrun	some kerosene
ša n udi	ša w wudi	ša w:udi	some butter
ša n iful:usn	ša y ful:usn	ša yful:usn	some chickens
ša n aγṛum	ša w γṛum	ša wγṛum	some bread
ša n aslix	ša w slix	ša wslix	some skin
ša n atfl	ša w tfl	ša wtfl	some snow
ša n aγanim	ša w γanim	ša wγanim	some reeds

However few nouns retain their /#a-/ and follow the rules of construct state of nouns.

ša n atay ⟶	ša w watay ⟶	ša w:atay	some tea
ša n awal ⟶	ša w wawal ⟶	ša w:awal	some talk

(e) <u>the noun follows the conjunction 'and' /d/ (N_1 and N_2)</u>:

lq:hwa dwatay (<atay)	coffee and tea
argaz t:mḍ:ut: (<tamḍ:ut)	the man and the lady

(n.b. /d/ assimilates to a following /t/ in the above example)

tamḍ:ut durgaz (<argaz)	the lady and the man
aγyul t:funast (tafunast)	the donkey and the cow

* * *

Notes on the Noun in Ayt Seghrouchen (A.S.)

1 The nominal affixes listed here for Ayt Ayache are the same for Ayt Seghrouchen.

2 Quite a number of the masculine singular nouns which in Ayt Ayache have initial /#a-/ appear in Ayt Seghrouchen without this /#a-/. The plurals of these A.S. nouns, however, are identical with those of A.A. Moreover, the construct state (see IV.7) of the A.S. nouns has /#u-/ as in A.A.

Examples:

Singular			Plural	
A.A.	A.S.	Construct	A.A. & A.S.	
aɣnim	ɣanim	uɣanim	iɣanimn	reed
afus	fus	ufus	ifas:n	hand
aḍaḍ	ḍad	uḍaḍ	iduḍan	finger
afud	fud	ufud	ifad:n	knee

3 This is another phonological difference between the two dialects; In A.S.,

/-r# + -n#/	/-rn#/
/-l# + -n#/	/-ln#/
/-n# + -n#/	/-n:#/ (same as A.A.)

Examples from A.S.:

adrḍur	iḍrḍurn	deaf
aγz:al	iγz:aln	stick
afṛ:an	ifṛ:an:	oven

4 As examples of lexical differences:

A.A.	A.S.	
ifd:iwž	aqz:iw	spark
isl:i	aẓṛu	stone
ixf	azl:if	head
tazlaft	ṭẓiwa	platter
tawrirt	tiš:ut	hill

5 In Ayt Seghrouchen we get /it-/ (m), /suyt/ /ist/ (f), e.g.:

ifgih	itlfgih	learned person
ʕt:i	suytʕt:i	my paternal aunt

6 The same nouns are here listed for A.S.:

Singular	Plural	
arba	lwašun	boy
tarbat:	tišir:atin	girl
tamṭ:ut:	tiʕy:alin	woman
tažmart	tiγal:in	mare
tixsi	ul:i	sheep
tiṭ:	al:n	eye

7 The same nouns are here listed for A.S.:

fus	tfust	small hand
ḍar	ḍ:art:	small foot
aγbalu	taγbalut:	small spring
ažrtil	tažrtilt	small mat

8 The same nouns here are listed for A.S.:

txant	axam	big tent
tašṭ:abt	ašṭ:ab	big room
tmart	mar	big beard
tabḥirt	abḥir	big garden

9 The same nouns are here listed for A.S.:

udi	butter
uz:al	iron
az:ar	hair
imndi	grain
ḍ:ṛa	corn
aγṛum	bread
aγi	milk
tadunt	grease, shortening, cooking fat
taḍuft	wool
tisnt	salt
tuža	grass
iγd	ashes

10 Plural Collective Nouns in A.S.:

aman	water
idam:n	blood
lflus	money
mid:n	people
irdn	wheat
taṛwa	offspring. children
tiγṛad	salary
imas:n	plough
timẓin	barley
timšṛad	scissors
imṛγan	sauce
ifsan	seeds

11 Noun of Unity in A.S.:

/bṣ/	onions	talbṣlt	an onion
/:imun/	oranges	talimunt	an orange
/xux/	peaches	talxuxt	a peach
/xiz:u/	carrots	taxiz:ut:	a carrot

Nouns of Unity achieved by the use of /aḥbub/ 'grain' in A.S.:

aḥbub	nṛ:uz	a grain of rice
aḥbub	nḍ:ṛa	a kernel of corn
aḥbub	w:aḍil	a grape

12 Such composed nouns in A.S. are:

u (son of)	of (ms)
ult (daughter of)	of (fs)
ulahl	parent, relative (ms)
ultlahl	parent, relative (fs)
bu (owner of)	of (ms)
ayt (owners of)	of (mp)
buyḥl:al	liar (ms)
ayt iḥl:al	liars (mp)
m: (mother of)	
suyt (mothers of)	
m:iḥl:al	liar (fs)
suytiḥl:al	liars (fp)

/bu/ and /m:/ can denote a trade or occupation :

buγaba	one in charge of a forest
bulḥm:am	public bath attendant (m)
m:lḥm:am	public bath attendant (f)

13 The construct state of the noun is the same in Ayt Seghrouchen as it is in Ayt Ayache.

V. Particles

This section discusses the Interrogative particles, Conjunctions, Prepositions, the Presentational particles, the Vocative particle and the Conditional particles in Ayt Ayache and Ayt Seghrouchen. Due to the fact that there is quite a difference between the two dialects in this domain of their lexicon, a full discussion of each of the headings mentioned above is given for Ayt Seghrouchen following that of Ayt Ayache.

V. Particles

V.1 Interrogative Particles (Ayt Ayache)

1) may ? — Who?

- mag:ms muḥa ? (may ims -→ mag:ms)	Who is Muha?
=muḥa amdaḳ:l nʕli ag:a	Muha is Ali's friend.
ms	to be related to (a verb of identification)
-may tms faḍma ?	Who is Fadma?
= faḍma mays nmuḥa ay tga	Fadma is Muha's mother

2) ma ~ may ? — What?

- ma dat:inid ?	What are you saying?
= walu	Nothing.
- may tn:id ?	What did you say?
= n:iγaš yaḷ:ah and:u γr tad:arṭ	I told you let us go home.
ini	to say
n:iγ	I said
n:iγaš	I said to you

3) mat:a ? — What? Which?

- mat:a was: ?	What day? (which day?)
= ltnayn	Monday.
- mat:a laswaq: n:a γr dat:d:ud ?	What markets do you go to?
= dant:sw:aq: midlt	We go to the Midelt market.

4) mi? — Who? What?

- šg: dmi ?	You and who?
= nk: dmuḥa	I and Muha.
- maṭiša dmi ?	Tomatoes and what?
= maṭiša dl:ubya	Tomatoes and green beans.

5) mani ? — Where?

- mani muḥa ? — Where is Muha?
= id:a γr s:uq: — He went to the market.
= il:a da — He is here.
= il:a din: — He is there.
= uril:i — He is not here.
= urs:inγ — I do not know.
= dγi ad:iʕayd — He will be back soon.

ili	to exist, to be
da	here
din:	there
dγi	now

6) maγr ? — Where?

- maγr id:a muḥa ? — Where did Muha go?
= id:a sigran — He went to the fields
- maγr td:id ? — Where are you going?
= d:iγ γr ʕari — I am going to the mountains.

7) mani luq:t ? — When?

- mani luq:t ay dit:ʕayad ʕli ? — What time will Aly be back?
= as:a — Today.
= ask:a — Tomorrow.
= adizri wask:a — The day after tomorrow.
= dγi — Now.

ʕayd	to return

8) milmi ? — When?

- milmi ay diʕayd muḥa ? — When did Muha come back ?
= urs:inγ — I do not know.
= iḍl:i — Yesterday.
- milmi ay dit:ʕayad muḥa ? — When will Muha be back?
= dγi ad:iʕayd — He will be back soon.

9) winmi (m) ?	Whose (m.)? (Notice: it is the object that is masculine)
- winmi igra ?	Whose field is this?
= winw	It's mine.
= win ʕli	It's Aly's
= wins	It's his/hers

10) tinmi (f) ?	Whose (f.)? (Notice: it is the object that is feminine)
- tinmi tad:arta ?	Whose house is this?
= tin ʕli	It's Aly's.
= tinw	mine
tinš	yours (m.s.)
tin:m	yours (f.s.)
tins	his/hers
tin:γ	ours
tin:un	yours (m.p.)
tin:ḳnt	theirs (m.)
tinsnt	theirs (f.)

11) milan ?	Whose?
- milan tad:arta ?	Whose house is this?
= tin muḥa	It's Muha's.

12) mimš ?	How?
- mimš ag:a ?	How is it?
= aml:al	White.
- mimš dat:g:ad iḍ:ʕam ?	How do you (s.) make couscous?
= urs:inγ	I don't know.

Notice: ag:a < ay iga (which it is)

13) šḥal ?	How many? How much?
~mšḥal ?	
~mšṭa ?	
- šḥal t:aman ?	What is the price?

=tlatin ryal	Thirty Rials
-ṣ̌hal tas:aˤt ?	What time is it?
=tsˤud dumnaṣf	9:30
-mšta l:wašun ay γurṣ̌	How many children do you have?
=γuṛi snat ntšir:atin	I have two girls.

14) max ?	Why?
max al:iy ?	Why ... ?
-max ?	Why?
=urs:inγ	I don't know.
-max al:iy did:a ?	Why did he come?
=t:afad adik: γr muḥa	In order to visit Muha.

15) mand:yịd ?	Which one (m or f)?
-mand:yid muha ag:d:an γr s:uq: ?	Which Muha went to the market?
=muha uˤq:a	Muha Ouakka.
-mand:yid fadma ag:d:an γr s:uq: ?	Which Fadma went to the market?
=faḍma usˤid	Fadma Ousaid.

Notice: (ag:d:an < ay id:an) 'who went'. id:an is the past participle of /d:u/ 'to go'. Whenever /ay + i ---> g:/ as in /ag:d:an/ this will be transcribed as one word.

16) mand:iyun ?	Which one of you (m)?
-mand:iyun ag:d:an γr s:uq: ?	Which one of you (m.) went to the market?
=muḥa ag:d:an	Muha.

17) mand:iknt ?	Which one of you (f)?
-mand:iknt ag:s:nwan aγṛum ?	Which one of you (f) baked the bread?
=faḍma	Fadma.
=nk:	I.

s:nw	to cook
18) mand:iynγ ?	Which one of us?
-mand:iynγ ay trid ?	Which one of us do you want?
=šg: amuḥa	You, Muha.
=šm: afaḍma	You, Fadma.
19) mand:iksn ?	Which one of them (m)?
-mand:iksn ay trid ?	Which one of them (m.) do you want?
=ʕli	Aly
-mand:iksn ag:swan atay ?	Which one of them (m) drank the tea?
=muḥa	Muha.
20) mand:iksnt ?	Which one of them (f.)?
-mand:iksnt ag:s:nwan aγṛum ?	Which one of them (f) baked the bread ?
=faḍma	Fadma.
21) is ?	Do-Have-Is/Are?
-istrid atay ?	Do you want tea?
=la . riγ lq:hwa	No, I want coffee.
-isid:a muḥa ?	Did Muha go?
=y:ih	Yes.
22) id: ?	Do-Have-Is/Will/Are?
-id: tad:artnš aya ?	Is this your house?
=y:ih	Yes.
-id: nt:a ?	Is it him?
-id: nt:at ?	Is it her?
=la	No.
-id:adixdm ?	Is he going to work? Will he work?
=la	No.

/id:/ is here transcribed as part of a verbal construction but autonomous from a following noun.

V.2 Interrogative Particles (Ayt Seghrouchen)

1. may — Who?

-mag:ms muḥnd ?	Who is Muhnd
-muḥnd amd:ak:l nˤli ag:žu	Mohamed is Aly's friend.
-maytms mam:a ?	Who is Mamma?
-mam:a im:as m:uhnd aytžu . (< n+muḥnd)	Mamma is Mohamed's mother.

2. may — What?

-may t:init ?	What are you saying?
-walu	Nothing
-may tn:it ?	What did you say?
-n:ixaš yal:ah an:raḥ ɣr tad:art .	I told you, "Let's go home."

3. mat:a — What, which

-mat:a was: ?	What,which day?
-lt:nayn	Monday
-mat:a laswaq: din ɣr tg:urt ?	Which market do you go to?
-l:atsw:aq:x sḳ:ura	I go to Skoura market.

4. mi — Who, what.

-šk: dmi ?	You and who (else) ?
-ntš dmuḥnd .	Muhnd and I.
-maṭiša dmi ?	Tomatoes and what?
-maṭiša dl:ubya	Tomatoes and green beans.

5. mani — Where?

mani muḥnd ?	Where is Muhnd?
-iraḥ ɣr s:uq:	He went to the market.
-il:a da - -	He is here.
-il:a din: - -	He is there.
-uril:i	He is not
-urs:inx	I do not know
-durt:x ad:iˤid	He will be back soon.

6. maγr	Why?
-maγr da tq:imt ?	Why are you staying here?
urufx mani γr γa raḥx	I do not know where to go.(Lit: I do not find where to go).
7. <u>mat:a luq:t</u>	When, What time.
mat:a luq:t ayd:γa iˁid ˁli ?	When is Aly coming back?
-iḍu	Today.
8. <u>mlmi ~ milmi</u>	When ?
-mlmi ayd:iˁid muḥnd	When did Muhnd come back?
-urs:inx	I do not know.
-idn:aṭ	Yesterday.
-mlmi ayd:γayˁid muḥnd	When is Muhnd coming back?
-durṭx ad:iˁid	He will be back soon.
9. <u>wim:i (< win + mi), wig:ilin</u>	Whose (m) ?
wig:ilin ižru ?	Whose field is this?
winw	Mine.
win ˁli	Aly's.
win:s	His.
10. tim:i ~ wig:ilin ? (< tin + mi)	Whose is...?
wig:ilin tad:artu ~ tim:i tad:artu	Whose house is this?
tinˁli	Aly's.
tin:š	Yours (ms).
tin:m	Yours (fs).
tin:s	His/ Hers.
tin:x	Ours.
tin:un	yours (mp).
tin:šnt	Yours (fp).
tin:sn	Theirs (mp).
tin:snt	Theirs (fp).

11. <u>wig:ilin</u>	Whose is...
wig:ilin tad:artu ?	Whose house is this?
tim:uḥnd (<tin + muḥnd)	It is Muhnd's.
12. <u>mism</u>	How
mism ag:žu ?	How is it?
aml:al	White.
mism ayt:g:t iwutšu ?	How do you do couscous?
13. <u>mšḥal ~ mšta</u> ?	How much, how many?
-mšḥal t:aman ?	How much is it? (liter. "How much is the price.
-tlatin ryal .	30 rials
-mšḥal tas:aˤt ?	What time is it?
-t:sˤa wnṣ:	9:30
-mšḥal l:wašun ayγ rš ?	How many children do you have?
-γri snat ntšir:atin	I have two girls.
14. <u>mah , mah azg:a</u>	Why?. Why....?
-mah ?	
-urs:inx	I do not know.
-mah azg:a d:iraḥ ?	Why did he come?
-t:af ad:ik: γr muḥnd .	So that he visits Muhnd.
15. <u>mandg:it</u> ?	
-mandg:it muḥnd ag:ṛaḥn γr s:uq: ?	Which Muhnd went to the market?
-muḥnd uˤq:a	Muhnd Ouakka.
16. <u>mandiwn</u>	Which one? (among you (m))
-mandiwn ag:raḥn γr s:uq: ?	Which one of you went to the market?
-muḥnd ag:raḥn	It is Muhnd who went.

17. <u>mandiwnt</u>	which one (of you (f)) ?
-mandiwnt ag:s:nwn aɣṛum ?	Which one of you cooked the bread?
-mam:a	Mamma.
-ntš .	I.
18. <u>mandinx</u>	who among us
-mandinx aytbɣit ?	
-šk: amuḥnd .	you, Muḥnd
-šm: amam:a .	you, Mamma
19. <u>mandisn</u>	who, which among them (m)
-mandisn aytbɣit ?	Who/ which one do you want?
-ʕli .	Aly.
-mandisn ag:swin at:ay ?	Who among them drank tea?
-muḥnd .	Muḥnd.
20. <u>mandisnt</u>	who/which one of them (f)
-mandisnt ag:s:nawn aɣṛum ?	Which one is cooking bread?
-mam:a	Mamma.
21. <u>is</u>	Interrogative particle
-is tbɣit at:ay ?	Do you want tea?
-la , bɣix lq:hwa .	No. I want coffee.
-is iṛaḥ muḥnd ?	Did Muḥnd go?
-y:ih .	Yes.
22. <u>isd</u>	Interrogative particle
-isdtad:artn:š ayu ? > ist:ad:artn:š ayu ?	Is this your house?
-y:ih	Yes.
-isd + nt:a --->isn:t:a	Is it him?
-isd + nt:at --->isn:t:at	Is it her?
-la	No.
-isd adixdm ?	Is he going to work?
-urs:inx	I do not know.

V.3 Conjunctions

V.3.1 Ayt Ayache

1)	l:iy	when
	ad:ay	
	nd:a l:iy did:a	When he came we left
	ad:ay nwin waman adᶜmrγ atay .	When the water boils, I will make tea.
2)	l:iy	while
	l:iy das:araγ žmᶜγ dᶜli .	While I was walking, I met Aly .
3)	γas an:axf γas	as soon as
	γas an:axf t:užadm nd:u	As soon as you (m.p.) are ready we will go
	γas adnwin waman adᶜm:rγ atay	As soon as the water boils I'll make tea.
4)	ay	who, which
	n:a	
	muḥa ag: d:an . (< ay id:an)	It's Muha who went.
	faḍma ag: d:an .	It's Fatma who went.
	tiṣ̌ir:atin ag: d:an .	It's the girls who went.
	argaz n:a yd:an , yma ag:a .	The man who went is my brother.
	l:una ay xṭarγ .	It's this color which I choose.
	l:un n:a xṭarγ aya .	This is the color which I choose.
	lᶜil n:a yran lk:as aya.	This is the boy who wants the glass.
	han lᶜil n:a yran lk:as.	There is the boy who wants the glass.
	tarb:at: n:a yran lk:as aya .	This is the girl who wants the glass.
	han tarb:at n:a yran lk:as .	There is the girl who wants the glass.
	tafunast n:a ytšan tuya aya .	This is the cow that ate the grass.

han tafunast n:a ytšan tuya .	There is the cow that ate the grass.
5) aḳ:ma	whatever
aḳ:mani	wherever
aḳ:milmi	whenever
aḳ:an:a	whatever
aḳ:un:a	whoever
aḳ:ma γr id:a, yaf žḥa .	Wherever he goes, he finds Jeha.
aḳ:mani γr id:a , yaf žha .	Wherever he goes, he finds Jeha.
ad:ud γur:γ aḳ:milmi	Come to see us, whenever (you want).
aḳ:an:a trid adaštšγ .	I'll give you whatever you want.
aḳ:wn:a did:an tšmas atay .	Give tea to whoever comes here.
6) d	and
id:a muḥa dᵊli γrs:uq: .	Muha and Ali went to the market.
7) walayn:i	but
walakn:i	
maša	
d:iγ walayn:i urn:ufiγ muḥa .	I went but I did not find Muha.
8) la ... ula ...	neither...nor...
urifhim la lmalik ula lwazirns	Neither the king nor
ayn:a yn:a žḥa .	his minister understood what Jeha said.
9) al:iy	until
al:	until
iq:ṛa al:iy iwḥl .	He studied until he got tired.

q:im al: did:u .	Stay until he comes.
10) t:afad	so that
ḥma	in order to
rb:aɣ tamaziɣt t:afad adsiwlɣ imd:n da .	I studied Berber so that I could talk to people here.
ṛb:aɣ tamaziɣt ḥma adsiwlɣ imd:n da .	I studied Berber so that I could talk to people here.
11) ʕlaḥq:	because
riɣt ʕlaḥq: iẓil .	I like him because he is nice.
12) mad	or
is trid lq:hwa mad atay ?	Do you want coffee or tea?

V.3.2 <u>Ayt Seghrouchen</u>

1) zg:a	when
ad:ay	
nṛaḥ zg:a d:iraḥ .	We left when he came.
ad:ay nun waman adʕm:ṛx at:ay	When the water boils, I will make tea.
2) zg:a	while
zg:a s:arix žmʕx dʕli .	I met Ali while I was walking.
3) xas , adinx	as soon as
xas adnun waman adʕm:ṛx at:ay .	I'll make tea as soon as the water is boiled.
adinx t:užidm an:ṛaḥ .	We will leave as soon as you are ready.
4) ay , din	who, which
muḥnd ag:ṛaḥn .	It is Muhnd who left.
lwašun ag:ṛaḥn	It is the kids who left.

mam:a ag:ṛaḥn	It is Mamma who left.
tišir:atin ag:ṛaḥn	It is the girls who left .
l:unu ayxṭarx .	It is this color I chose.
l:un din xṭarx ayu .	This is the color I chose.
arba din ibγan lkas ayu .	That is the boy who wants the glass.
haš arba din ibγan lkas .	There is the boy who wants the glass.
tarbat: din ibγan lkas ayu.	This is the girl who wants the glass.
hašn: tarbat: din ibγan lkas .	There is the girl who wants the glass.
tafunast din itšin tuža ayu .	This is the cow which ate the grass.
hašn: tafunast din itšin tuža .	There is the cow which ate the grass.
haš aryaz din γr sγix ižru .	This is the man from whom I bought the field.

5) ak:adin — whatever

ak:mani — wherever

ak:adin in:a žḥa iṭṣ lmalik: .	The king laughed at anything Jeha said.
ak:mani γr iṛaḥ ižmɤ džḥa .	He meets Jeha wherever he goes.

6) d — and, with

iṛaḥ muḥa dɤli γr s:uq:	Muha and Ali went to the market.

7) walayn:i , walakayn:i , maša — but

rahx {walayn:i / walakayn:i / maša} urn:ufix muḥnd

8) la ----ula — neither, nor

urifhim la lmalik: ula lwazirn:s adin in:a žḥa .	Neither the king nor his minister understood what Jeha said.

ul:it:t:x la lbṣl la tiš:rt — I eat neither onions nor garlic.

9) azg:a — till, until

al:

iq:ṛa azg:a ywḥl — He studied until he got tired.

q:im al: d:iṛaḥ . — Stay until he comes.

10) t:af — in order to, so that.

žm:ʕ lflus t:af at:aft mas γatsγt ṭ:unubiḷ . — Save money so that you buy a car. (Lit: so that you find what to buy a car with.)

11) ʕlaḥq: — because

bγixt ʕlaḥq: iʕdl . — I like him because he is nice.

12) mad — or

is tbγit lq:hwa mad at:ay ? — Do you want coffee or tea?

V.4 Prepositions

V.4.1 Ayt Ayache

1) s , γr , i — to (for)

id:a sasif — He went to the river.

id:a γr s:uq: — He went to the market.

šasd ṣ:init imuḥa adiʕm:ṛ . — Give Muha the tray (and the tea pot & glasses) so that he can make tea.

ts:nwa faḍma aγṛum imuḥa . — Fadma baked bread for Muha.

2) γr / --Noun — at

γuṛ/ -- Pronoun

insa ḥd:u γr muḥa . — Haddu spent the night at Muha's place.

3) y — in

il:a ytad:art . — He is home (in the house).

Notice: y + i --->g:

y + a --->g̣:

y irdn ------->g:irdn — in the wheat

y abrid ------>g̣:brid — in the road

4) s — with (instrumental)

yumẓt: sufus — He held it (f.) with the hand.

5) s — to (Directional)

id:a sasif — He went to the river.

Notice: A noun is in the Construct State after instrumental /s/ but not after directional /s/.

6) xf / --- Noun — on

ɣif / ---Pronoun

tl:a xf ḍ:bla — It (f.) is on the table.

tl:a ɣifs . — It (f.) is on it.

7) tf:ir — behind

ḍar

il:a tf:ir ntad:art . — He is behind the house.

tl:a ḍar ntad:artns . — She is behind her house.

8) dat — in front of

il:a dat ntad:art — He is in front of the house.

9) zy — from

id:ad zy midlt . — He came from Midelt.

td:ad tbrat: zymuḥa . — A letter came from Muha.

10) n — of

ha tasarut: ntad:art . — Here is the key for the house.

Notice: <u>phonological</u> <u>changes</u> of /n/

n + lbab -------> l:bab		of the door .
n + atay -------> w:atay		of tea
n + iful:usn ---> yful:usn		of chickens
n + z:itun -----> nz:itun		of olives

11) ingr — between

am:as — in the middle of

tl:a ingr tiwṛiq:in l:kṇ:aš — It (f.) is between the pages of the notebook.

tl:a am:as l:kṇ:aš . — It (f.) is in the middle of the note book.

12) qbl — before

id:ad qbl tifawt . — He came before dawn.

13) tf:ir — after

id:ad tf:ir l:xṭubt . — He came after the Friday prayer.

14) d:aw — under

tl:a d:aw nḍ:bla . — It (f.) is under the table.

V.4.2 <u>Ayt Seghrouchen</u>

1) γr , i — to

iṛaḥ γr iγzr . — He went to the river.

iṛaḥ γr s:uq: . — He went to the market.

ušd: ṣ:iny:a imuḥnd adiˤm:ṛ . — Give Mohand the tray (and the tea pot and glasses) so that he will make tea.

ts:nu mam:a aγṛum imuhnd . — Mamma baked bread for Mohand.

2) γr — at (chez in French)

insu ḥd:u γr muḥa . — Haddou spent the night at Moha's place.

3) y — in

il:a ytad:art — He is home (in the house)

Notice: y + i ---->g:
y + a ---->g:

y + irdn ---------->g:irdn — in the wheat

y + abrid --------> g:brid — in the road

4) s — with (instrumental)

it:ft: sufus . — He held it (f.) with the hand.

5) x — on

tl:a xt:bla — It (f.) is on the table.

tl:a xs . — It (f.) is on it.

Notice: xfi = on me

6) df:ir — behind

il:a df:ir ntad:art . — He is behind the house.

7) zdat — in front of

il:a zdat ntad:art . — He is in front of the house.

8) zy — from

irahd: zy midlt . — He came from Midelt.

trahd: tbrat: zy muha . — A letter came from Muha.

9) n — of

ha tsarut: ntad:art . — Here is the key for the house.

Notice: phonological changes of /n/

n + lbab --------> l:bab — of the door

n + at:ay --------> w:at:ay — of tea

n + udi ---------> w:udi — of the butter

n + ifilan -------> y:filan — of the threads

10) žar between

am:as in the middle

tl:a žar tiwṛiqin l:ḳn:aš . It (f.) is between the pages of the notebook.

11) qbl , zdat before

iṛaḥd: zdat l:fžr . He came before dawn.

12) df:ir after

iṛaḥd: df:ir l:xŭḍbt . He came after the Friday prayer.

13) d:aw under

tl:a d:aw nṭ:bla . It (f.) is under the table.

V.5 The Presentational Particles.

1) ha (A.A. and A.S.) must be followed by a noun: Here...is, Here...are

ha muḥa id:ad Here comes Muha (A.A)

ha muḥnd iraḥd: Here comes Muha (A.S)

2) han (A.A.) followed by a noun

hat (A.A.) followed by a verbal form

haš (A.S.) followed by a noun

haš (A.S.) plus a third person pronominal suffix

han muḥa id:ad Here comes Muha (A.A.)

hat id:ad . Here he comes (A.A.)

haš muḥnd iraḥd: Here comes Muha (A.S.)

hašt Here he is

hašt: Here she is.

haštn Here they are (m.)

haštnt Here they (f.) are.

V.6 Vocative Particle

a — vocative particle (Oh, you)

This is the same both in Ayt Ayache and Ayt Seghrouchen.

ad:ud amuḥa . — Come here Muha. (Ayt Ayache)

awru anmuḥnd . — Come here Muha (Ayt Seghrouchen)

V.7 Conditional Particles

(1) mš (A.A.,A.S.) — if (possible, probable)

mš dḥr: isignaw adwit ụṇẓaṛ (A.A.) .
If clouds appear, it rains.

mš imṛḍ ḥd: layt:waʕad aḍbib (A.S.) .
If somebody is sick, he sees the doctor.

(2) mšur (A.A.,A.S.) — if not (possible, probable)

mšur did:i ask:a , add:uɣ ɣrmidlt (A.A.) .
mšur d:irah dutša , adraḥx ɣmidlt (A.S.) .
If he does not come tomorrow, I'll go to Midelt.

(3) mr (A.A., A.S.) — if (contrary to fact, impossible)

mr ɣuri l:in lflus iḍl:i , l:asɣiɣ igran nʕli (A.A.) .
If I had had the money yesterday, I would have bought Aly's fields.

mr d:iṛaḥ . l:awšixas lḥžab (A.S.).
Had he come, I would have given him the amulet.

(4) mrid: (A.A.), mlid: (A.S.) if (contrary to fact, impossible)

mrid: ša yaḍn , urit:awy taqb:uta sql:mn sbˁmysat ryal (A.A.)
If it were somebody else, I would not have given him the djellaba for less than 700 Ryals.

mrid: isuridawa ḍ:aḷb lˁil , l:aym:ut . (A.A.)
Had the Sheikh not cured the boy, he would have died.

mlid: ḥd: ḍnin yurit:awy taqb:ut:u sql: mnsbˁmy:at ryal (A.S.) .
It it were somebody else, I would not have given him the djellaba for less than 700 Ryals.

mlid: isuridawi t:alb arba l:aym:ut (A.S.) .
Had the Sheikh not cured the boy, he would have died.

VI. Grammar of the Verb

This section treats the grammar of the verb in Ayt Ayache in an exhaustive manner. It discusses Verb Stems (both basic and derived) as well as Noun Stems (Verbal Nouns). It also discusses Temporal and Modal derivations. Examples and rules for all the derivations are included in this section. A morphophonemic sketch stating forty-four possible changes appears at the end of this section.

Notes on the grammar of the verb in Ayt Seghrouchen, showing differences from Ayt Ayache with ample examples, appear before Appendices A and B. Appendix A is a Verb Sample Appendix for Ayt Ayache. It is followed by a verb list of 450 verbs from that dialect. Appendix B is a Verb Sample Appendix for Ayt Seghrouchen.

VI. Grammar of the Verb

VI.1 Basic and Derived Verb Stems

VI.1.1 Basic Verb Stems

All unaugmented stems (1-77) appearing in position a) in the Verb Sample Appendix A (pp. 245-261) are basic verb stems (V). As is seen from the examples, some basic verb stems (V) are clearly borrowings from Arabic. However, these stems are now considered an integral part of Tamazight verb lexicon, since they conform completely to the derivational and inflectional patterns of the native stems: e.g., Basic verb stems 45 /zdm/* 'collect wood'** (Native or Berber) and 44 /xdm/ 'work' (Arabic loan), derive the following nouns of agent : /azd:am/, /izd:amn/, /tazd:amt/, /tizd:amin/ and /axd:am/, /ixd:amn/, /taxd:amt/, /tixd:amin/ (ms, mp, fs, fp respectively for each set). Temporal and Modal derivations and even native ablaut (see VI.3.1) that apply to V45 /zdm/ (Berber) apply to V44 /xdm/ (Arabic): e.g., /zdmγ/ 'I collected wood', /xdmγ/ 'I worked'; /urnzdim/ 'we did not collect wood' and /urnxdim/ 'we did not work'.

VI.1.2 Derived Verb Stems

All augmented verb stems appearing in position a) in

---

* A number preceding a form (or a stem) refers to the place of V (Basic Verb Stem) in the Verb Sample Appendix A pp. 245-261

** Meanings of V's are glossed as infinitives without "to".

the Verb Sample Appendix are derived stems (Causative SV, Reciprocal MV, Recipro-Causative MSV, and Passive TuV). To support the statement made in VI.1.1 above about the conformity of borrowed stems to native derivational patterns, the following examples are here cited using derivatives of stems /γus /,/ʕum / and /kmz/, /frs/:

V		SV	MSV
γus	'be burnt' (Berber)	sγus	m:sγus
ʕum	'swim' (Arabic loan)	sʕum	m:sʕum
V		MV	TuV
kmz	'scratch' (Berber)	m:kmaz	t:ukmz
frs	'attack' (Arabic loan)	m:fras	t:ufrs

VI.2 Verb Affixes

Verb affixes are either movable or fixed affixes.

VI.2.1 Movable Affixes

A movable affix is one that is now pre-verbal, (i.e. prefixed to the stem), now post-verbal (i.e. suffixed to the stem). This section discusses two sets of affixes, the Orientational Affixes and the Object Pronominal Affixes.

The Orientational Affixes are: /d/[1] denoting proximity, and /n:/ denoting remoteness. Thus from 71 /d:u/ 'go' we get: /i-d:a/ 'he went', /i-d:a-d/ 'he came', /i-d:a-n:/ 'he went there'.[1] (For Comparative Notes, see pp. 216-239)

Included as movable affixes are object pronominal affixes.

The positions of /d/ and /n:/ as well as that of the object pronominal affixes have been stated in III.3 pp. 44-46 Pronominal Systems under the heading Pronominal Affixes for Verbs and Prepositions.

VI.2.2 Fixed Affixes

A fixed affix is either a prefix, a suffix, or a discontinuous morpheme.

a) Prefixes:

1) Derived Stem Prefixes. This group is prefixed either to a basic verb stem (V) to form a derived verb stem (SV, MV, MSV, TuV) or to a derived verb stem to form its habitual verb stem (SVH, MVH, MSVH, TuVH). VH, the habitual verb stem of unaugmented V, is also derived by the realization of T (see No. 5 below; also see VI.4.2)

These prefixes are here symbolized as

1. S - for causative derivation SV
2. M - for reciprocal derivation MV
3. MS - for recipro-causative derivation MSV
4. Tu - for passive derivation TuV
5. T - for habitual derivation HV, SVH, MVH, MSVH, TuVH

A rare but possible derivation is a TuSV derivation which is a passive derived from a causative stem e.g. 33 /t:usfrḥ/.

2) Temporal and Modal Affixes. This group of Tense and Mode prefixes derives the future and present tenses and their negative and interrogative modes as well as the modes of the past tense.

(i) Temporal Prefixes. There are two temporal prefixes (one for future tense and one for present tense derivations) and an aspectual prefix that derives a progressive or inchoative action.

Future Tense Prefix /ad-/: This prefix derives a future tense from V, SV, MV, MSV or TuV: e.g. 11 /ʕum/ 'swim', /ad-ʕum-γ / 'I will swim'.

Present Tense Prefix /da-/ ~ /l:a-/.[2] This prefix derives a present tense from VH, SVH, MVH, MSVH, or TuVH: e.g., 11 /ʕum/ 'swim' /t:ʕum/ VH, /da-t:ʕum-γ / /l:a-t:ʕum-γ / 'I swim'.

Progressive or Inchoative Action Prefix /ar-/.[3] This prefix derives a progressive or inchoative action from VH, SVH, MVH, MSVH or TuVH: e.g., 11 /ʕum/ 'swim', /t:ʕum/ VH, /ar-t:ʕum-γ / 'I started to swim, I began to swim'.

(ii) Modal Prefixes. This section discusses the derivation of the negative and/or interrogative modes of the verb listing the prefixes used in such derivatives with examples illustrating the generated structure.

Interrogative: /id:-/[4] occurs before the temporal prefix /ad-/ to derive an interrogative future construction: e.g., 11 /ʕum/ 'swim' /ad-ʕum-ɣ/ 'I will swim', /id:-ad-ʕum-ɣ / 'Will I swim?'

Interrogative: /is-/[5] occurs before a V, SV, MV, MSV, or TuV inflected for person-number-gender to derive a past tense interrogative construction or before /da-/ (see (i) above) to derive an interrogative present construction:e.g., 11 /ʕum/ 'swim' /ʕum-ɣ / 'I swam' /is-ʕum-ɣ / 'did I swim?' /t:ʕum/ VH, /da-t:ʕum- ɣ/ 'I swim' /is-da-t:ʕum-ɣ / 'do I swim?'

Negative: /ur-/[6] occurs before an affirmative construction to derive a negative one: e.g. 11 /ʕum /'swim' /t:ʕum/ VH, /ʕum-ɣ/ 'I swam', /ur-ʕumɣ/ 'I did not swim' /da-t:ʕum -ɣ/ 'I swim', /ur-da-t:ʕum-ɣ/ 'I do not swim'.

Negative-Interrogative: A negative construction derived by the prefix /ur-/ may be preceded by the in errogative prefix /is-/ to derive a negative interrogative construction:

e.g.,	/ʕum/ 'swim'	/ur-ʕum-ɣ/	I did not swim.
		/is-ur-ʕum-ɣ/	Didn't I swim?
	/t:ʕum/ VH	/ur-da-t:ʕum-ɣ/	I do not swim.
		/is-ur-da-t:ʕum-ɣ/	Don't I swim?

b) Suffixes

There are two sets of suffixes, both of which are used for Imperative Derivations.

Imperative Mode Derivational Suffixes: The suffixes shown in Table 1 derive (second person) imperative constructions whereas the suffixes in Table 2, derive hortatory (first person) constructions. Notice that person-dual occurs only in the hortatory construction in this dialect. The negative imperative is derived by prefixation of /adur-/ to VH, SVH or MVH and suffixation of -PNG set shown in Table 1.

PNG	Imper. Suffix
2 s m	-Ø
2 s f	-Ø
2 p m	-at
2 p f	-nt

Table 1

Second Person Imperative Suffixes 7

PNG	Imper. Suffix
1 d m	-aγ
1 d f	-am
1 p m	-ataγ
1 p f	-ntaγ

Table 2

Hortatory Suffixes 7

c) Person-Number-Gender Affixes

There is only one set for the inflection for /-PNG-/ in ALL TENSES in Tamazight (See Table 3.).

P N G	Inflectional Affix
1 s	______ɣ
2 s	t______d
3 s m	i______
3 s f	t______
1 p	n______
2 p m	t______m
2 p f	t______nt
3 p m	______n
3 p f	______nt

Table 3

Ayt Ayache /-PNG-/ Affixes 8

Another morpheme that should be mentioned here is the Participle Morpheme /-n/. Since the realization of -PNG- effects a change in the stem of certain verb classes in the past tense, therefore the participle rule must be applied after the realization of the features for $P_3N_sG_m$ and the Modal prefix to allow for the occurrence of the ablaut. (See VI.3.1)

The suffix /-n/ is common to the three participles: Present, Past and Future participles

(See also Tables 11-39 A.S. pp. 220-237)

VI.3 Classification of Verb Stems[9]

This section discusses the grouping of unaugmented verb stem into two types, four classes and nine sub-classes as is done in the Sample Appendix.

The underlying structure of the verb stem in Tamazight is ‖ABCD‖ . Here ‖A‖ represents the first radical, ‖B‖ represents the second radical and so forth. If ‖B‖, for example, is a [+tense] radical (e.g., t:, d:, m:, etc.), it is referred to as ‖B:‖ and to the stem as ‖AB:CD‖; if it is a vowel, it is referred to as ‖V‖ and to the stem as ‖AVCD‖.

The classification of Tamzzight verb stems is based primarily on an ablaut that occurs in the past tense for particular classes (see VI.3.1) and secondarily on the derivational processes of derived verb stems (Causative, Reciprocal and Passive verb stems and their Habitual stems; see VI.4. The sub-classification is based on several factors shown in VI.3.2.

Tamazight verb stems may then be classified into two types: Ablauted and Non-Ablauted. The ablauted type is characterized by having all its members with third radical ‖C‖ = ‖ø‖ in their underlying structures whereas the unablauted type does not have a ‖ø‖ as third radical (See VI. 3.1) The general structure of the unablauted type is

‖AB(C)(D)‖ whereas that of the ablauted type is ‖(A)B(:)Ø(D)‖ In more detail the structure of the ablauted type is $\left\{ \begin{array}{l} \|AB(:)\emptyset(D)\| \\ \|OB(:)\emptyset(D)\| \end{array} \right\}$ The positing of a null radical for ‖ A ‖ symbolized as ‖O‖ accounts for the structure of such ablauted stems as 66 /g/ 'be, do', 68 /g̣:/ 'knead', 69 /k:/ 'pass' and 57 /f:r/ 'hide' with the underlying structures /OgØ/, /Og̣:Ø/, /Ok:Ø/ and /Of:Ør/ respectively.

VI.3.1 The Different Ablauts

Ablaut occurs (for some verb classes) only in the affirmative and/or negative past. The ablaut of the interrogative past follows that of the affirmative past; the negative-interrogative ablaut is the same as the negative past. For this reason we will refer only to affirmative and negative past and mark them as [-Negative] and [+ Negative]: e.g., 70 /ls/ 'get dressed': /i-lsa/ 'he got dressed', /is-ilsa/ 'did he get dressed?', /ur-i-lsi/ 'he did not get dressed', /isur-ilsi/ 'didn't he get dressed?'.

The following discussion is meant to show the kinds of ablauts that occur in Tamazight and the rules governing their occurrence.

VI.3.1.1 Zero Ablaut /Ø/

We must distinguish between zero and no ablaut. The

latter is a characteristic of such verb stems as 1 - 25 in the Appendix that do <u>not</u> have an underlying structure with ‖C‖ = ‖Ø‖ . Zero ablaut, /Ø/, is characteristic of the others (25 - 77 with ‖C‖ = ‖Ø‖): e.g., 9 /sal/ 'ask' has no ablaut as in /sal-γ/ 'I asked', /ur-sal-γ/ 'I did not ask'; whereas 70 /ls/ (underlying form /lsØ/) 'get dressed' is ablauted and thus gives: /lsi-γ/ 'I got dressed' and /ur-lsi-γ/ 'I did not get dressed'.

The following examples of verb stems, both in their underlying and surface structures, show the occurrence of /Ø/ as the ‖C‖ radical of certain sub-classes to which this grammar refers as ablauted. Also included in the examples are unablauted verb stems whose ‖C‖ radicals are not /Ø/.

	Underlying Structure ABCD	Surface Structure	
3	fa	fa	'yawn'
6	šk:a	šk:a	'doubt'
1	dawa	dawa	'cure'
9	sal	sal	'ask'
18	xṭar	xṭar	'choose'
21	ḥudr	ḥudr	'bend, be low'
33	frØḥ	frḥ	'be happy'
34	fs:Ør	fs:r	'explain'

52	amØẓ	amẓ	'take'
57	Of:Ør	f:r	'hide'
62	afØ	af	'find'
63	aš:Øk	aš:k	'be lost'
64	arØr	rar	'return'
66	OgØ	g	'be, do'
70	lsØ	ls	'get dressed'
71	Od:Øu	d:u	'go'
77	irØi	iri	'want'

Thus the major distinction is whether the underlying structure of the stem has its ||C|| radical as ||Ø|| (e.g., 26-77 in the Verb Appendix) or not (e.g., 1-25 in the Verb Appendix). Based on this distinction, Tamazight verb stems are classified into two types:

A - Unablauted (1-25 in Verb Appendix)

B - Ablauted (26-77 in Verb Appendix)

VI.3.1.2 [Ø:i/a] Ablaut

The most distinctive ablaut is the change of /Ø/ referred to in VI.3.1.1 above to /i/ in the Past$_{[-Negative]}$ for $P_1N_sG_{m\&f}$, $P_2N_sG_{m\&f}$ and to /a/ in the Past$_{[-Negative]}$ for PNG other than these mentioned here.

Using this feature, the Ablauted Type (26-77) is classified into two classes:

- [Ø:i/a] +

-	+
/frØḥ/	/af/
/fs:Ør/	/aš:Øk/
/amØz/	/arØr/
/Of:Ør/	/lsØ/
	/Od:Øu/
	/irØi/

[Ø:O] and [Ø:i/a] Classes of Ablauted Verb Stems

Examples of [Ø:i/a] Ablaut: (For complete conjugations of ablauted and unablauted verb stems, see Tables 4,5, and 6)

70 /ls/ (< /lsØ/)

lsiγ	'I got dressed'
tlsid	'you (s) got dressed'
ilsa	'he got dressed'
tlsa	'she got dressed'

Examples of [- Ø:i/a] (which will be referred to as [Ø:O], i.e. zero: null ablaut):

33 frḥ (< frØḥ)

frḥγ	'I was happy'
tfrḥd	'you were happy'
ifrḥ	'he was happy'
tfrḥ	'she was happy'

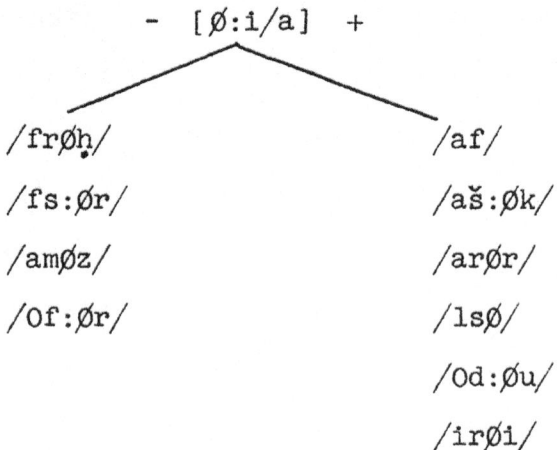

VI.3.1.3 Predictable Ablauts

Two other predictable ablauts are: [Ø:i] ablaut and [a:u] ablaut.

VI.3.1.3-a [Ø:i] Ablaut

This is a change of /Ø/ to /i/ in the past for <u>all</u> PNG. This is, of course, a general ablaut since it occurs with all ablauted stems: e.g., 70 /ls/ (</lsØ/): /lsiɣ/ 'I got dressed', /urlsiɣ/ 'I did not get dressed', /ilsa/ 'he got dressed', /urilsi/ 'he did not get dressed'; 33 /frḥ/: /frḥɣ/ 'I was happy', /urfriḥɣ/ 'I was not happy', /ifrḥ/ 'he was happy', /urifriḥ/ 'he was not happy'.

VI.3.1.3-b [a:u] Ablaut

This is a change of /a/ to /u/ (for ablauted stems). Thus any stem with ‖A‖ = /a/ and ‖C‖ = /Ø/ undergoes this change of /a/ ⟶ /u/ in the Past [±Neg]. This accounts for the fact that such stems as 12 /an:ay/ 'see' and 13 /aẓum/ 'fast' are classified as unablauted since their ‖C‖ is not /Ø/ : e.g., 62 /af/ (/afØ/) 'find': /ufiɣ/ 'I found', /urufiɣ/ 'I didn't find', /yufa/ 'he found', /uryufi/ 'he did not find'.

VI.3.1.4 Metathesis

The role of metathesis is important in stating the

structure of certain sub-classes of verbs in Tamazight. A look at 9 /sal/ 'ask' and 64 /rar/ 'return' shows that they have identical surface structures. However, their underlying structures are different: 9 /sal/ has /sal/ as underlying structure whereas the underlying struc ure of 64 /rar/ is /arØr/.

A verb base (i.e. the underlying structure of the verb stem) may be marked for [±Metathesis] which affects its ‖AB‖ and/or ‖ØD‖ radicals: e.g., /arØr/ ⟶ /rarØ/; /as:Øk/ ⟶ /as:kØ/; or its ‖B"Ø‖ radicals: e.g., /grØ/ ⟶ /gØr/. Stems marked for double metathesis (i.e. the /arØr/ ⟶ /rarØ/structure) are rare in this dialect. Lexicons and dictionaries of Tamazight list three to five verbs with this particular structure. Stems of the /as:Øk/ ⟶ /as:kØ/ and the /grØ/ ⟶ /gØr/ structures are rare also.

VI.3.1.5 Predictable Changes in the Sub-class /d:u/ - /iri/

This sub-class is characterized by having ‖D‖ = ‖V‖ where ‖V‖ is either /u/ or /i/ but not /a/. A predictable change occurs with the realization of person-number-gender in the Past$_{[\pm \text{Negative}]}$ to the members of this sub-class whose structure (whether /bdu/, /d:u/, /ˁd:u/, or /iri/). This is $\| (A)B\emptyset V\| \longrightarrow \| (A)B\emptyset / \_\_ V = \left\{ \begin{matrix} u \\ i \end{matrix} \right\}$.

In addition another rule that is necessary for any stem with ‖A‖ = /#i-/ whether ablauted or not (e.e. 77 or 15) is one that deletes initial /#i-/ before the realization of /-PNG-/ in the $\text{Past}_{[\pm\text{Negative}]}$. It will thus operate on unablauted 15 /iẓil/ 'be nice' as well as on ablauted 77 /iri/ 'want'.

Examples of the above-mentioned changes are: /šmu/ (< /šmØu/) 'smoke': /šmiγ/ 'I smoked', /uršmiγ/ 'I did not smoke', /išma/ 'he smoked', /urišmi/ 'he did not smoke' and 77 /iri/ (< /irØi/) 'want': /riγ/ 'I wanted', /ur:iγ/ 'I did not want', /ira/ 'he wanted/, /uriri/ 'he did not want'. (See full paradigms in Tables 5 and 6.)

VI.3.2 Classes and Sub-classes of the Two Types of Tamazight Verb Stems

This section discusses the bases of the classification of Tamazight verb stems into two types, four classes and nine sub-classes.

VI.3.2.1 Ablauted and Unablauted Types

Based on the occurrence or non-occurrence of a ‖Ø‖ as the ‖C‖ radical of their underlying structures, Tamazight verb stems are classified into two types:

A Ablauted (with ‖C‖ = ‖Ø‖ in the underlying structure)

B Unablauted (with no ‖Ø‖ in the underlying structure)

This information is shown here in the following figure:

- [‖C‖ = ‖Ø‖] +

A Unablauted

‖AB(C)(D)‖

1 - 25

B Ablauted

‖(A)B(:)Ø(D)‖

26 - 77

Ablauted and Unablauted Types of Tamazight Verb Stems

VI.3.2.2 Classes of the Ablauted Type

Based on the change [Ø:i/a] referred to in VI.3.1.2 ablauted stems (26-77) are classified into two classes: B-i and B-ii. B-i (26-61) is referred to as [-Ø:i/a] (or [Ø:0]); B-ii (62-77) is referred to as [+Ø:i/a]. This is illustrated in the following figure:

- [Ø:i/a] +

B-i { ‖AB(:)ØD‖ ; ‖aBØD‖ ; ‖OB:ØD‖ }

B-ii { ‖aB Ø(D)‖ [±Met] [±Met] ; ‖(A)B(:) Ø‖ [±Met] ; ‖A(:)B(:)Ø{i, u}‖ }

Classes of the Ablauted Type

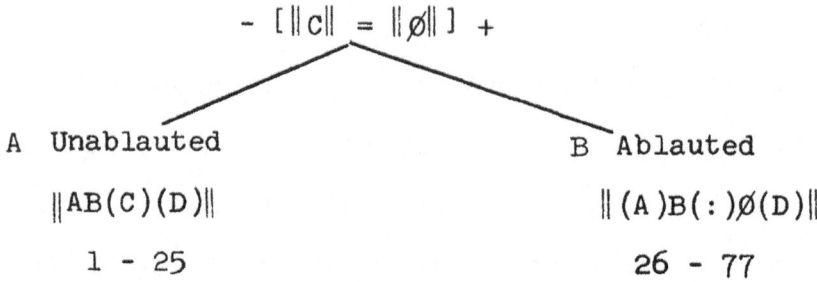

VI.3.2.3 Classes of the Unablauted Type

The members of the unablauted type do not undergo any change with the realization of person-number-gender in the past. However, classification into two classes: A-i and A-ii is necessary for the statement of particular derivations. All members of the unablauted type are characterized by a structure that does not have ‖C‖ as ‖Ø‖ and that necessarily has ‖V‖ as either radical ‖B‖, ‖C‖ or ‖D‖. The position of ‖V‖ is the basis of the classification of unablauted stems into A-i and A-ii. All members of the A-ii class have the structure ‖AVCD‖ (referred to as /ḥaḍr, d:irz, ḥudr/).

Based on whether the stem has ‖B‖ = ‖V‖ followed by ‖CD‖, the two classes of the unablauted type are shown in the following figure:

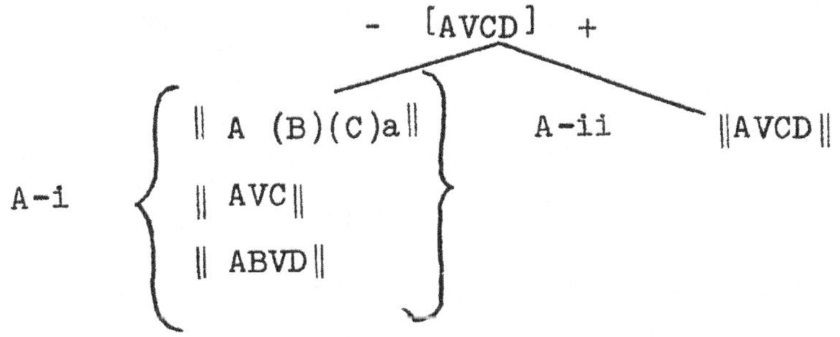

Classes of the Unablauted Type

VI.3.2.4 Sub-classification of Tamazight Verb Stems

This section groups together the information stated in VI.3.2.1 to VI.3.2.3 above showing types A and their four classes: A-i, A-ii and B-i, B-ii, their nine sub-classes: A-i (1-3), B-i (1-3) and B-ii (1-3) as well as the bases of this classification.

$$- \quad [C = \emptyset] \quad +$$

A $\|AB(C)(D)\|$ 　　　　　　B $\|(A)B(:)\emptyset D\|$

　1-25　　　　　　　　　　　　26-77

$$- \quad [\|AVCD\|] \quad +$$　　　　　$$- \quad [\emptyset : i/a] \quad +$$

　　1 $\|A(B)(C)a\|$　　　　　　　　　　　1 $\|AB(:)\emptyset D\|$　　　1 $\|aB \underset{[+Met]}{} \underset{[+Met]}{\emptyset(D)}\|$

A-i　2 $\|AVC\|$　　　A $-B\|AVCD\|$　　B-i　2 $\|aB\emptyset D\|$　　B-ii　2 $\|(A)B(:) \underset{[+Met]}{\emptyset}\|$

　　3 $\|ABVD\|$　　　　　　　　　　　　3 $\|OB:\emptyset D\|$　　　3 $\|(A(:))B(:)\emptyset \{{u \atop i}\}\|$

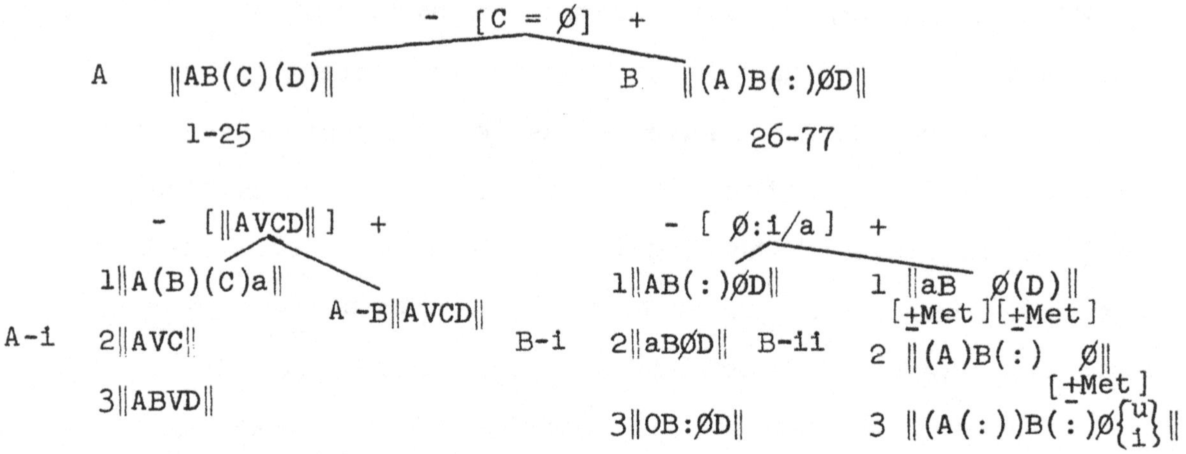

Sub-Classes of Tamazight Verb Stems

VI.3.3 Illustrative Examples of Conjugation of Verbs Representing the Various Sub-Classes of Tamazight Verb Stems

In this section fourteen verb stems representing the various structures of the sub-classes of verb stems discussed above are used to exemplify the Surface Structure (SS) forms resulting from the realization of person-number-gender (PNG) in the Past$_{[\pm\text{Negative}]}$. Some verbs are inflected for all persons-numbers- and genders. Ohters with the same structure and/or belonging to the same category of ablaut are inflected only for $P_1 N_s$ and $P_3 N_s G_f$. All forms in Tables 4, 5, and 6 appear in their <u>surface structure (SS)</u>, i.e. after the operation of the morphophonemic rules. Meanings are only listed for the Affirmative Past.

PNG	Stem		Affirmative Past		Negative Past
	dawa	'cure'			
1s			dawaγ	'I cured'	urdawaγ
2s			tdawad	'you cured'	urtdawad
3sm			idawa	'he cured'	uridawa
3sf			tdawa	'she cured'	urtdawa
1p			ndawa	'we cured'	urndawa
2pm			tdawam	'you cured'	urtdawam
2pf			tdawant	'you cured'	urtdawant
3pm			dawan	'they cured'	urdawan
3pf			dawant	'they cured'	urdawant
	sal	'ask'			
1s			salγ	'I asked'	ursalγ
3sf			tsal	'she asked'	urtsal
	xṭar	'choose'			
1s			xṭarγ	'I chose'	urxṭarγ
3sf			txṭar	'she chose'	urtxṭar
	ḥaḍr	'be present'			
1s			ḥaḍrγ	'I was present'	urḥaḍrγ
3sf			tḥaḍr	'she was present'	urtḥaḍr

TABLE 4 - Person-Number-Gender Paradigms for Unablauted Stems

PNG	Stem	Affirmative Past		Negative Past
	frḥ 'be happy'			
1s		frḥγ	'I was happy'	urfriḥγ
2s		tfrḥd	'you were happy'	urtfriḥd
3sm		ifrḥ	'he was happy'	urifriḥ
3sf		tfrḥ	'she was happy'	urtfriḥ
1p		nfrḥ	'we were happy'	urnfriḥ
2pm		tfrḥm	'you were happy'	urtfriḥm
2pf		tfrḥnt	'you were happy'	urtfriḥnt
3pm		frḥn	'they were happy'	urfriḥn
3pf		frḥnt	'they were happy'	urfriḥnt
	fs:r 'explain'			
1s		fs:rγ	'I explained'	urfs:irγ
3sf		tfs:r	'she explained'	urtfs:ir
	amẓ 'take'			
1s		umẓγ	'I took'	urumiẓγ
2s		tumẓd	'you took'	urtumiẓd
3sm		yumẓ	'he took'	uryumiẓ
3sf		tumẓ	'she took'	urtumiẓ
1p		numẓ	'we took'	urnumiẓ
2pm		tumẓm	'you took'	urtumiẓm
2pf		tumẓnt	'you took'	urtumiẓnt
3pm		umẓn	'they took'	urumiẓn
3pf		umẓnt	'they took'	urumiẓnt
	f:r 'hide'			
1s		f:rγ	'I hid'	urf:irγ
3sf		tf:r	'she his'	urtf:ir

TABLE 5 - Person-Number-Gender Paradigms for [Ø:0] Ablauted Stems

PNG	Stem	Affirmative Past		Negative Past
	af 'find'			
1s		ufiɣ	'I found'	urufiɣ
2s		tufid	'you found'	urtufid
3sm		yufa	'he found'	uryufi
3sf		tufa	'she found'	urtufi
1p		nufa	'we found'	urnufi
2pm		tufam	'you found'	urtufim
2pf		tufant	'you found'	urtufint
3pm		ufan	'they found'	urufin
3pf		ufant	'they found'	urufint
	as:k 'be lost'			
1s		uš:kiɣ	'I was lost'	uruš:kiɣ
3sf		tuš:ka	'she was lost'	urtuš:ki
	rar 'return'			
1s		ruriɣ	'I returned'	ur:uriɣ
3sf		trura	'she returned'	urtruri
	ls 'get dressed'			
1s		lsiɣ	'I got dressed'	urlsiɣ
2s		tlsid	'you got dressed'	urtslid
3sm		ilsa	'he got dressed'	urilsi
3sf		tlsa	'she got dressed'	urtlsi
1p		nlsa	'we got dressed'	urnlsi
2pm		tlsam	'you got dressed'	urtlsim
2pf		tlsant	'you got dressed'	urtlsint
3pm		lsan	'they got dressed'	urlsin
3pf		lsant	'they got dressed'	urlsint
	bdu 'begin'			
1s		bdiɣ	'I began'	urbdiɣ
2s		tbdid	'you began'	urtbdid
3sm		ibda	'he began'	uribdi
3sf		tbda	'she began'	urtbdi
1p		nbda	'we began'	urnbdi
2pm		tbdam	'you began'	urtbdim
2pf		tbdant	'you began'	urtbdint
3pm		bdan	'they began'	urbdin
3pf		bdant	'they began'	urbdint
	iri 'want'			
1s		riɣ	'I wanted'	ur:iɣ
2s		trid	'you wanted'	urtrid
3sm		ira	'he wanted'	uriri
3sf		tra	'she wanted'	urtri
1p		nra	'we wanted'	urnri
2pm		tram	'you wanted'	urtrim
2pf		trant	'you wanted'	urtrint
3pm		ran	'they wanted'	ur:in
3pf		rant	'they wanted'	ur:int

TABLE 6 - Person-Number-Gender Paradigms for [Ø:i/a]Ablauted Stems

VI.4 Derivational Processes [10]

VI.4.1 Introduction

Derivations are of two kinds: Stem Derivations and Temporal/Modal Derivations. Derived Stems are either Verb Stems or Noun Stems. The Derived Verb Stems include the Causative SV, the Reciprocal MV, the Recipro-Causative MSV, and the Passive TuV as well as their Habitual Stems (SVH, MVH,MSVH,TuVH respectively) and the habitual VH of the unaugmented Verb Stem V. Derived Noun Stems include the stems of such nouns as the ones appearing in postiions c), d) and e) in the Sample Appendix(Noun of Action, Agent, Instrument, Place or Occupation also see the Grammar of the Noun.) The following are the main Temporal and Modal derivations of the unaugmented verb stem V and its habitual stem VH: Aorist (Aor.), Affirmative Past (Aff. Past), Negative Past (Neg. Past), Interrogative Past (Interr. Past), Negative-Interrogative Past (Neg-Interr. Past),Affirmative Future (Aff. Fut.), Negative Future (Neg. Fut.), Interrogative Future (Interr. Fut.), Affirmative Present (Aff. Pres.), Negative Present (Neg. Pres.), Interrogative Present (Interr, Pres.), Negative-Interrogative Present (Neg-Interr. Pres.), Imperative (Imp.), Negative Imperative (Neg. Imp.), Past Participle (Past Part.), Present Participle (Pres. Part.), and Future Participle (Fut. Part.). Most of the above-mentioned temporal and modal structures generated from V and its VH may also be generated from SV, MV, MSV and their habitual stems SVH,MVH,and MSVH. Fewer structures are generated from TuV and its habitual stem TuVH.

The purpose of this chapter is to characterize how a native speaker of Tamazight can generate all the forms referred to here. This is represented in a series of discussions. Section VI.4.2 discusses the derivation of VH i.e. the habitual of the unaugmented stem . Sections VI.4.3 VI.4.4 and VI.4.5 discuss the derivations of the Causative, Reciprocal and Passive stems respectively. The discussion of the derivation of the habitual of a particular derived stem is included with it in the same section: e.g. Section VI.4. discusses SV and SVH derivations. Section VI.4.6 is an informal discussion of derived noun stems and nouns. Section VI.4.7 shows the derivations of the different tenses and their modes as well as the participles with examples shown in Tables 7-29. Rules are formulated for each temporal and modal derivation and a summary of the rules appears in VI.4.7.8.

Throughout Section VI.4 DSR refers to a deep structure rule which generates a form with its morpheme boundary /-/ whereas SSR refers to a surface structure rule that deletes /-/ and realizes other changes stated for the generated structure. SSR's of a particular derivation follow DSR's of the same derivation except for general SSR's which are grouped in Section VI.5.

VI.4.2 Derivation of the Habitual VH of the Unaugmented Stem

VH is the stem used in the derivation of the present tense with its different modes, the progressive and inchoative actions, the negative and the energetic imperatives, and the present and future participles. The VH is derived from unaugmented V; theoretically each V has a VH.

Prefix /t:-/ is used to derive the habitual stem of any V of type A-i (1-73)[*] /t:____*a*V-/ derives habitual stems from V's of the type A-ii. (74-115). /-*a*V-/[**] is an alpha rule that adds a vowel that is identical to the stem vowel (see examples for A-ii below).

Examples

		V		VH
A-i	3	fa	'yawn'	t:fa
	37	sal	'ask'	t:sal
	46	ʕum	'swim'	t:ʕum
	72	zwiɣ	'be red'	t:zwiɣ

* Numerals refer to number of verb stem in Verb List at the end of this chapter. (pp. 262-282)

** For a more elaborate description of the habitual derivational processes see Abdel-Massih, Ernest, Tamazight Verb Structure: A Generative Approach, Indiana University: Bloomington, Indiana, 1971.

A-ii 77 ḥaḍr 'be present' t:ḥaḍar

74 d:irz 'step back' t:diriz

83 ḥudr 'bend' t:ḥudur

B.i.1 To derive the habitual of V of type B.i.1. (116-315) observe the following:

a) All verbs of the /fs:r/ (‖AB:ØD‖) sub-group derive their habitual stems by prefix /t:-/ and ‖Ø‖ ⟶ /-a-/, i.e.

162 fs:r 'to explain' ⟶ t:fs:ar (VH)

b) All V's marked native (i.e. not Arabic) derive their VH's thus: ‖B‖ ⟶ ‖B:‖ e.g.

225 rẓm 'to open' ⟶ rẓ:m (VH)

c) V's marked 'Arabic loan' derive their VH's by prefix /t:-/ and ‖-Ø-‖ ⟶ /a-/ if ‖B‖ is not /r/ nor /d, t, s, z, s, or z/, e.g.

126 bˤd 'be far' ⟶ t:bˤad (VH)

144 fhm 'understand' ⟶ t:fham (VH)

d) If ‖B‖ is /r/ we may get VH's as variants of both forms mentioned in b) and c) above, e.g.

149 frḥ 'be happy' ⟶ fr:ḥ

t:fraḥ (VH)

e) If ‖B‖ is /d, t, s, z, s or z/ VH is formed as in b) above.

271 xdm 'work ⟶ xd:m (VH)

B.i.2 To derive VH's of B.i.2 (316-337) and B.i.3 (338-360) the prefix /t:-/ is used: e.g.,

325	amẓ	'take'	⟶	t:amẓ	(VH)
340	f:r	'hide'	⟶	t:f:r	(VH)

/t:____a#/ is the derivational affix of members of B.ii.1 (361-370), e.g.

362	af	'find'	⟶	t:afa	(VH)
361	adž	'let'	⟶	t:adža	(VH)
369	rar	'return, give back'		t:rara	(VH)

As for B.ii.2 (371-397), /t:____a#/ derives a VH of the structures /0gØ/⟶g, bd:Ø⟶bd: whereas lsØ⟶ls derives the VH as ls:a and gØr⟶grØ⟶gr derives the VH as g:ar. This means that /Ø/⟶/a/ and the radical preceding /Ø/⟶[+tense], e.g.

	V		VH
377	g̣:	'knead'	t:g̣:a
371	bd:	'stand up'	t:bd:a
388	ls	'get dressed'	ls:a
376	gr	'throw away'	g:ar

B.ii.3 (398-450) derive their VH's mainly by the prefix /t:-/. Stems with ‖B‖ as /n/ derive their VH's by ‖B‖⟶‖B:‖. Stems with ‖B‖ as /m/ derive their VH's by variants of both processes mentioned above, e.g.

401	dˤu	'pray for'	⟶	t:dˤu	(VH)
400	bnu	'build'	⟶	bn:u	(VH)
412	ḥmu	'be hot weather'	⟶	{tḥmu / ḥm:u}	(VH)

VI.4.3 Causative Stem Derivation

The Verb Appendix shows, where the semantic features of V permit, two causative stems appearing in positions a) and b). The stem in position a) is referred to as SV; i.e. causative stem and the one in position b) is referred to as SVH, i.e. habitual of the causative stem. SV is used for past and future tense derivations, for imperative and past participle derivations. SVH is used for present tense, negative imperative and present and future participle derivations. In general SV corresponds to V (in derivational power) whereas SVH corresponds to VH.

SV is derived from V by the causative prefix $\left\{\begin{matrix}/s\text{-}/\\ /s{:}\text{-}/\end{matrix}\right\}$.

SVH is derived from SV by an infix (/-V-/), e.g.

	V		SV	SVH
3	fa	'yawn'	sfa	sfa
83	ḥudr	'bend'	sḥudr	sḥudur
173	ḥml	'flood'	s:ḥml	s:hmal
426	ṣfu	'be clean'	ṣ:fu	ṣ:fu

VI.4.4 Reciprocal Verb Stem Derivation

The Verb Appendix shows, where the semantic features of V permit, two reciprocal stems in positions a) and b). The stem in position a) is referred to as MV, i.e. Reciprocal Verb Stem; whereas the stem in position b) is referred to as

MVH, i.e. habitual of the reciprocal stem. Stems with reciprocal and causative connotation (Recipro-Causative) appear partly in the Causative and partly in the Reciprocal columns and are referred to as: a) MSV, b) MSVH. This section states the derivation of Recip. and Recipro-Caus. stems. This is done because some V's derive Recipro-Causative stems in spite of the fact that the semantic features of V do not permit the derivation of a causative stem. Such cases are not numerous; e.g. 383 /nγ/ 'kill' does not derive a causative, however, it derives recipro-causative: MSV /msnγa/ and MSVH /t:msnγa/. Some V's derive variants, i.e. reciprocals and recipro-causatives: e.g.

	V		SV	SV	MV
47	bd:l	'change'	sbd:l		mbd:al
			sbd:al		t:mbd:al
				msbd:al	
				t:msbd:al	

where the MV means 'to exchange or change with one another' and the MSV means 'to cause one another to exchange. MV and MVH correspond to V as far as Temporal and Modal derivations are concerned, whereas MVH and MSVH correspond to VH.

MV* is derived from V by the reciprocal prefix {/m-/, /m:-/},

---

* For a more elaborate description of the phonological rules governing the shape of the causative and/or reciprocal prefix, see Abdel-Massih, Ernest, Tamazight Verb Structure: A Generative Approach, Indiana University: Bloomington, Indiana, 1971.

MSV is derived by prefixing {/-ms-/, /-m:s-/} to V. A vowel infix is added if the stem has a consonant cluster as its final two radicals. MVH and MSVH are derived from MV and MSV respectively by prefix /t:-/: e.g.

	V		MV/MSV	MVH/MSVH
37	sal	'ask'	m:sal	t:msal
46	ʕum	'swim'	m:sʕum	t:m:sʕum
95	ṭalb	'demand'	mṭalab	t:mṭalab
144	fhm	'understand'	msfham	t:msfham

VI.4.5 Passive Verb Stem Derivation

The Verb Appendix shows two passives: TuV, i.e. passive stem appearing in position a) and TuVH, i.e. the habitual of the passive stem appearing in position b). TuV is derived from V. Stems 149 and 152 in Appendix derive their passives (TuSV) from SV

TuV is the stem that derives past and future tenses and their modes; TuVH is the stem that derives the present tense and its modes. The derivation of TuV from V (most common passive) or SV (very rare passive) is achieved by the passive derivational prefix /t:u-/ and the derivation of TuVH from TuV by an optional infix (/-V-/)*, e.g.

* For a more elaborate description see Abdel-Massih, Ernest , op. cit.

		V	TuV	TuVH
11	ḥn:a	'pity'	t:uḥn:a	t:uḥn:a
37	sal	'ask'	t:usal	t:usal
88	saʕd	'help'	t:usaʕd	t:usaʕad
116	bdr	'mention'	t:ubdr	t:ubdar

VI.4.6 Derived Noun Stems and Nouns

VI.4.6.1 Introduction

It was stated before that noun stems would be discussed though not fully. This section attempts to show the relation between nouns of action, of agent and other derived nouns and their V's in terms of derivations. The statements are very simple. For more elaborate discussion see the Grammar of the Noun

VI.4.6.2 Noun Stem Derivation

Most noun stems are derived from V's; however, few nouns of action may be derived from SV, MV or MSV. Many noun stems are identical with their V's (SV's, MV's or MSV's): e.g.

		V	N-act.	N-agt (m,s)*
84	kašf	'foretell'	a-kašf-	am-kašf-
		V	SV	N-act
7	ḥn:a	'be peaceful'	sḥn:a	a-sḥn:a-

* Throughout this section, Noun Stems will be underlined.

	V		MV	N-act
81	ḥasb	'count'	mḥasab	a-<u>mḥasab</u>-

In many cases the stem of the noun of action is derived from V by change of ‖Ø‖ to /-a-/ and the noun of agent stem is derived from that of N-act by change of ‖B‖ ⟶ ‖B:‖ ([-tense] ⟶ [+tense]). This is characteristic of stems with underlying structure ‖ABØD‖: e.g.

	V		N-act	N-agt (m,s)
167	hdm	'demolish'	a-<u>hdam</u>-	a-<u>hd:am</u>-

Most V's with underlying structures ‖AB:ØD‖ derive their N-agt stems by change of ‖Ø‖ ⟶ /a-/. This particular sub-class has (in most cases) identical V's and N-act stems: e.g.

	V		N-act	N-agt (m,s)
123	bš:r	'give good news'	a-<u>bš:r</u>-	a-<u>bš:ar</u>-

The sub-class of verb stems with the underlying structure ‖OB:ØD‖ derives its N-act stems by change ‖Ø‖ ⟶ /-u-/ and of ‖B:‖ ⟶ ‖B‖ ([+tense] ⟶ [-tense]). This is characteristic of the sub-class with ‖A‖ = ‖O‖ (‖O‖ ⟶ /u-/), e.g.

	V		N-act
338	b:y	'cut'	u-<u>buy</u>-
341	f:ɣ	'go out'	u-<u>fuɣ</u>-

The sub-class of verb stems with the underlying structure ‖ABØ‖ derives stems of N-act and N-agt by change of ‖Ø‖ ⟶ ‖V‖.

This sub-class of verbs is characterized by deriving most of its N-acts by the affix /m____t/. If ‖V‖ is /-i-/ then it ⟶ /-iw-/.

	V		N-act	N-agt (m,s)
379	ks	'tend sheep'	ta-ks:a-	am-ksa-
380	ls	'dress'	m-lsiw-t	
381	ns	'spend the night'	m-nsiw-t	
383	ṛɣ	'warm oneself'	m-ṛɣiw-t	
385	sɣ	'buy'	m-sɣiw-t	
392	ẓḍ	'weave'	m-ẓḍiw-t	am-ẓḍa-

The sub-class of verbs with the underlying structure ‖ABóV‖ shows a number of N-act and N-agt which (together with their stems) are derived from V on the pattern of a corresponding Arabic noun. Mention should be made of the fact that when a noun is derived (whether of this sub-class or any other sub-class) on an Arabic noun pattern, the shape of the Berber noun is not easily predictable. Examples given below show noun stems derived from the different classes of V stems that follow an Arabic pattern:

	V		N-act
81	ḥasb	'count'	l-ḥsab-
95	ṭalb	'demand'	ṭ:alab (l-ṭalab-)
422	ržu	'hope'	r:ža (l-rža-)
427	ṣḥu	'be healthy'	ṣ:aḥt (l-ṣaḥt-)

440	ʕfu	'forgive'	l-ʕfu-
265	wq:r	'respect'	l-uq:r-

	V		N-agt (m,s)
400	bnu	'build'	a-bn:ay-
179	ḥšm	'govern'	l-ḥak:m-
264	wk:l	'appoint as representative'	l-ušil-

VI.4.7 Temporal and Modal Derivation

VI.4.7.1 Introduction

This section discusses the derivation of the different tenses and modes of the verb in Tamazight. The discussion includes the following derivations from unaugmented V: the imperative, the Aorist, the past tense with its different modes: affirmative, interrogative, negative and negative-interrogative; the future tense with its two modes: affirmative and interrogative - "Will" type as well as the derivation of the past participle and a variant of the future participle. From VH the following derivations are discussed: energetic imperative, negative imperative, interrogative future - Q type, negative future, the present tense with its different modes: affirmative, interrogative, negative and negative-interrogative, as well as the present and future participles.

The derivations referred to above are all achieved by using V and VH. Moreover, SV, MV or MSV can generate most of the structures that a V does and SVH, MVH or MSVH can generate most of the structures that a VH does. Fewer structures are generated from the passive stem TuV and its habitual TuVH.

VI.4.7.2 Derivation of Imperative Structures

Tamazight has different imperative structures that will be referred to as 2-a, 2-b and 1-a, 1-b, 1-c. Structures 2-a and 2-b are second person imperatives where 2-b is the negative imperative. 1-a, 1-b and 1-c are hortatory or cohortative constructions expressing an exhortation or suggestion for first person. The negative imperative and the energetic imperative are derived from VH. The other imperative structures are derived from V. /-PNG/* of the imperatives are all suffixes (see Tables 1 and 2).

Imperative 2-a is derived simply by affixation of /-PNG/ (suffixes) shown in Table 1 to either V to derive second person imperative or to VH to derive the energetic imperative which for /ʕum/ 'swim' may be translated as either 'get in the habit of swimming' or 'do swim'. Imperative 2-b is derived by prefixation of the negative imperative derivational prefix /adur-/ to VH and the realization of imperative /-PNG_2/ suffixes referred to above. Imperative 1-a is derived by the suffixation of /-PNG_1/ set shown in Table 2. Imperatives 1-b and 1-c differ from 1-a both in meaning and in structure. All the three structures mean 'let us...', except that 1-b and 1-c have the added feature [+movement]. The difference

---

* This study refers to the suffixed PNG of the imperative as /-PNG/ or /-$PNG\{{1 \atop 2}\}$/ where /-PNG_2/ means second person suffixes and /-PNG_1/ is hortatory suffixes. It will also refer to the affixed PNG of the different tenses as /-PNG-/.

in structure lies in the fact that /-PNG_1/ are added to the V to derive 1-a, whereas in deriving 1-b they are added to the V /k:r/ 'get up' and in 1-c /-PNG_1/ are added to /yal:ah/ a particle meaning 'let us'.

$$\left\{\begin{array}{lll} /k{:}r/ & + & /\text{-}PNG_1/ \\ /yal{:}ah/ & + & /\text{-}PNG_1/ \end{array}\right\}$$ are both followed by the desired V + /-PNG-/ + future prefix /ad-/: e.g. /ʕum-aɣ / 'let us (both) swim', /k:r-a ad-n-ʕum/ 'let us (both) go and swim'[/ad-n-ʕum/ (DS) ⟶ /an-ʕum/ (SS)]. Another structural difference is that 1-a does not distinguish between G_m and G_f in P_d whereas 1-b and 1-c do.

Imperative structures with the movable affixes /-d-/ of proximity, /-n:-/ of remoteness and the pronominal affixes occur with the affix post-$\text{Imperative}_{[\text{-Negative}]}$ and in the order: $\text{Imper}_{[\text{-Negative}]}$+ (I.Obj.) + (D.Obj.) + (orientational affix) or pre-$\text{Imperative}_{[\text{+Negative}]}$ and in the order: Neg, Imper. Prefix + (I.Obj.) + (D.Obj.) + (orientational affix) + Imperative.

Causative and Reciprocal Imperatives are derived in the same way the imperatives of a V and its VH are derived; Causative and reciprocal imperative structures with the movable affixes are also derived in the same way referred to in the previous paragraph. Not all imperative constructions with the movable affixes occur with the derived verb stems (Caus. and Recip.).

Rules for the Generation of the Different Imperative Structures (from V and VH)

Imper-DSR_1 Imperative $\longrightarrow$ V + /-PNG_2/

Imper-DSR_2 Energetic Imper. $\longrightarrow$ VH + /-PNG_2/

Imper-DSR_3 Negative Imper. $\rightarrow$ /adur-/ + VH + /-PNG_2/

Imper-DSR_4 Hortatory $\longrightarrow$ V + /-PNG_1/

Imper-DSR_5 $Hortatory_{[+Movement]}$ $\longrightarrow$

$$\left\{\begin{matrix} /k{:}r/ \\ /yal{:}ah/ \end{matrix}\right\} +/\text{-}PNG_1/+/ad\text{-}/+/\text{-}P_1N_p\text{-}/+V$$

Imper-DSR_6 Movable Affix $\longrightarrow$

$$\left\{\begin{matrix} V + /\text{-}PNG_2/+(I.Obj.) + (D.Obj.) + (Orient.Aff.) \\ /adur\text{-}/+(I.Obj.)+(D.Obj.)+(Orient.Aff.)+ \\ VH + /\text{-}PNG_2/ \end{matrix}\right\}$$

Note on Imper-DSR_6: This rule states the position of the movable affixes in relation to the imperative. (This is true of all rules concerning Movable Affixes in the following sections.)

Examples of Imperative structures generated by the above rules are shown in Tables 7-13 in their (SS) form.

	2-a		2-b
PNG	Imperative	Energetic Imperative	Negative Imperative
2smf	ʕum	t:ʕum	adurt:ʕum
2pm	ʕumat	t:ʕumat	adurt:ʕumat
2pf	ʕumnt	t:ʕumnt	adurt:ʕumnt

TABLE 7 - Imperatives 2-a and 2-b of /ʕum/ (SS)

	Hortatory	Hortatory [+Movement]	
PNG	1-a	1-b	1-c
1dm	ʕumaɣ	k:raɣ anʕum	yaḷ:ahaɣ anʕum
1df	ʕumaɣ	k:ram anʕum	yaḷ:aham anʕum
1pm	ʕumataɣ	k:rataɣ anʕum	yaḷ:ahataɣ anʕum
1pf	ʕumntaɣ	k:rntaɣ anʕum	yaḷ:ahntaɣ anʕum

TABLE 8 - Imperatives 1-a, 1-b, and 1-c of /ʕum/ (SS)

	2-a		2-b
PNG	Imperative	Energetic Imperative	Negative Imperative
2smf	awid	t:awid	adurt:awy
2pm	awyad:	t:awyad:	adurt:awyat
2pf	awind:	t:awind:	adurdt:awint

TABLE 9 - Imperatives 2-a and 2-b /awy/ in combination with the proximity affix /-d-/ (SS)

	2-a		2-b
PNG	Imperative	Energetic Imperative	Negative Imperative
2smf	sḥudr	sḥudur	adursḥudur
2pm	sḥudrat	sḥudurat	adursḥudurat
2pf	sḥudrnt	sḥudurnt	adursḥudurnt

TABLE 10 - Imperatives 2-a and 2-b of /sḥudr/, causative of /ḥudr/ (SS)

	Hortatory	Hortatory [+Movement]	
PNG	1-a	1-b	1-c
1dm	sḥudraɣ	k:raɣ ansḥudr	yaḷ:ahaɣ ansḥudr
1df	sḥudraɣ	k:ram ansḥudr	yaḷ:aham ansḥudr
1pm	sḥudrataɣ	k:rataɣ ansḥudr	yaḷ:ahataɣ ansḥudr
1pf	sḥudrntaɣ	k:rntaɣ ansḥudr	yaḷ:ahntaɣ ansḥudr

TABLE 11 - Imperatives 1-a, 1-b, 1-c of /sḥudr/, causative of /ḥudr/ (SS)

	2-a		2-b
PNG	Imperative	Energetic Imperative	Negative Imperative
2smf	mʕawan	t:mʕawan	adurt:mʕawan
2pm	mʕawanat	t:mʕawanat	adurt:mʕawanat
2pf	mʕawannt	t:mʕawannt	adurt:mʕawannt

TABLE 12 - Imperatives 2-a and 2-b of /mʕawn/, reciprocal of /ʕawn/ (SS)

	Hortatory	Hortatory$_{[+Movement]}$	
PNG	1-a	1-b	1-c
1dm	mˤawanaγ	k:raγ anmˤawan	yaḷ:ahaγ anmˤawan
1df	mˤawanaγ	k:ram anmˤawan	yaḷ:aham anmˤawan
1pm	mˤawanataγ	k:rataγ anmˤawan	yaḷ:ahataγ anmˤawan
1pf	mˤawanntaγ	k:rntaγ anmˤawan	yaḷ:ahntaγ anmˤawan

TABLE 13 - Imperatives 1-a, 1-b, 1-c of /mˤawan/, reciprocal of /ˤawn/ (SS)

VI.4.7.3 Derivation of the Past Tense and Its Different Modes

The past tense is derived from V by the realization of /-PNG-/ shown in Table 3. As stated before, /-PNG-/affixes are the same no matter what the temporal (past, present, future) structure is. Its different modes are derived by the modal prefixes discussed in VI.2.2 above. The realization of /-PNG-/ in the past effects a change in the verb stem of certain classes. This was discussed in VI.3 and was referred to as ablaut (Abl) and to the stems as ablauted stems.

Rules for the Derivation of the Different Modes of the Past Tense: (from V)

Past-DSR$_1$ Affirm. Past ⟶ V + /-PNG-/ + (Abl)

Past-DSR$_2$ Interrog. Past ⟶ /is-/ + Affirm. Past

Past-DSR$_3$	Neg. Past ⟶ /ur-/ + V + /-PNG-/ + (Abl)
Past-DSR$_4$	Neg-Interrog. Past ⟶ /is-/ + Neg. Past
Past-DSR$_5$	Movable Affix ⟶ { Post-Verbal / Affirm. Past___ ; Pre-Verbal / ___Non-Affirm. Past }

Examples of the products of the above rules are shown in Tables 14-17. All forms have as subject /-$P_3N_sG_m$-/ (prefix /i-/). Blank boxes indicate that the form does not occur.

Examples of Past Tense Structures

	Past	Past, Prox. Affix	Past, I.Obj., Prox. Affix
Affirm.	iʕawn	iʕawnd	iʕawnasd
Interr.	isiʕawn	isdiʕawn	isasdiʕawn
Neg.	uriʕawn	urdiʕawn	urasdiʕawn
Neg-Int.	isuriʕawn	isurdiʕawn	isurasdiʕawn

TABLE 14 - Structures generated from V /ʕawn/ in the past (SS)

	Past	Past, Prox. Affix	Past, I.Obj. Prox. Affix
Affirm.	isˁawn	isˁawnd	isˁawnasd
Interr.	isisˁawn	isdsˁawn	isasdisˁawn
Neg.	urisˁawn	urdsˁawn	urasdisˁawn
Neg.Int.	isurisˁawn	isurdsˁawn	isurasdisˁawn

TABLE 15 - Structures generated from /sˁawn/, Causative of /ʕawn/ in the past (SS)

	Past	Past, Prox. Affix	Past, I.Obj., Prox. Affix
Affirm.	imˁawan	imˁawand	
Interr.	isimˁawan	isdmˁawan	
Neg.	urimˁawan	urdimˁawan	
Neg.Int.	isurimˁawan	isurdimˁawan	

TABLE 16 - Structures generated from /mˁawan/, Reciprocal of /ʕawn/ in the past (SS)

	Past	Past, Prox. Affix.	Past, I.Obj., Prox. Affix
Affirm.	it:uˁawn	it:uˁawnd	it:uˁawnasd
Interr.	isit:uˁawn	isdit:uˁawn	isasdit:uˁawn
Neg.	urit:uˁawn	urdit:uˁawn	urasdit:uˁawn
Neg.Int.	isurit:uˁawn	isurdit:uˁawn	isurasdit:uˁawn

TABLE 17 - Structures generated from /t:uˁawn/, Passive of /ʕawn/ in the past (SS)

VI.4.7.4 Derivation of the Future Tense and Its Different Modes

The structures generated for the future tense are: affirmative future, interrogative future (Will type), negative future and interrogative future (Q type).

Rules for the Generation of the Different Future Modes (from V and VH)

Fut-DSR_1	Affirm-Fut ⟶ /ad-/ + V + /-PNG-/
Fut-DSR_2	$\text{Interr-Fut}_{\text{will}}$ ⟶ /id:-/ + Affirmative Future
Fut-DSR_3	Negative Fut ⟶ /ur-/ + VH + /-PNG-/
Fut-DSR_4	Interr. Fut_{Q} ⟶ QW + VH + /-PNG-/
Fut-DSR_5	Movable Affixes ⟶ Pre-Verbal

Most of the above-mentioned structures may be derived for the causative, reciprocal, recipro-causative and passive where SV, MV, MSV, amd TuV are used in place of V; and SVH, MVH, MSVH, and TuVH are used in place of VH.

Examples of the results of the above rules are shown in Tables 18-21. All forms are generated with -$P_3N_sG_m$- (Prefix /-i/). Blank boxes indicate that the form does not occur.

	Future	Future, Prox. Affix	Future, I.Obj., Prox. Affix
Affirm.	adiˤawn	ad:iˤawn	adasdiˤawn
Interr.	id:adiˤawn	id:ad:iˤawn	id:adasdiˤawn
Neg.	urit:ˤawan	urit:ˤawan	urasdit:ˤawan
Neg.Int.	milmi yt:ˤawan	milmi dit:ˤawan	milmi asdit:ˤawan

TABLE 18 - Structures generated from V /ˤawn/ and its VH /t:ˤawan/ in the future - (SS)

	Future	Future, Prox. Affix	Future, I.Obj., Prox. Affix
Affirm.	adisˤawn	ad:isˤawn	adasdisˤawn
Interr.	id:adisˤawn	id:ad:isˤawn	id:adasdisˤawn
Neg.	urisˤawan	urdisˤawan	urasdisˤawan
Neg.Int.	milmi ysˤawan	milmi disˤawan	milmi asdisˤawan

TABLE 19 - Structures generated from the causatives a) /sˤawn/ and b) /sˤawan/ in the future - (SS)

	Future	Future, Prox. Affix	Future, I.Obj., Prox. Affix
Affirm.	adimˤawan	ad:imˤawan	
Interr.	id:adimˤawan	id:ad:imˤawan	
Neg.	urit:mˤawan	urdimˤawan	
Neg. Int.	milmi yt:mˤawan	milmi dit:mˤawan	

TABLE 20 - Structures generated from the reciprocals a) /mˤawan/ and b) /t:mˤawan/ in the future - (SS)

	Future	Future, Prox. Affix	Future, I.Obj., Prox. Affix
Affirm.	adit:uˤawn		adasdit:uˤawn
Interr.	id:adit:uˤawn		id:adasdit:uˤawn
Neg.	urit:uˤawan		urasdit:uˤawan
Neg.Int.	milmi it:uˤawan		milmi asdit:uˤawan

TABLE 21 - Structures generated from the passives a) /t:uˤawn/ and b) /t:uˤawan/ in the future - (SS)

VI.4.7.5 Derivation of the Present Tense and Its Different Modes

The present tense with its different modes is derived from VH (or SVH, MVH, MSVH, TuVH).

Rules for the Generation of the Present Tense (from VH)

Pres-DSR$_1$	Affirm. Pres. $\longrightarrow \left\{\begin{matrix} \text{da-} \\ \text{l:a-} \end{matrix}\right\}$ + VH + /-PNG-/
Pres-DSR$_2$	Interrog. Pres. $\longrightarrow$ /is-/ + Affirm. Pres.
Pres-DSR$_3$	Neg. Pres. $\longrightarrow$ /ur-/ + Affirm. Pres.
Pres-DSR$_4$	Neg-Interrog. Pres. $\longrightarrow$ /is-/ + Neg. Pres.
Pres-DSR$_5$	Movable Affix $\longrightarrow$ Pre-Verbal

Examples of present tense structures generated by the above rules are shown in Tables 22-25. All forms are generated with -$P_3N_sG_m$- (prefix /i-/). Blank boxes indicate the form does not occur.

	Present	Pres., Prox. Affix	Pres., I.Obj., Prox. Affix
Affirm.	dayt:ˤawan	dadit:ˤawan	dasdit:ˤawan
Interrog.	isdayt:ˤawan	isdadit:ˤawan	isdasdit:ˤawn
Neg.	urdayt:ˤawan	urdadit:ˤawan	urdasdit:ˤawan
Neg. Int.	isurdayt:ˤawan	isurdadit:ˤawan	isurdadit:ˤawan

TABLE 22 - Structures generated from /t:ˤawan/, VH of /ʕawn/ in the present (SS)

	Present	Pres., Prox. Affix	Pres., I.Obj., Prox. Affix
Affirm.	daysˤawan	dadisˤawan	dasdisˤawan
Interrog.	isdaysˤawan	isdadisˤawan	isdasdisˤawan
Neg.	urdaysˤawan	urdadisˤawan	urdasdisˤawan
Neg. Int.	isurdaysˤawan	isurdadisˤawan	isurdasdisˤawan

TABLE 23 - Structures generated from /sˤawan/, SVH of /ʕawn/ in the present (SS)

	Present	Pres., Prox. Affix	Pres., I.Obj., Prox. Affix
Affirm.	dayt:mˤawan	dadit:mˤawan	
Interrog.	isdayt:mˤawan	isdadit:mˤawan	
Neg.	urdayt:mˤawan	urdadit:mˤawan	
Neg. Int.	isurdayt:mˤawan	isurdadit:mˤawan	

TABLE 24 - Structures generated from /t:mˤawan/, MVH of /ʕawn/ in the present (SS)

	Present	Pres., Prox. Affix	Pres., I.Obj., Prox. Affix
Affirm.	dayt:uˤawan		dasdit:uˤawan
Interrog.	isdayt:uˤawan		isdasdit:uˤawan
Neg.	urdayt:uˤawan		urdasdit:uˤawan
Neg. Int.	isurdayt:uˤawan		isurdasdit:uˤawan

TABLE 25 - Structures generated from /t:uˤawan/, TuVH of /ʢawn/ in the present (SS)

VI.4.7.6 Derivation of the Aorist

The aorist is a dependent tense that does not occur as sentence initial. It is formed from V (SV or MV) simply by the realization of /-PNG-/.

Rules for the Generation of the Aorist (from V):

Aor-DSR$_1$ Aorist ⟶ V + /-PNG-/

Aor-DSR$_2$ Movable Affixes ⟶ Post-Verbal

Aorist forms are identical with past tense forms of unablauted stems but differ from those of the ablauted stems by the ablaut.

Aorists generated by the above rules are shown in Table 26 for SS forms. All forms are generated with -$P_3N_sG_m$- (prefix /i-/).

	Aorist	Aorist, Prox. Affix	Aorist,I.Obj.,Prox.Aff.
V	iʕawn	iʕawnd	iʕawnasd
SV	isʕawn	isʕawnd	isʕawnasd
MV	imʕawan	imʕawand	

TABLE 26 - Aorists of /ʕawn/, its SV and MV (SS)

VI.4.7.7 <u>Derivation of the Participles</u>

This section discusses the derivation of past, present, and future participles both affirmative and negative.

The past participle is formed by suffixation of the participle suffix /-n/ to a derived past in $-P_3N_sG_m-$. Prefixation of /ur-/ gives the negative participle. Either of these two participles is used with subjects of any number or gender. A plural past participle formed by suffixation of /-in/ to past in $-P_3N_pG_m-$ is used only with plural (m,f) subjects.

The present participle is formed by suffixation of the participle suffix /-n/ to a derived present structure in $-P_3N_sG_m-$. Prefixation of /ur-/ gives its negative participle.

The future participle is derived by suffixation of the participle suffix /-n/ to a VH after the realization of $-P_3N_sG_m-$. Prefixation of /ur-/ gives its negative participle. A variant affirmative future participle (which has no negative) may be derived by suffixation of the participle suffix /-n/ to a derived aorist in $-P_3N_sG_m-$.

Rules for the Generation of the Participles

Part-DSR_1 (Neg) Past Part. $\longrightarrow$ (/ur-/) + $Past_{[-P_3N_sG_m-]}$ + /-n/

Part-DSR_2 Plural Past Part. $\longrightarrow$ $Past_{[-P_3N_pG_m-]}$ + /-n/

Part-DSR_3 (Neg) Fut.Part. $\longrightarrow$ (/ur-/) + $Pres_{[-P_3N_sG_m-]}$ + /-n/

Part-DSR_4 (Neg) Fut.Part. $\longrightarrow$ (/ur-/) + $VH_{[-P_3N_sG_m-]}$ + /-n/

Part-DSR_5 Variant Fut. Part. $\longrightarrow$ $Aor_{[-P_3N_sG_m-]}$ + /-n/

Part-DSR_6 Movable Affix $\longrightarrow$ Pre-Participle

Participles derived by the above rules for the V 25 /ˤawn/ are shown in Tables 27-29 for SS forms.

All participles occur in structures using the relative pronouns /n:a/ 'who, that' or /aɣra/ 'who will, that will': e.g., /n:a yˤawn:/ means 'who helped', /n:a dayt:ˤawan:/ means 'who is helping' and /aɣra yt:ˤawan:/ means 'who will help'.

	Past. Partic.	Past Part., Prox. Affix	Past Part., I.Obj., Prox. Affix
Affirm.	iˤawn:	diˤawn:	asdiˤawn:
Neg.	uriˤawn:	urdiˤawn:	urasdiˤawn:
Plural	ˤawn:in	dˤawn:in	asdˤawn:in

TABLE 27 - Past Participles of /ˤawn/ (SS)

	Pres.Part.	Pres.Part., Prox. Affix	Pres.Part.,I.Obj., Prox. Affix
Affirm	dayt:ˁawan:	dadit:ˁawan:	dasdit:ˁawan:
Neg.	urdayt:ˁawan:	urdadit:ˁawan:	urdasdit:ˁawan:

TABLE 28 - Present Participles of /t:ˁawan/, VH of /ˁawn/ (SS)

	Fut. Part.	Fut. Part., Prox. Affix	Fut.Part.,I.Obj., Prox. Affix
Affirm.	it:ˁawan:	dit:ˁawan:	asdi :ˁawan:
Neg.	urit:ˁawan:	urdit:ˁawan:	urasdit:ˁawan:
Variant Form	iˁawn:	diˁawn:	asdiˁawn:

TABLE 29 - Future Participles of /ˁawn/ and its VH /t:ˁawan/ (SS)

VI.4.7.8 Summary of DSR's for Temporal, Modal and Participle Derivations (T/M-P)[11]

T/M-P-DSR_1 Imperative → $\left\{\begin{array}{l}V\\SV\\MV\\MSV\end{array}\right\}$ + /-PNG_2/

T/M-P-DSR_2 Energetic Imperative → $\left\{\begin{array}{l}VH\\SVH\\MVH\\MSVH\end{array}\right\}$ + /-PNG_2/

T/M-P-DSR_3 Neg. Imper. ⟶ /adur-/ + $\left\{\begin{array}{l}VH\\SVH\\MVH\\MSVH\end{array}\right\}$ + /-PNG_2/

T/M-P-DSR_4 Hortatory ⟶ $\left\{\begin{array}{l}V\\SV\\MV\\MSV\end{array}\right\}$ + /-PNG_1/

T/M-P-DSR_5 $Hortatory_{[+Movement]}$ ⟶

$\left\{\begin{array}{l}/k{:}r/\\/ya\d{l}{:}ah/\end{array}\right\}$ + /-PNG_1/ + /ad-/ + /-P_1N_p-/ + $\left\{\begin{array}{l}V\\SV\\MV\\MSV\end{array}\right\}$

T/M-P-DSR$_6$

$$\text{Affirm. Past} \longrightarrow \left\{\begin{matrix}\text{V}\\ \text{SV}\\ \text{MV}\\ \text{MSV}\\ \text{TuV}\end{matrix}\right\} + \text{/-PNG-/} + \text{(Abl)}$$

T/M-P-DSR$_7$

$$\text{Interrog. Past} \longrightarrow \text{/is-/} + \text{Affirm. Past}$$

T/M-P-DSR$_8$

$$\text{Neg. Past} \longrightarrow \text{/ur-/} + \left\{\begin{matrix}\text{V}\\ \text{SV}\\ \text{MV}\\ \text{MSV}\\ \text{TuV}\end{matrix}\right\} + \text{/-PNG-/} + \text{(Abl)}$$

T/M-P-DSR$_9$

$$\text{Neg-Interrog. Past} \longrightarrow \text{/is-/} + \text{Neg. Past}$$

T/M-P-DSR$_{10}$

$$\text{Affirm. Fut.} \longrightarrow \text{/ad-/} + \left\{\begin{matrix}\text{V}\\ \text{SV}\\ \text{MV}\\ \text{MSV}\\ \text{TuV}\end{matrix}\right\} + \text{/-PNG-/}$$

T/M-P-DSR$_{11}$

$$\text{Interrog. Fut} \xrightarrow[\text{"will"}]{} \text{/id:-/} + \text{Affirm. Fut.}$$

T/M-P-DSR$_{12}$

$$\text{Neg.Fut.} \longrightarrow \text{/ur-/} + \left\{\begin{matrix}\text{VH}\\ \text{SVH}\\ \text{MVH}\\ \text{MSVH}\\ \text{TuVH}\end{matrix}\right\} + \text{/-PNG-/}$$

$T/M\text{-}P\text{-}DSR_{13}$ Interrog. Fut. $\xrightarrow[\text{"Q"}]{}$ Qw + $\left\{\begin{array}{l} \text{VH} \\ \text{SVH} \\ \text{MVH} \\ \text{MSVH} \\ \text{TuVH} \end{array}\right\}$ + /-PNG-/

$T/M\text{-}P\text{-}DSR_{14}$ Affirm. Pres. $\longrightarrow \left\{\begin{array}{l} \text{/da-/} \\ \text{/l:a-/} \end{array}\right\}$ + $\left\{\begin{array}{l} \text{VH} \\ \text{SVH} \\ \text{MVH} \\ \text{MSVH} \\ \text{TuVH} \end{array}\right\}$ + /-PNG-/

$T/M\text{-}P\text{-}DSR_{15}$ Interrog. Pres. $\longrightarrow$ /is-/ + Affirm. Pres.

$T/M\text{-}P\text{-}DSR_{16}$ Neg. Present $\longrightarrow$ /ur-/ + Affirm. Pres.

$T/M\text{-}P\text{-}DSR_{17}$ Neg-Interr. Pres. $\longrightarrow$ /is-/ + /ur-/ + Affirm. Pres.

$T/M\text{-}P\text{-}DSR_{18}$ Aorist $\longrightarrow \left\{\begin{array}{l} \text{V} \\ \text{SV} \\ \text{MV} \\ \text{MSV} \end{array}\right\}$ + /-PNG-/

$T/M\text{-}P\text{-}DSR_{19}$ Past Part. $\longrightarrow \left\{\begin{array}{l} \text{(/ur-/) + Past}_{[-P_3N_sG_m-]} + \text{/-n/} \\ \text{Past}_{[-P\ N\ G\ -]} + \text{/-in/ Plural} \end{array}\right\}$

$T/M\text{-}P\text{-}DSR_{20}$ Present Part. $\longrightarrow$ (/ur-/) + $\text{Pres}_{[-P_3N_sG_m-]}$ + /-n/

$T/M\text{-}P\text{-}DSR_{21}$ Fut. Part. $\rightarrow \left\{ \begin{array}{l} (/ur\text{-}/) + SVH_{[P_3 N_s G_m\text{-}]} + /\text{-}n/ \\ Aor_{[\text{-}P_3 N_s G_m\text{-}]} + /\text{-}n/ \quad \text{Affirm.} \end{array} \right\}$

$T/M\text{-}P\text{-}DSR_{22}$ Movable Affix $\rightarrow \left\{ \begin{array}{l} \text{Post-Verbal} \,/\, [\text{-Temporal, Modal prefix or preposition}] \\ \text{Pre-Verbal} \,/\, [\text{+Temp/Mod pref. or prep.}] \\ \text{Pre-Participle} \end{array} \right\}$

VI.5 Morphophonemic Sketch

VI.5.1 Introduction

The morphophonemic changes which occur in the dialect under consideration, mainly in verb derivations, may be divided into six classes: voicing assimilation, reduction, hiatus, and change of vowel to glide: (V ⟶ G).

This section states the morphophonemic changes in phonemic symbols* (in VI.5.2) and then (in VI.5.3) gives examples of these changes using verbs from the Verb List and the end of this chapter. Phonemic symbols are written between slashes / /; hyphen /-/ represents morpheme boundary; /#/ word boundary.

VI.5.2 General Rules of Tamazight Verb Morphophonemics [12]

The following rules apply to /-PNG-/ inflection and combination of verb with temporal and modal prefixes. These rules are referred to as General Surface Structure Rules (Gen-SSR's) since they affect the shape of any verbal derivation in contexts specified in the examples given in VI.5.3.

---

* For a more elaborate description of verb morphophonemics see Abdel-Massih, Ernest, Tamazight Verb Structure: A Generative Approach, Indiana University Press: Bloomington, Indiana, 1971.

	Sequence	Voicing Assimilation	Flatness Assimilation	Articulatory Assimilation	Reduction
Gen-SSR$_1$	/t-d/	dd			d:
Gen-SSR$_2$	/t-ḍ/	dḍ	ḍḍ		ḍ:
Gen-SSR$_3$	/d-t/	tt			t:
Gen-SSR$_4$	/ḍ-t/	ṭt	ṭṭ		ṭ:
Gen-SSR$_5$	/ḍ-t:/	ṭt:	ṭṭ:		ṭ:
Gen-SSR$_6$	/ḍ-d/		ḍḍ		ḍ:
Gen-SSR$_7$	/t-t:/				t:
Gen-SSR$_8$	/t:-t/				t:
Gen-SSR$_9$	/t-t/				t:
Gen-SSR$_{10}$	/d-d/				d:
Gen-SSR$_{11}$	/t-ṭ/		ṭṭ		ṭ:
Gen-SSR$_{12}$	/γ-t/	xt			
Gen-SSR$_{13}$	/γ-γ/	qq			q:
Gen-SSR$_{14}$	{/n-n#/ /n-n-v-/}				{n:# n:v-}
Gen-SSR$_{15}$	/m-m#/				m:
Gen-SSR$_{16}$	/r-r/				r:
Gen-SSR$_{17}$	/r-n#/			rr	r:
Gen-SSR$_{18}$	/l-n#/			ll	l:
Gen-SSR$_{19}$	/n-m#/			mm	m:
Gen-SSR$_{20}$	/d-š/			kk	k:
Gen-SSR$_{21}$	/d-ḳ/			ḳḳ	ḳ:
Gen-SSR$_{22}$	/d-n/			n	
Gen-SSR$_{23}$	/s-s/				s:
Gen-SSR$_{24}$	/s-ṣ/		ṣṣ		ṣ:

	Sequence	Voicing Assimilation	Flatness Assimilation	Articulatory Assimilation	Reduction
Gen-SSR$_{25}$	/s-ž/	zž		žž	ž:
Gen-SSR$_{26}$	/s-š/			šš	š:
Gen-SSR$_{27}$	/s-z/	zz			z:
Gen-SSR$_{28}$	/s-ẓ/	zẓ	ẓẓ		ẓ:
Gen-SSR$_{29}$	/s-d/	zd			
Gen-SSR$_{30}$	/z-t/	st			
Gen-SSR$_{31}$	/ẓ-t/	ṣt	ṣṭ		
Gen-SSR$_{32}$	/t-z/	dz			
Gen-SSR$_{33}$	/ṭ-ž/	ḍž			

	Sequence	Hiatus	V ⟶ G	Reduction
Gen-SSR$_{34}$	/i-i/	iyi		
Gen-SSR$_{35}$	/i-a/	iya		
Gen-SSR$_{36}$	/u-a/	uya		
Gen-SSR$_{37}$	/u-i/	uyi		
Gen-SSR$_{38}$	/u-u/	uyu		
Gen-SSR$_{39}$	/a/a/			a
Gen-SSR$_{40}$	/#i-i/		yi	
Gen-SSR$_{41}$	/#i-a/		ya	
Gen-SSR$_{42}$	/#i-u/		yu	
Gen-SSR$_{43}$	/-i-i-/		iy	
Gen-SSR$_{44}$	/-a-i/		ay	

VI.5.3 Examples

Rule 1

129	/t-db:r-d/[*] → /d:b:rd/		'you (s) managed'
129	/t-db:r/ → /d:b:r/		'she managed'
251	/t-šm:t-d/ → /tšm:d:/		'you (s) cheated'
251	/i-šm:t-d/ → /išm:d:/		'he cheated'

Rule 2

138	/t-ḍr:ˤ/ → /ḍ:r:ˤ/		'she screamed'
136	/ṭ-ḍl:ˤ-d/ → /ḍ:l:ˤd/		'you (s) flattened bread'

Rule 3

251	/ad-t-šm:t/ → /at:šm:t/		'she will cheat'
251	/ad-t-šm:t-nt/ → /at:šm:tnt/		'you (fp) will cheat'

Rule 4

300	/i-ˤrḍ-t/ → /iˤrṭ:/		'he invited him'

Rule 5

300	/i-ˤrḍ-t:/ → /iˤrṭ:/		'he invited her'

Rule 6

238	/t-ṣfḍ-d/ → /tsfḍ:/		'you (s) wiped'
197	/i-nṣḍ-d/ → /insḍ:/		'he blew his nose' (+ prox.)

---

* A numeral preceding an example refers to the number of the simple verb stem in the Verb List from which the form is derived (see Verb List, pp. 262-282).

Rule 7

46 /da-t-t:ʕum-d/→/dat:ʕumd/ 'you (s) swim'

113 /da-t-t:ʕawan/→/dat:ʕawan/ 'she helps'

Rule 8

88 /da-t:-t-t:saʕad/→/dat:t:saʕad/ 'she helps her'

Rule 9

378 /da-t-t-ks:a-d/→/dat:ks:ad/ 'you tend it (m)'

Rule 10

88 /i-saʕd-d/——→ /isaʕd:/ 'he helped' (+ proximity)

113 /ad-d-ʕawn-γ/→/ad:ʕawnγ/ 'I'll help' (+ proximity)

Rule 11

261 /t-ṭfṣ/——→ /ṭ:fṣ/ 'she folded'

262 /t-ṭrẓ-d/——→ /ṭ:rẓd/ 'you (s) embroidered'

Rule 12

104 /zayd-γ-t/——→/zaydxt/ 'I added it'

Rule 13

341 /f:γ-γ/——→ /f:q:/ 'I went out'

157 /da-t:fr:aγ-γ/→/dat:fr:aq:/ 'I am pouring'

Rule 14

113	/ʕawn-n/ ⟶	/ʕawn:/	'they (m) helped'
113	/ʕawn-nt/ ⟶	/ʕawnnt/	'they (f) helped'
113	/ʕawn-n-in/ ⟶	/ʕawn:in/	plural participle of /ʕawn/

Rule 15

311	/t-ɣṛ:m-m/ ⟶	/tɣṛ:m:/	'you (mp) indemnified'
311	/t-ɣṛ:m-m-t/ ⟶	/tɣṛ:mmt/	'you (mp) indemnified'

Rule 16

450	/ur-riɣ/ ⟶	/ur:iɣ/	'I do not want'

Rule 17

296	/ʕm:ṛ-n/ ⟶	/ʕm:r:/	'they (m) filled'
296	/ʕm:ṛ-nt/ ⟶	/ʕm:rnt/	'they (f) filled'

Rule 18

63	/slil-n/ ⟶	/slil:/	'they (m) rinsed'
63	/slil-nt/ ⟶	/slilnt/	'they (f) rinsed'

Rule 19

375	/ad-t-gn-m/ ⟶	/at:gm:/	'you (mp) will sleep'
279	/t-xzn-m-t/ ⟶	/txznmt/	'you (mp) stored it'

Rule 20

37 /ad-š-i-sal/ ⟶ /ak:isal/ 'he will ask you (ms)'

Rule 21

37 /ad-kn-i-sal/ ⟶ /aḳ:nisal/ 'he will ask you (mp)'

Rule 22

37 /ad-n-sal/ ⟶ /ansal/ 'we will ask'

200 /ad-n-ntl/ ⟶ /anntl/ 'we will hide'

200 /ad-ntl-γ/ ⟶ /adntlγ/ 'I will hide'

Rule 23

62 /sdid/ 'be thin' : SV /s-sdid/ —— /s:did/

232 /is-sl:m-n/ ⟶ /is:l:mn/ 'did they (m) greet?'

Rule 24

65 /ṣmid/ 'be cold' : SV /s-ṣmid/ ⟶ /ṣ:mid/

245 /is-ṣy:f-n/ ⟶ /iṣ:y:fn/ 'did they harvest the summer crops?'

Rule 25

438 /žru/ 'happen' : SV /s-žru/ ⟶ /ž:ru/

289 /is-žbr-n/ ⟶ /iž:br:/ 'did they (m) come back?'

Rule 26

428 /šḍu/ 'smell' : SV /s-šḍu/ → /š:ḍu/

18 /is-šk:a-n/ → /iš:k:an/ 'did they (m) doubt?'

Rule 27

436 /zwu/ 'dry' : SV /s-zwu/ → /z:wu/

103 /is-zawg:-n/ → /iz:awg:n/ 'did they (m) ask protection?'

Rule 28

106 /is-ẓawḍ-n/ → /iẓ:awḍn/ 'did they (m) throw away?'

Rule 29

132 /is-dlš-n/ → /izdlšn/ 'did they (m) massage?'

113 /is-d-i-ʕawn/ → /izdiʕawn/ 'did he help?' (+ prox.)

113 /is-da-t:ʕawan-n/ → /izdat:ʕawan:/ 'are they (m) helping?'

Rule 30

79 /i-ḥarz-t/ → /iḥarst/ 'he forbade him'

Rule 31

325 /i-amẓ-t/ → /yumṣṭ/ 'he took it (m)'

Rule 32

280 /t-zdm-d/ → /dzdmd/ 'you (s) collected wood'

Rule 33

289	/t-žbr-d/ ⟶ /džbrd/	'you (s) came back'

Rules 34- 39

/i-i/	449	/ini-i/ ⟶ /iniyi/	'tell me'
/i-a/	449	/ini-as/ ⟶ /iniyas/	'tell him'
/u-a/	402	/d:u-at/ ⟶ /d:uyat/	'go (mp)'
/u-i/	431	/šru-i/ ⟶ /šruyi/	'rent (for) me'
/u-u/	364	/it:u-us:a/ ⟶ /it:uyus:a/	'it was tied'
/a-a/ ⟶ /a/			
	18	/šk:a-at/ ⟶ /šk:at/	'doubt (mp)!'
	113	/da-as-i-t:ˁawan/ ⟶ /dasit:ˁawan/	'he helps him'
	113	/da-aγ-i-t:sal/ ⟶ /daγit:sal/	'he asks us'

Rules 40-43

51	/i-aẓum/ ⟶ /yaẓum/	'he fasted'
57	/i-iẓil/ ⟶ /yiẓil/	'he was nice'
362	/i-ufa/ ⟶ /yufa/	'he found'

Rule 44

89	/t-saˁf-š-d/ ⟶ /tsaˁfšid/	'she was patient with you (s)' (+ prox.)
89	/t-saˁf-t-d/ ⟶ /tsaˁftid/	'she was patient with him' (+ prox.)
89	/t-saˁf-aγ-d/ ⟶ /tsaˁfaγd/	'she was patient with us' (+ prox.)

* * *

Notes on the Verb in Ayt Seghrouchen (A.S.)

Only differences from Ayt Ayache (A.A.) grammar are discussed here.

1 These are /d:/ and /n:/ in A.S., e.g.,

/ṛaḥ/	to go
/i-ṛaḥ-d:/	he came
/i-ṛaḥ-n:/	he went there

2 In A.S. the present tense prefix is only /l:a-/, e.g.,

/l:a-i-t:ʕum:/	he is swimming

3 In A.S. the progressive or inchoative prefix is /al-/, e.g.,

/al-i-t:ʕum:/	he started to swim

4 In A.S. this morpheme is /is-/ which is the Interrogative particle. In most cases in future construction /is-/ is followed by /-d-/, a particle of emphasis, e.g.,

/is-d-ad-i-ʕum:/	will he swim?

5 The particle is /is-/ but it precedes a verb stem in the Habitual form without a present tense prefix; e.g.,

/is-i-t:ʕum:/	is he swimming? does he swim?

6 In A.S. there are two negative particles:
(a) /ur-/ before V, SV, ... in the past and before VH in the formation of the future negative and (b) /ul:i-/ before VH, SVH, ... (present); e.g.,

/i-ʕum:/	he swam
/ur-i-ʕum:/	he did not swim
/l:a-i-t:ʕum:/	he is swimming
/ul:i-i-t:ʕum:/	he is not swimming
/adiʕum:/	he will swim
/urit:ʕum:/	he will not swim

7

-PNG	Imper. Suffix
2sm	-∅
2sf	-∅
2pm	-m
2pf	-nt

TABLE 1 - Second Person Imperative Suffixes (A.S.).

-PNG	Imper. Suffix
1dm	-ax
1df	-ntax
1pm	-max
1pf	-ntax

TABLE 2 - Hortatory Suffixes (A.S.).

8

-PNG-	Inflectional Affix
1s	___x
2s	t___t
3sm	i___
3sf	t___
1p	n___
2pm	t___m
2pf	t___nt
3pm	___n
3pf	___nt

TABLE 3 - Ayt Seghrouchen -PNG- Affixes

9 Ablaut in Ayt Seghrouchen may be summed up as follows:

i. Unablauted stems: show no ablaut (neither in affirmative not negative) and are represented by the verb stems /ʕum:/ 'to swim' of the structure ‖AVC‖ , /barš/ 'to congratulate' of the structure ‖AVCD‖ , /bd:/ 'to stand up' of the structure ‖AB:‖ , /dž:/ 'to let', /f:u/ 'to dawn', and /bḍu/ 'to divide' of the structure ‖ABV‖. For conjugations see Table #4 -11 (A.S.).

ii. Ablauted Stems:

(a) Ø:0 ablaut are stems which have no ablaut in Affirmative past but have /i/ ablaut in the negative. This is represented by /fṛḥ/ 'to be happy' /bry/'to grind' (see Table 16 (A.S.) for changes in /-y#/ of this type). /qṛ:r/ 'to decide', /bndq/ 'to bow', /l:γ̣m/ 'to twist' and /ẓ:ʕ/ 'to dismiss' of the structure ‖A(:)B(:)(C)(D)‖ . For conjugations see Tables #12 - 23 (A.S.).

(b) i/a ablaut for members of the ‖ABa#‖ structure represented here by /bda/ 'to start'. This group has /i/ ablaut for first and second person singular and /a/ for the rest of the PNG paradigm. This is the only group that is ablauted in the future. For conjugations see Tables #24 - 27 (A.S.).

(c) i/u ablaut occurs with verbs as /iž/ 'to do', /k:/ 'to pass' /ls/ 'to shear' of the structure ‖A(:)‖ or ‖AB‖ . /i/ occurs with PNG: 1s, 2s, 2pm,f and 3pm,f. /u/ occurs with PNG: 3m,f and 1p. For conjugations see Tables #28 - 31 (A.S.).

(d) a - u ablaut refers to change of a to u, e.g., /adf/ 'to enter' or /džal:/ 'to swear' of the structure ‖aBC‖ or ‖(A)BaD‖ . For conjugations see Tables #32 - 35 (A.S.).

(e) a - i ablaut refers to change of a to i for only two verbs, namely /awḍ/ ' to reach', /awy/ 'to take away'. See conjugations in Tables #36 - 39 (A.S.).

-PNG-	Affirm.	Neg.	Interr.	Neg. Interr.
1s	ʕum:x	urʕum:x	isʕum:x	isurʕum:x
2s	tʕum:t	urtʕum:t	istʕum:t	isurtʕum:t
3sm	iʕum:	uriʕum:	isiʕum:	isuriʕum:
3sf	tʕum:	urtʕum:	istʕum:	isurtʕum:
1p	nʕum:	urnʕum:	isnʕum:	isurnʕum:
2pm	tʕum:m	urtʕum:m	istʕum:m	isurtʕum:m
2pf	tʕum:nt	urtʕum:nt	istʕum:nt	isurtʕum:nt
3pm	ʕum:n	urʕum:n	isʕum:n	isurʕum:n
3pf	ʕum:nt	urʕum:nt	isʕum:nt	isurʕum:nt

TABLE 4 (A.S.) - /-PNG-/ paradigms for unablauted /ʕum:/ 'to swim' in the past.

-PNG-	Affirm.	Neg.	Interr.	Neg. Interr.
1s	adʕum:x	urt:ʕum:x	isad:ʕum:x	isurt:ʕum:x
2s	at:ʕum:t	urt:ʕum:t	isat:ʕum:t	isurt:ʕum:t
3sm	adiʕum:	urit:ʕum:	isadiʕum:	isurit:ʕum:
3sf	at:ʕum:	urt:ʕum:	isat:ʕum:	isurt:ʕum:
1p	an:ʕum:	urnt:ʕum:	isan:ʕum:	isurnt:ʕum:
2pm	at:ʕum:m	urt:ʕum:m	isat:ʕum:m	isurt:ʕum:m
2pf	at:ʕum:nt	urt:ʕum:nt	isat:ʕum:nt	isurt:ʕum:nt
3pm	adʕum:n	urt:ʕum:n	isadʕum:n	isurt:ʕum:n
3pf	adʕum:nt	urt:ʕum:nt	isadʕum:nt	isurt:ʕum:nt

TABLE 5 (A.S.) - /-PNG-/ paradigms for unablauted /ʕum:/ 'to swim' in the future.

-PNG-	Affirm.	Neg.	Interrog.	Neg.Interr.
1s	l:at:ʕum:x	ul:it:ʕum:x	ist:ʕum:x	isul:it:ʕum:x
2s	l:at:ʕum:t	ul:it:ʕum:t	ist:ʕum:t	isul:it:ʕum:t
3sm	l:ayt:ʕum:	ul:iyt:ʕum:	isit:ʕum:	isul:iyt:ʕum:
3sf	l:at:ʕum:	ul:it:ʕum:	ist:ʕum:	isul:it:ʕum:
1p	l:ant:ʕum:	ul:int:ʕum:	isnt:ʕum:	isul:int:ʕum:
2pm	l:at:ʕum:m	ul:it:ʕum:m	ist:ʕum:m	isul:it:ʕum:m
2pf	l:at:ʕum:nt	ul:it:ʕum:nt	ist:ʕum:nt	isul:itʕum:nt
3pm	l:at:ʕum:n	ul:it:ʕum:n	ist:ʕum:n	isul:it:ʕum:n
3pf	l:at:ʕum:nt	ul:it:ʕum:nt	ist:ʕum:nt	isul:it:ʕum:nt

TABLE 6 (A.S.) - /-PNG-/ paradigms for unablauted /ʕum:/ in the present.

-PNG#	Imper.	Energetic Imper.	Neg. Imper.
2s	ʕum:	t:ʕum:	adurt:ʕum:
2pm	ʕum:m	t:ʕum:m	adurt:ʕum:m
2sf	ʕum:nt	t:ʕum:nt	adurt:ʕum:nt

TABLE 7 (A.S.) - Imperative structures for unablauted /ʕum:/

-PNG-	Affirm.	Neg.	Interrog.	Neg. Interr.
1s	bd:x	urbd:x	isbd:x	isurbd:x
2s	tbd:t	urtbd:t	istbd:t	isurtbd:t
3sm	ibd:	uribd:	isibd:	isuribd:
3sf	tbd:	urtbd:	istbd:	isurtbd:
1p	nbd:	urnbd:	isnbd:	isurnbd:
2pm	tbd:m	urtbd:m	istbd:m	isurtbd:m
2pf	tbd:nt	urtbd:nt	ustbd:nt	isurtbd:nt
3pm	bd:n	urbd:n	isbd:n	isurbd:n
3pf	bd:nt	urbd:nt	isbd:nt	isurbd:nt

TABLE 8 (A.S.) - /-PNG-/ paradigms for unablauted /bd:/ 'to stand up' in the past.

-PNG-	Affirm.	Neg.	Interrog.	Neg. Interr.
1s	adbd:x	urt:bid:idx	isadbd:x	isurt:bid:idx
2s	at:bd:t	urt:bid:it:	isatbd:t	isurt:bid:it:
3sm	adibd:	urit:bid:id	isadibd:	isurit:bid:id
3sf	at:bd:	urt:bid:id	isadtbd:	isurt:bid:id
1p	an:bd:	urnt:bid:id	isadnbd:	isurnt:bid:id
2pm	at:bd:m	urt:bid:idm	isadtbd:m	isurt:bid:idm
2pf	at:bd:nt	urt:bid:idnt	isadtbd:nt	isurt:bid:idnt
3pm	adbd:n	urt:bid:idn	isadbd:n	isurt:bid:idn
3pf	adbd:nt	urt:bid:idn	isadbd:nt	isurt:bid:idnt

TABLE 9 (A.S.) - /-PNG-/ paradigms for unablauted /bd:/ 'to stand up' in the future.

-PNG-	Affirm.	Neg.	Interrog.	Neg.Interr.
1s	l:at:bid:idx	ul:it:bid:idx	ist:bid:idx	isul:it:bid:idx
2s	l:at:bid:it:	ul:it:bid:it:	ist:bid:it:	isul:it:bid:it:
3sm	l:ayt:bid:id	ul:iyt:bid:id	isit:bid:id	isul:iyt:bid:id
3sf	l:at:bid:id	ul:it:bid:id	ist:bid:id	isul:it:bid:id
1p	l:ant:bid:id	ul:int:bid:id	isnt:bid:id	isul:int:bid:id
2pm	l:at:bid:idm	ul:it:bid:idm	ist:bid:idm	isul:it:bid:idm
2pf	l:at:bid:idnt	ul:it:bid:idnt	ist:bid:idnt	isul:it:bid:idnt
3pm	l:at:bid:idn	ul:it:bid:idn	ist:bid:idn	isul:it:bid:idn
3pf	l:at:bid:idnt	ul:it:bid:idnt	ist:bid:idnt	isul:it:bid:idnt

TABLE 10 (A.S.) - /-PNG-/ paradigms for unablauted /bd:/ 'to stand up' in the present

-PNG#	Imper.	Energetic Imper.	Neg. Imper.
2s	bd:	t:bid:id	adurt:bid:id
2pm	bd:m	t:bid:idm	adurt:bid:idm
2pf	bd:nt	t:bid:idnt	adurt:bid:idnt

TABLE 11 (A.S.) - Imperative structures for unablauted /bd:/ 'to stand up'.

-PNG-	Affirm.	Neg.	Interrog.	Neg. Interr.
1s	fṛḥx	urfrihx	isfṛḥx	isurfrihx
2s	tfṛḥt	urtfṛiḥt	istfṛḥt	isurtfṛiḥt
3pm	ifṛḥ	urifṛiḥ	isifṛḥ	isurifrih
3pf	tfṛḥ	urtfṛiḥ	istfṛḥ	isurtfṛiḥ
1p	nfṛḥ	un:fṛiḥ	isnfṛḥ	isun:fṛiḥ
2pm	tfṛḥm	urtfṛiḥm	istfṛḥm	isurtfṛiḥm
2pf	tfṛḥnt	urtfṛiḥnt	istfṛḥnt	isurtfṛiḥnt
3pm	fṛḥn	urfṛiḥn	isfṛḥn	isurfṛiḥn
3pf	fṛḥnt	urfṛiḥnt	isfṛḥnt	isurfṛiḥnt

TABLE 12 (A.S.) - /-PNG-/ paradigms for /fṛḥ/ 'to be happy' of the Ø:0 ablaut in the past

-PNG-	Affirm.	Neg.	Interrog.	Neg. Interr.
1s	adfṛḥx	urfṛ:ḥx	isadfṛx	isurfṛ:ḥx
2s	at:fṛḥt	urtfṛ:ḥt	isat:fṛḥt	isurtfṛ:ḥt
3sm	adifṛḥ	urifṛ:ḥ	isadifṛḥ	isurifṛ:ḥ
3sf	at:fṛḥ	urtfṛ:ḥ	isat:fṛḥ	isurtfṛ:ḥ
1p	an:fṛḥ	urnfṛ:ḥ	isan:fṛḥ	isurnfṛ:ḥ
2pm	at:fṛḥm	urtfṛ:ḥm	isat:fṛḥm	isurtfṛ:ḥm
2pf	at:fṛḥnt	urtfṛ:ḥnt	isat:fṛḥnt	isurtfṛ:ḥnt
3pm	adfṛḥn	urfṛ:ḥn	isadfṛḥn	isurfṛ:ḥn
3pf	adfṛḥnt	urfṛ:ḥnt	isadfṛḥnt	isurfṛ:ḥnt

TABLE 13 (A.S.) - /-PNG-/ paradigms for /fṛḥ/ 'to be happy' in the future

-PNG-	Affirm.	Neg.	Interrog.	Neg. Interr.
1s	l:afṛ:ḥx	ul:ifṛ:ḥx	isfṛ:ḥx	isul:ifṛ:ḥx
2s	l:atfṛ:ḥt	ul:itfṛ:ḥt	istfṛ:ḥt	isul:itfṛ:ḥt
3sm	l:ayfṛ:ḥ	ul:iyfṛ:ḥ	isifṛ:ḥ	isul:iyfṛ:ḥ
3sf	l:atfṛ:ḥ	ul:tfṛ:ḥ	istfṛ:ḥ	isul:itfṛ:ḥ
1p	l:anfṛ:ḥ	ul:infṛ:ḥ	isnfṛ:ḥ	isul:infṛ:ḥ
2pm	l:atfṛ:ḥm	ul:itfṛ:ḥm	istfṛ:ḥm	isul:itfṛ:ḥm
2pf	l:atfṛ:ḥnt	ul:itfṛ:ḥnt	istfṛ:ḥnt	isul:itfṛ:ḥnt
3pm	l:afṛ:ḥn	ul:ifṛ:ḥn	isfṛ:ḥn	isul:ifṛ:ḥn
3pf	l:afṛ:ḥnt	ul:ifṛ:ḥnt	isfṛ:ḥnt	isul:ifṛ:ḥnt

TABLE 14 (A.S.) - /-PNG-/ paradigms for /fṛḥ/ 'to be happy' in the present.

-PNG#	Imper.	Energetic Imper.	Neg. Imper.
2s	fṛḥ	fṛ:ḥ	adurfṛ:ḥ
2pm	fṛḥm	fṛ:ḥm	adurfṛ:ḥm
2pf	fṛḥnt	fṛ:ḥnt	adurfṛ:ḥnt

TABLE 15 (A.S.) - Imperative structures for ablauted /fṛḥ/ 'to be happy'.

-PNG-	Affirm.	Neg.	Interrog.	Neg. Interr.
1s	brix	urbrix	isbrix	isurbrix
2sm	tbrit	urtbrit	istbrit	isurtbrit
2sm	ibry	uribriy	isibry	isuribriy
3sf	tbriy	urtbriy	istbry	isurtbriy
1p	nbry	urnbriy	isnbry	isurnbriy
2pm	tbrim	urtbrim	istbrim	isurtbrim
2pf	tbrint	urtbrint	istbrint	isurtbrint
3pm	brin	urbriyn	isbrin	isurbrin
3pf	brint	urbriynt	isbrint	isurbrint

TABLE 16 (A.S.) - /-PNG-/ for /bry/ 'to grind' of the Ø:0 ablaut in the past.

-PNG-	Affirm.	Neg.	Interrog.	Neg. Interr.
1s	adbrix	urbr:ix	isadbrix	isurbr:ix
2s	at:brit	urtbr:it	idat:brit	isurtbr:it
3sm	adibriy	uribr:y	isadibry	isuribr:i
3sf	at:bry	urtbr:y	isat:bry	isurtbr:i
1p	an:bry	urnbr:y	isan:bry	isurnbr:i
2pm	at:brim	urtbr:im	isat:brim	isurtbr:im
2pf	at:brint	urtbr:int	isat:brint	isurtbr:int
3pm	adbrin	urbr:in	isatdbrin	isurbr:in
3pf	adbrint	urbr:int	isadbrint	isurbr:int

TABLE 17 (A.S.) - /-PNG-/ paradigms for /bry/ 'to grind' in the future.

-PNG-	Affirm.	Neg.	Interrog.	Neg. Interr.
1s	l:abr:ix	ul:ibr:ix	isbr:ix	isul:ibr:ix
2s	l:atbr:it	ul:itbr:it	isibr:it	isul:itbr:it
3sm	l:aybr:y	ul:iybr:y	isibr:y	isul:iybr:y
3sf	l:atbr:y	ul:itbr:y	istbr:y	isul:itbr:y
1p	l:anbr:y	ul:ibr:ix	isnbr:i	isul:inbr:im
2pm	l:atbr:im	ul:itbr:it	istbr:im	isul:itbr:im
2pf	l:atbr:int	ul:iybr:iy	istbr:int	isul:itbr:int
3pm	l:abr:in	ul:itbr:y	isbr:in	isul:ibr:in
3pf	l:abr:int	ul:itbr:int	isbr:int	isul:ibr:int

TABLE 18 (A.S.) - /-PNG-/ paradigms for /bry/ 'to grind' in the present.

-PNG#	Imper.	Energetic Imper.	Neg. Imper.
2s	bry	br:y	adurbr:y
2pm	brim	br:im	adurbr:im
2pf	brint	br:int	adurbr:int

TABLE 19 (A.S.) - Imperative structures for /bry/ 'to grind'.

-PNG-	Affirm.	Neg.	Interr.	Neg. Interr.
1s	ẓ:ʕx	urẓ:iʕx	isẓ:ʕx	isurẓ:iʕx
2s	tẓ:ʕt	urtẓ:iʕt	istẓ:ʕt	isurtẓ:iʕt
3sm	iẓ:ʕ	uriẓ:iʕ	isiẓ:ʕ	isuriẓ:iʕ
3sf	tẓ:ʕ	urtẓ:iʕ	istẓ:ʕ	isurtẓ:iʕ
1p	nẓ:ʕ	urnẓ:iʕ	isnẓ:ʕ	isurnẓ:iʕ
2pm	tẓ:ʕm	urtẓ:iʕm	istẓ:ʕm	isurtẓ:iʕm
2pf	tẓ:ʕnt	urtẓ:iʕnt	istẓ:ʕnt	isurtẓ:iʕnt
3pm	ẓ:ʕn	urẓ:iʕn	isẓ:ʕn	isurẓ:iʕn
3pf	ẓ:ʕnt	urẓ:iʕnt	isẓ:ʕnt	isurẓ:iʕnt

TABLE 20 (A.S.) - /-PNG-/ paradigms for /ẓ:ʕ/ 'to chase' of the Ø:0 ablaut in the past.

-PNG-	Affirm.	Neg.	Interr.	Neg. Interr.
1s	adẓ:ʕx	urt:ẓʕx	isẓ:ʕx	isurẓ:iʕx
2s	at:ẓ:ʕt	urt:ẓʕt	istẓ:ʕt	isurtẓ:iʕt
3sm	adiẓ:ʕ	urit:ẓʕ	isiẓ:ʕ	isuriẓ:iʕ
3sf	at:ẓ:ʕ	urt:ẓ:ʕ	istẓ:ʕ	isurtẓ:iʕ
1p	an:ẓ:ʕ	urnt:ẓ:ʕ	isnẓ:ʕ	isurnẓ:iʕ
2pm	at:ẓ:ʕm	urt:ẓ:ʕm	istẓ:ʕm	isurtẓ:iʕm
2pf	at:ẓ:ʕnt	urt:ẓ:ʕnt	istẓ:ʕnt	isurtẓ:iʕnt
3pm	adẓ:ʕn	urt:ẓ:ʕn	istẓ:ʕn	isurẓ:iʕn
3pf	adẓ:ʕnt	urt:ẓ:ʕnt	isẓ:ʕnt	isurẓ:iʕnt

TABLE 21 (A.S.) - /-PNG-/ paradigms for /ẓ:ʕ/ 'to chase' in the future.

-PNG-	Affirm.	Neg.	Interr.	Neg. Interr.
1s	l:at:ẓ	ul:it:ẓ:ˤx	ist:ẓ:ˤx	isul:it:ẓ:ˤx
2s	l:at:ẓ:ˤt	ul:it:ẓ:ˤt	ist:ẓ:ˤt	isul:it:ẓ:ˤt
3sm	l:ayt:ẓ:ˤ	ul:iyt:ẓ:ˤ	isit:ẓ:ˤ	isul:iyt:ẓ:ˤ
3sf	l:at:ẓ:ˤ	ul:it:ẓ:ˤ	ist:ẓ:ˤ	isul:it:ẓ:ˤ
1p	l:ant:ẓ:ˤ	ul:int:ẓ:ˤ	isnt:ẓ:ˤ	isul:int:ẓ:ˤ
2pm	l:at:ẓ:ˤm	ul:it:ẓ:ˤm	ist:ẓ:ˤm	isul:it:ẓ:ˤm
2pf	l:at:ẓ:ˤnt	ul:it:ẓ:ˤnt	ist:ẓ:ˤnt	isul:it:ẓ:ˤnt
3pm	l:at:ẓ:ˤn	ul:it:ẓ:ˤn	ist:ẓ:ˤn	isul:it:ẓ:ˤn
3pf	l:at:ẓ:ˤnt	ul:it:ẓ:ˤnt	ist:ẓ:ˤnt	isul:it:ẓ:ˤnt

TABLE 22 (A.S.) - /-PNG-/ paradigms for /ẓ:ˤ/ 'to chase' in the present.

-PNG#	Imper.	Energetic Imper.	Neg. Imper.
2s	ẓ:ˤ	t:ẓ:ˤ	adurt:ẓ:ˤ
2pm	ẓ:ˤm	t:ẓ:ˤm	adurt:ẓ:ˤm
2pf	ẓ:ˤnt	t:ẓ:ˤnt	adurt:ẓ:ˤnt

TABLE 23 (A.S.) - Imperative structures for /ẓ:ˤ/ 'to chase'.

-PNG-	Affirm.	Neg.	Interr.	Neg. Interr.
1s	bdix	urbdix	isbdix	isurbdix
2s	tbdit	urtbdit	istbdit	isurtbdit
3sm	ibda	uribdi	isibda	isuribdi
3sf	tbda	urtbdi	istbda	isurtbdi
1p	nbda	un:bdi	isnbda	isurnbdi
2pm	tbdam	urtbdim	istbdam	isurtbdim
2pf	tbdant	urtbdint	istbdant	isurtbdint
3pm	bdan	urbdin	isbdan	isurbdin
3pf	bdant	urbdint	isbdant	isurbdint

TABLE 24 (A.S.) - /-PNG-/ paradigms for /bda/ 'to begin' of the i/a ablaut in the past.

-PNG-	Affirm.	Neg.	Interr.	Neg. Interr.
1s	adbdix	urbd:ix	isadbdix	isurbd:ix
2s	at:bdit	urtbd:it	isat:bdit	isurtbd:it
3sm	adibda	uribd:a	isadibda	isuribd:a
3sf	at:bda	urtbd:a	isat:bda	isurtbd:a
1p	an:bda	urnbd:a	isan:bda	isurnbd:a
2pm	at:bdam	urtbd:am	isat:bdam	isurtbd:am
2pf	at:bdant	urtbd:ant	isat:bdant	isurtbd:ant
3pm	adbdan	urbd:an	isadbdan	isurbd:an
3pf	adbdant	urbd:ant	isadbdant	isurbd:ant

TABLE 25 (A.S.) - /-PNG-/ paradigms for /bda/ 'to begin' of the i/a (only type ablauted) in the future.

-PNG-	Affirm.	Neg.	Interr.	Neg. Interr.
1s	l:abd:ix	ul:ibd:ix	isbd:ix	isul:ibd:ix
2s	l:atbd:it	ul:itbd:it	istbd:it	isul:itbd:it
3sm	l:aybd:a	ul:iybd:a	isibd:a	isul:iybd:a
3sf	l:atbd:a	ul:itbd:a	istbd:a	isul:itbd:a
1p	l:anbd:a	ul:inbd:a	isnbd:a	isul:inbd:a
2pm	l:atbd:am	ul:itbd:am	istbd:am	isul:itbd:am
2pf	l:atbd:ant	ul:itbd:ant	istbd:ant	isul:itbd:ant
3pm	l:abd:an	ul:ibd:an	isbd:an	isul:ibd:an
3pf	l:abd:ant	ul:ibd:ant	isbd:ant	isul:ibd:ant

TABLE 26 (A.S.) - /-PNG-/ paradigms for /bda/ 'to begin' in the present.

-PNG#	Imper.	Energetic Imper.	Neg. Imper.
2s	bda	bd:a	adurbd:a
2pm	bdam	bd:am	adurbd:am
2pf	bdant	bd:ant	adurbd:ant

TABLE 27 (A.S.) - Imperative structures of /bda/ 'to begin'.

-PNG-	Affirm.	Neg.	Interr.	Neg. Interr.
1s	dlix	urdlix	isdlix	isurdlix
2s	tdlit	urd:lit	isd:lit	isurd:lit
3sm	idlu	uridli	isidlu	isuridli
3sf	tdlu	urd:li	isd:lu	isurd:li
1p	ndlu	urndli	isndlu	isurndli
2pm	d:lim	urd:lim	isd:lim	isurd:lim
2pf	d:lint	urd:lint	isd:lint	isurd:lint
3pm	dlin	urdlin	isdlin	isurdlin
3pf	dlint	urdlint	isdlint	isurdlint

TABLE 28 (A.S.) - /-PNG-/ paradigms for /dl/ 'to cover' of the i/u ablaut in the past.

-PNG-	Affirm.	Neg.	Interr.	Neg. Interr.
1s	ad:lx	urd:alx	isad:lx	isurd:alx
2s	at:dlt	urtd:alt	isat:dlt	isurtd:alt
3sm	adidl	urid:al	isadidl	isurid:al
3sf	at:dl	urtd:al	isat:dl	isurtd:al
1p	an:dl	urnd:al	isan:dl	isurnd:al
2pm	at:dlm	urtd:alm	isat:dlm	isurtd:alm
2pf	at:dlnt	urtd:alnt	isat:dlnt	isurtd:alnt
3pm	ad:ln	urd:aln	isad:ln	isurd:aln
3pf	ad:lnt	urd:alnt	isad:lnt	isurd:alnt

TABLE 29 (A.S.) - /-PNG-/ paradigms for /dl/ 'to cover' in the future.

-PNG-	Affirm.	Neg.	Interr.	Neg. Interr.
1s	l:ad:alx	ul:id:alx	isd:alx	isul:id:alx
2s	l:atd:alt	ul:itd:alt	istd:alt	isul:itd:alt
3sm	l:ayd:al	ul:iyd:al	isid:al	isul:iyd:al
3sf	l:atd:al	ul:itd:al	istd:al	isul:itd:al
1p	l:and:al	ul:ind:al	isnd:al	isul:ind:al
2pm	l:atd:alm	ul:itd:alm	istd:alm	isul:itd:alm
2pf	l:atd:alnt	ul:itd:alnt	istd:alnt	isul:itd:alnt
3pm	l:ad:aln	ul:id:aln	isd:aln	isul:id:aln
3pf	l:ad:alnt	ul:id:alnt	isd:alnt	isul:id:alnt

TABLE 30 (A.S.) - /-PNG-/ paradigms for /dl/ 'to cover' in the present.

-PNG#	Imper.	Energetic Imper.	Neg. Imper
2s	dl	d:al	adurd:al
2pm	dlm	d:alm	adurd:alm
2pf	dlnt	d:alnt	adurd:alnt

TABLE 31 (A.S.) - Imperative structures for /dl/ 'to cover'.

-PNG-	Affirm.	Neg.	Interr.	Neg. Interr.
1s	udfx	urudfx	isudfx	isurudfx
2s	tudft	urtudft	istudft	isurtudft
3sm	yudf	uryudf	isyudf	isuryudf
3sf	tudf	urtudf	istudf	isurtudf
1p	nudf	un:udf	isnudf	isun:udf
2pm	tudfm	urtudfm	istudfm	isurtudfm
2pf	tudfnt	urtudfnt	istudfnt	isurtudfnt
3pm	udfn	urudfn	isudfn	isurudfn
3pf	udfnt	urudfnt	isudfnt	isurudfnt

TABLE 32 (A.S.) - /-PNG-/ paradigms for /adf/ 'to enter' of the a - u ablaut in the past.

-PNG-	Affirm.	Neg.	Interr.	Neg. Interr.
1s	adadfx	urt:adfx	isadadfx	isurt:adfx
2s	at:adft	urt:adft	isat:adft	isurt:adft
3sm	adyadf	urit:adf	isadyadf	isur:t:adf
3sf	at:adf	urt:adf	isat:adf	isurt:adf
1p	an:adf	urnt:adf	isan:adf	isurnt:adf
2pm	at:adfm	urt:adfm	isat:adfm	isurt:adfm
2pf	at:adfnt	urt:adfnt	isat:adfnt	isurt:adfnt
3pm	adadfn	urt:adfn	isadadfn	isurt:adfn
3pf	adadfnt	urt:adfnt	isadadfnt	isurt:adfnt

TABLE 33 (A.S.) - /-PNG-/ paradigms for /adf/ 'to enter' in the future.

-PNG-	Affirm.	Neg.	Interr.	Neg. Interr.
1s	l:at:adfx	ul:it:adfx	ist:adfx	isul:it:adfx
2s	l:at:adft	ul:it:adft	ist:adft	isul:it:adft
3sm	l:ayt:adf	ul:iyt:adf	isit:adf	isul:iyt:adf
3sf	l:at:adf	ul:it:adf	ist:adf	isul:it:adf
1p	l:ant:adf	ul:int:adf	isnt:adf	isul:int:adf
2pm	l:at:adfm	ul:it:adfm	ist:adfm	isul:it:adfm
2pf	l:at:adfnt	ul:it:adfnt	ist:adfnt	isul:it:adfnt
3pm	l:at:adfn	ul:it:adfn	ist:adfn	isul:it:adfn
3pf	l:at:adfnt	ul:it:adfnt	ist:adfnt	isul:it:adfnt

TABLE 34 (A.S.) - /-PNG-/ paradigms for /adf/ 'to enter' in the present.

-PNG#	Imper.	Energetic Imper.	Neg. Imper.
2s	adf	t:adf	adurt:adf
2pm	adfm	t:adfm	adurt:adfm
2pf	adfnt	t:adfnt	adurt:adfnt

TABLE 35 (A.S.) - Imperative structures for /adf/ 'to enter'.

-PNG-	Affirm.	Neg.	Interr.	Neg. Interr.
1s	iwḍx	uriwḍx	isiwḍx	isuriwḍx
2s	tiwṭ:	urtiwṭ:	istiwṭ:	isurtiwṭ:
3sm	yiwḍ	uryiwḍ	isyiwḍ	isuryiwḍ
3sf	tiwḍ	urtiwḍ	istiwḍ	isurtiwḍ
1p	niwḍ	urniwḍ	isniwḍ	isurniwḍ
2pm	tiwḍm	urtiwḍm	istiwḍm	isurtiwḍm
2pf	tiwḍnt	urtiwḍnt	istiwḍnt	isurtiwḍnt
3pm	iwḍn	uriwḍn	isiwḍn	isuriwḍn
3pf	iwḍnt	uriwḍnt	isiwḍnt	isuriwḍnt

TABLE 36 (A.S.) - /-PNG-/ paradigms of /awḍ/ 'to reach' of the a - i ablaut in the past.

-PNG-	Affirm.	Neg.	Interr.	Neg. Interr.
1s	adawḍx	urt:awḍx	isadawḍx	isurt:awḍx
2s	at:awṭ:	urt:awṭ:	isat:awṭ:	isurt:awṭ:
3sm	adyawḍ	urit:awḍ	isadyawḍ	isurit:awḍ
3sf	at:awḍ	urt:awḍ	isat:awḍ	isurt:awḍ
1p	an:awḍ	urnt:awḍ	isan:awḍ	isurnt:awḍ
2pm	at:awḍm	urt:awḍm	isat:awḍm	isurt:awḍm
2pf	at:awḍnt	urt:awḍnt	isat:awḍnt	isurt:awḍnt
3pm	adawḍn	urt:awḍn	isadawḍn	isurt:awḍn
3pf	adawḍnt	urt:awḍnt	isadawḍnt	isurt:awḍnt

TABLE 37 (A.S.) - /-PNG-/ paradigms of /awḍ/ 'to reach' in the future.

-PNG-	Affirm.	Neg.	Interr.	Neg. Interr.
1s	l:at:awḍx	ul:it:awḍx	ist:awḍx	isul:it:awḍx
2s	l:at:awṭ:	ul:it:awṭ:	ist:awṭ:	isul:it:awṭ:
3sm	l:ayt:awḍ	ul:iyt:awḍ	isit:awḍ	isul:iyt:awḍ
3sf	l:at:awḍ	ul:it:awḍ	ist:awḍ	isul: it:awḍ
1p	l:ant:awḍ	ul:int:awd	isnt:awḍ	isul:int:awd
2pm	l:at:awḍm	ul:it:awḍm	ist:awḍn	isul:it:awḍm
2pf	l:at:awḍnt	ul:it:awḍnt	ist:awḍnt	isul:it:awḍnt
3pm	l:at:awḍn	ul:it:awḍn	ist:awḍn	isul:it:awḍn
3pf	l:at:awḍnt	ul:it:awḍnt	ist:awḍnt	isul:it:awḍnt

TABLE 38 (A.S.) - /-PNG-/ paradigms for /awḍ/ 'to reach' in the present.

-PNG#	Imper.	Energetic Imper.	Neg. Imper.
2s	awḍ	t:awḍ	adurt:awḍ
2pm	awḍm	t:awḍm	adurt:awḍm
2pf	awḍnt	t:awḍnt	adurt:awḍnt

TABLE 39 (A.S.) - Imperative paradigms of /awḍ/ 'to reach'.

10 Stem derivations in Ayt Seghrouchen differ slightly in their realization from those in Ayt Ayache. (See Sample Appendix B.)

11 Rules for Temporal Modal and Participle derivations in A.S. are identical with those of A.A. except for the difference in Temp-Mod Affixes mentioned in #2 - 6 above.

12 Differences in Verb Morphophonemics are here listed for A.S.:

Rule 5	/ḍ-ṭ:/	→	ḍṭ:	
	/i-ʕaṛḍ-ṭ:/	→	iʕaṛḍṭ:	he invited her
Rule 10	/-d-d#/	→	dd:	
	/-d-d-/	→	d:	
	/i-waʕ d-d/	→	iwaʕ dd:	he came (+ proximity)
	/ad-d-ʕawn-γ/	→	ad:ʕawnγ	I'll help (+ proximity)
Rule 13	/-γ-x#/	→	/x:/	
	/f:γ-x/	→	f:x:	I went out
Rule 17	/ṛ-n#/	→	/ṛn#/	
	/ʕm:ṛ-n/	→	ʕm:ṛn	they (m) filled
Rule 18	/l-n#/	→	/-ln#/	
	/s:lil-n/	→	s:liln	they (m) rinsed
Rule 19	/-n-m#/	→	/-nm#/	
	/ad-t-žn-m/	→	atžnm	
Rule 20	/d-š/	→	/š:/	
	/ad-š-i-sal	→	aš:isal	he will ask you (ms)

Rule 22	/d-n/	⟶	n:	
	/ad-n-sal/	⟶	an:sal	we will ask
Rule 25	/-s-ž-/	⟶	/-sž-/	
	/s-žru/	⟶	/sžru/	SV of /žru/
Similarly, 26. 27 :	/s-š/	⟶	/sš/	
	/s-z/	⟶	/sz/	

Verb Sample Appendices and List

Introduction to Appendix A (from Ayt Ayache)

Appendix A contains 77 unaugmented verb stems and their derivatives arranged alphabetically according to the class or sub-class to which V belongs (see Chapter 4 for classification of verb stems). The alphabetical order for classes and sub-classes both in the Appendix and the verb list is:

a b b: d d: ḍ ḍ: f f: g g: g̣ g̣: h ḥ ḥ: i k k: ḳ ḳ:
l l: ḷ ḷ: m m: n n: q q: q̣ q̣: r r: ṛ ṛ: s s: ṣ ṣ:
š š: t t: ṭ ṭ: u w w: x x: x̣ y y: z z: ẓ ẓ: ž ž:
ʕ ɣ ɣ: ɣ̣

Each of the numbers 1-77 in Appendix A and 1-450 in the verb list refers to an unaugmented verb stem and its derivatives.

The 450 verb stems represent the verbs of the corpus of the research on the Ayt Ayache dialect. As they appear in the verb list, they are grouped into two types: A - unablauted (1-115), B - ablauted (116-450). Each type has two classes, A and B, which in turn are grouped into sub-classes with an Arabic numeral preceding each sub-class. At the beginning of each class in the Appendix appears the general underlying structure of its sub-classes; at the beginning of each sub-class appear the maximum possibilities for its underlying structure with an illustrative example or examples used to name the sub-class: e.g., in the Appendix Class I of type A appears as

Unablauted
1. A(B)(C)a
2. AVC
3. ABVC

and sub-class I appears as

1.	Aa	fa
	AB(C)a	šk:a, štka
	AVCa	dawa, fuk:a

Sometimes more examples are shown listed in the Appendix.

There are two major sets for any listing (V and its derivatives) in the Appendix. One set is that of unaugmented forms, the other of augmented forms. A maximum of five listings a) to e) appears, in most cases, for each set.

For the unaugmented set:

a) lists V followed by an English translation as infinitive without 'to'. Next to the meaning the symbol 'ar' means Arabic loan, 'ma' Moroccan Arabic loan; no symbol means native or Tamazight.* Finally "t" means transitive, "i" intransitive, "n" (i.e. neutral) both transitive and intransitive.

b) lists the habitual form of the simple stem VH

c) lists a noun of action derived from the simple stem: N-act. Parenthesis show a plural if it exists: e.g. 5 c) afuk:a (ifuk:atn)**; or a plural suffix 9 c) s:wal (-at)

d) lists a noun of agent. If no further information follows, this means that the noun under consideration is a "Sound" masculine singular (ms) noun which follows a regular pattern in deriving a masculine plural (mp), a feminine singular (fs) and a feminine plural (fp): e.g. 22 d) /amkašf/ 'fortune-teller' (ms) derives: /imkašfn/ (mp), /tamkašft/ (fs), /timkašfin/ (fp). If the derivations do not follow the above pattern, they are listed with plurals (or plural prefixes) in parenthesis: e.g.

---

* This information is, of course, debatable. However, the author's native knowledge of Arabic, the discussion of these verb stems and their derivatives with the informant and the consultation of various dictionaries, such as Wehr's and Harrell's lead the author to the conclusions shown in this Appendix.

** Numbers refer to the place of V in Appendix A.

36 d) bulḥm:am (id-)
m:lḥm:am (ist-)

Some nouns are followed by *f which means that mp is a possible derivation whereas fs and fp are not:
e.g. 28 d) abr:aḥ ; *f

e) lists a noun (ms or fs) followed by (instr.) if it is a noun of instrument, (loc.) if it is a noun of place, or (occup.) if it is a noun of occupation:
e.g.
36 e) lḥm:am (loc.)
46 e) lʕbra (instr.)

Plurals appear in parenthesis if they exist.

Augmented stems appear in this order: Causative, Reciprocal, and Passive. The maximum number of forms that any augmented stem can show is three a) to c) where

a) lists causative SV, reciprocal MV, passive TuV which are all derived from unaugmented V

b) lists habitual forms of causative SVH, of reciprocal MVH, of passive TuVH.

c) lists a N-act derived from the causative SV or the reciprocal MV (rather then from V): e.g.
25 c) amʕawan

a) and b) of the recipro-causative forms appear partly in the causative and partly in the reciprocal columns. These are:
a) MSV
b) MSVH

e.g. 4 a) msfafa
b) t:msfafa

Appendix A is compiled on the basis of derivation and

occurrence.* That is, V is the starting formative from which the other forms are derived by rules of generative grammar.

The justification of the horizontal order,

a) V SV MSV MV TuV

is based on derivation of all augmented forms from V. Note that some MSV's can occur without corresponding SV's which shows they are derived from V's: e.g.

43 a) msl:am

b) t:msl:am

The order SV MSV MV is justified by the derivation of MSV from SV. The Passive is the form with the least occurrence and the one the least used even when it occurs. The informant said that it is preferrable to use the active rather than the passive as much as possible. Its main occurrence is with the third person, however it may occur with other persons. Sometimes a passive is derived from SV; e.g. 33 TuSV (t:usfrḥ); for these reasons, the passive form is put last.

The justification of the vertical order is that all forms on lines b) and c) are derived from a). Forms on line d) are derived (in many instances) from c): e.g.

29 a) bš:r

b) t:bš:ar

c) abš:r

d) abš:ar

Frequency of occurrence is also an important factor (see footnote).

---

* For percentages of occurrence, see Abdel-Massih, Ernest, Tamazight Verb Structure: A Generative Approach, University of Indiana:Bloomington, 1971, Table 97. The total number of the unaugmented verb stems (450) comprises the 100% shown in the table; the other percentages listed are based on the total number of the unaugmented verb stems (450 = 100%). The percentage of SV is 35.11, MV 31.11, MSV 13.55, TuV 31.77, N-act 78.22, N-agt 19.33 and N-instr, loc, occup 3.33.

The system shown in Appendix A is an open system. Thus, for example, 20 /ḥaḍr/ 'be present' has /sḥaḍr/ - SV, /sḥaḍar/ - SVH whereas 78 /kašf/ 'foretell' has no causative stems. The causative of /kašf/ is left blank, however, if a native speaker of Tamazight supplies a causative for this stem it will be one that the generative rules for causative derivation have stated in VI.4.3. The same is true for other derivations.

Throughout the Appendix transitivity is marked only for V and VH. SV's (and SVH's) are necessarily transitive whether or not the underlying V is transitive. TuV's are mainly derived from transitive V's; however, TuV's (and TuVH's) are intransitive and have as their subject the direct object of V's.

All the above information applies to Appendix B (from Ayt Seghrouchen), except that Appendix B is not followed by a Verb List as is Appendix A.

Verb Sample Appendix A (Ayt Ayache)

A. Unablauted

1. 1. ‖ A(B)(C)a ‖

2. ‖ AVC ‖

3. ‖ ABVD ‖

1. { ‖ Aa ‖, ‖ AB(C)a ‖, ‖ AVCa ‖ }

fa
šk:a , štka
dawa , fuk:a

	Unaugmented		Augmented	
		Causative	Reciprocal	Passive
1	a) dawa 'cure' ar t	sdawa		t:udawa
	b) t:dawa	sdawa		t:udawa
	c) adawa (idawatn)			
2	a) ḍr:a 'do harm' ar t			t:uḍr:a
	b) t:ḍr:a			t:uḍr:a
	c) ḍ:arar (id-)			
3	a) fa 'yawn' i	sfa		
	b) t:fa	sfa		

4	a) fafa 'wake up' i	sfafa		
	b) t:fafa	sfafa		
		a) msfafa		
		b) t:msfafa		
5	a) fuk:a 'undo, get someone out of trouble' ar t	sfuk:a		
	b) t:fuk:a	sfuk:a		
	c) afuk:a (ifuk:atn)			
		a) msfuk:a		
		b) t:msfuk:a		
6	a) šk:a 'doubt' ar i		mšk:a	t:ušk:a
	b) t:šk:a		t:mšk:a	t:ušk:a
	c) š:k:			
7	a) štka 'complain' ar i			t:uštka
	b) t:štka			t:uštka
	c) aštka (ištkatn)			

2. ||AVC|| sal, šib, ˤum

8	a) q:is	'tell stories'	ar t		m:q:is	
	b) t:q:is				t:mq:is	
9	a) sal	'ask'	ar t		m:sal	t:usal
	b) t:sal				t:msal	t:usal
	c) s:wal (-at)					
10	a) šib	'become white-haired'	ar i			
	b) t:šib					
	c) š:ib					
	) ašiban; * fp					
11	a) ˤum	'swim'	ar i	sˤum		
	b) t:ˤum			sˤum̄		
	c) taˤumt					
	d) aˤw:am					
				a) m:sˤum *		
				b) t:m:sˤum		

* 'bathe'

3. ||ABVD|| xṭar, slil, gzul

12	a) an:ay 'see' t		myan:ay	t:uyan:ay
	b) t:an:ay		t:myan:ay	t:uyan:ay
13	a) aẓum 'fast' ar t			
	b) t:aẓum			
14	a) gzul 'be short' i	s:gzul		
	b) t:gzul	s:gzul		
	c) tagzli			
15	a) iẓil 'be nice' i	s:iẓil		
	b) t:iẓil	s:iẓil		
	c) t:aẓ:lt			
16	a) slil 'rinse' t			t:uslil
	b) t:slil			t:uslil
	c) aslil			
17	a) ṭšar 'make dirty' t			t:uṭšar
	b) t:ṭšar			t:uṭšar
18	a) xṭar 'choose' ar t	s:xṭar		t:uxṭar
	b) t:xṭar	s:xṭar		t:uxṭar

ii. ||AVCD|| ḥaḍr, d:irz, ḥudr

19	a) d:irz 'step back' i	sd:irz		
	b) t:diriz	sd:iriz		
20	a) ḥaḍr 'be present' ar i	sḥaḍr		
	b) t:ḥaḍar	sḥaḍar		
	c) aḥaḍr			
21	a) ḥudr 'bend, be low' i	sḥudr		
	b) t:ḥudur	sḥudur		
	c) aḥudr			
22	a) kašf 'foretell' ar i			t:ukašf
	b) t:kašaf			t:ukašaf
	c) akašf			
	d) amkašf			
23	a) safr 'travel' ar i			
	b) t:safar			
	c) s:fr			
	d) amsafr			

24	a) žawr 'be neighbor' ar t		mžawar	
	b) t:žawar		t:mžawar	
	c) ažawr			
	d) ad:žar			
25	a) ʕawn 'help' ar n	sʕawn	mʕawan	t:uʕawn
	b) t:ʕawan	sʕawan	t:mʕawan	t:uʕawan
	c) aʕawn		amʕawan	
	d) amʕawn			

B. Ablauted

i. [Ø : O]

1. ‖AB(:)ØD‖

2. ‖aBØD‖

3. ‖OB:ØD‖

1. ‖AB(:)ØD‖ frØḥ ⟶ frḥ , fs:Ør ⟶ fs:r

	Unaugmented	Augmented		
		Causative	Reciprocal	Passive
26	a) bdr 'mention' t	s:bdr		t:ubdr
	b) bd:r	s:bdar		t:ubdar

27	a) bd:l 'change'	ar t	sbd:l	mbd:al	t:ubd:l
	b) t:bd:al		sbd:al	t:mbd:al	t:ubd:al
	c) abd:l				
			a) msbd:al		
			b) t:msbd:al		
28	a) br:ḥ 'announce'	ma i			
	b) t:br:aḥ				
	c) abr:ḥ				
	d) abr:aḥ ; * f				
29	a) bš:r 'give good news'	ar i	sbš:r	mbš:ar	t:ubš:r
	b) t:bš:ar		sbš:ar	t:mbš:ar	t:ubš:ar
	c) abš:r				
	d) abš:ar				
30	a) bᶜd 'be far'	ar i	s:bᶜd		
	b) t:bᶜad		s:bᶜad		
	c) abᶜad (~lbᶜd)				
			a) msbᶜad		
			b) t:msbᶜad		

31	a) dhn	'rub ointment'	ar t		m:dhan	t:udhn
	b) t:dhan				t:m:dhan	t:udhan
	c) adhan					
32	a) fḍr	'take lunch'	ar i	s:fḍr		
	b) fḍ:r			s:fḍar		
	c) lfḍur					
				a) msfḍar		
				b) t:msfḍar		
33	a) frḥ	'be happy'	ar i	s:frḥ		t:ufrḥ
	b) t:fraḥ ~ fr:ḥ			s:fraḥ		t:ufraḥ
	c) afraḥ					t:usfrḥ*
						t:usfraḥ
				a) msfrah		
				b) t:msfrah		
34	a) fs:r	'explain'	ar t		mfs:ar	t:ufs:r
	b) t:fs:ar				t:mfs:ar	t:ufs:ar
	c) afs:r					

* this passive is derived from the causative rather than from the unaugmented verb stem

35	a) ḥbs 'imprison' ar t			t:uḥbs
	b) t:ḥbas			t:uḥbas
	c)			
	d) aḥb:as			
	e) lḥbs (loc.)			
36	a) ḥm:m 'bathe' ar i	sḥm:m		
	b) t:ḥm:am	sḥm:am		
	c) aḥm:m			
	d) bulḥm:am (id-) m:lḥm:am (ist-)			
	e) lḥm:am (id-) (loc.)			
37	a) ḥšm 'govern, judge' ar i			t:uḥšm
	b) t:ḥšam			t:uḥšam
	c) lḥšam			
	d) lḥak:m (lḥḳ:am)			
38	a) ḥz:m 'wear a belt' ar i		mḥz:am	
	b) t:ḥz:am		t:mḥz:am	
	c) aḥz:m			
	d) lḥzam (id-) (instr.)			

39	a) nṣb	'make stew'	ma i			
	b) t:nṣab					
	c) anṣab					
40	a) nšr	'saw'	ar t			t:unšr
	b) nš:r					t:unšar
	c) anšar					
	d)					
	e) lmnšar (id-)	(instr.)				
41	a) rgm	'insult'	ar t		m:rgam	t:urgm
	b) rg:m				t:mrgam	t:urgam
	c) argam					
42	a) sl:k	'give a reasonable price'	ar t			
	b) t:sl:ak					
	c) asl:k					
	d) amsl:k					
				a) msl:ak*		
				b) t:msl:ak		
43	a) sl:m	'greet'	ar i		msl:am	
	b) t:sl:am				t:msl:am	
	c) sl:am					

* 'be tolerant'

44	a) xdm	'work'	ar n	s:xdm		t:uxdm
	b) xd:m			s:xdam		t:uxdam
	c) lxdmt					
	d) axd:am					
					a) msxdam	
					b) t:msxdam	
45	a)zdm	'collect wood'	t			
	b) zd:m					
	c) azdam					
	d) azd:am					
46	a)ʕbr	'measure, weigh'	ar t			t:uʕbr
	b) t:ʕbar					t:uʕbar
	c) lʕbar					
	d) aʕb:ar ; * f					
	e) lʕbra (-t) (instr.)					
47	a)ʕm:r	'fill'	ar t		mʕm:ar	
	b) t:ʕm:ar				t:mʕm:ar	
	c) aʕm:r					

48	a) γ̣l:f 'wrap' ar t			t:uγl:f
	b) t:γ̣l:af			t:uγl:af
	c) aγ̣l:f			

2. ‖aBØD‖ amØẓ ⟶ amẓ

49	a) agm 'bring water from a well' t			
	b) t:agm			
50	a) amn 'believe' ar n		myaman	
	b) t:amn		t:myaman	
51	a) amr 'order' ar i			
	b) t:amr			
	c) lamr (lamır)			
52	a) amẓ 'take' t		myamaẓ	t:uyumẓ
	b) t:amẓ		t:myamaẓ	t:uyamaẓ
	c) umıẓ ~ umẓ ~ imẓ			
53	a) asy 'carry' t	s:isy	myasay	t:uyusy
	b) t:asy	s:asay	t:myasay	t:uyasay
	c) isy			

54	a) awḍ	'reach'	n	s:iwḍ	myawaḍ	
	b) t:awḍ			s:awaḍ	t:myawaḍ	
55	a) awy	'take away'	t	s:iwy	myaway	
	b) t:awy			s:away	t:myaway	

3. ‖OB:ØD‖ Of:Ør ⟶ f:r

56	a) b:y	'cut'	t		myab:ay	
	b) t:b:y				t:myab:ay	
	c) ubuy					
57	a) f:r	'hide'	t		myaf:ar	
	b) t:f:r				t:myaf:ar	
	c) tufra					
58	a) f:γ	'go out'	i	s:ufγ		
	b) t:f:γ			s:ufuγ		
	c) ufuγ					
59	a) k:r	'get up'	i			
	b) t:k:r					

60	a) ẓ:y 'milk'	t			
	b) t:ẓ:y				
61	a) ẓ:ʕ 'dismiss'	t		myaẓ:aʕ	t:uẓ:ʕ
	b) t:ẓ:ʕ			t:myaẓ:aʕ	t:uyaẓ:aʕ

ii. ∅:i/a

1. ‖aB ∅(D)‖
    [±Met] [±Met]

2. ‖(A)B(:)∅‖
              [+Met]

3. ‖(A(:))B(:)∅V‖
                 [+diff]

1. { ‖aB ∅‖   af∅ ⟶ af
        [-Met] [-Met]

      ‖aB ∅D‖   aš:Ok ⟶ aš:k∅ ⟶ aš:k
        [-Met] [+Met]

      ‖aB ∅D‖   arør ⟶ rarø ⟶ rar
        [+Met] [+Met] }

62	a) af 'find'	t		myafa	t:uyufa
	b) t:afa			t:myafa	t:uyafa
63	a) aš:k 'be lost'	i		myaš:ka	
	b) t:aš:ka			t:myaš:ka	
	c) uš:ki				

64	a) rar 'return, give back'	n		mrara		
	b) t:rara			t:mrara		
	c) tararit:					

2. $\left\{ \begin{array}{l} \| \text{OB}(:)\ \underset{[-\text{Met}]}{\emptyset} \| \\ \| \text{AB}(:)\ \underset{[-\text{Met}]}{\emptyset} \| \\ \| \text{AB}\ \underset{[+\text{Met}]}{\emptyset} \| \end{array} \right\}$ OgØ ⟶ g , Og̣:Ø ⟶ g:Ø; lsØ ⟶ ls , bd:Ø ⟶ bd:; gØr ⟶ gr

65	a) bd: 'stand up'	i	sbd:			
	b) t:bd:a		sbd:a			
	c) ibd:i					
66	a) g 'be, do'	n		myag:a		
	b) t:g:a			t:myag:a		
67	a) gr 'throw away'	t		m:gar		
	b) g:ar			t:m:gar		
	c) tag̣uri					
68	a) g̣: 'knead'	t				
	b) t:g̣:a					
	c) tig̣:it					

69	a) k: 'pass, visit' t	s:ik:		
	b) t:k:a	s:ak:a		
	c) tik:it			
			a) msak:a	
			b) t:msak:a	
70	a) ls 'get dressed' t	s:ls		t:ulsa
	b) ls:a	s:lsa		t:ulsa
	c) mlsiwt			

3. { ‖OB:Øu‖, ‖A(:)BØu‖, ‖AB:Øu‖, ‖iBØi‖ }

Od:Øu ⟶ d:u

g:rØu ⟶ g:ru , šmØu ⟶ šmu

ɛd:Øu ⟶ ɛd:u

irØi ⟶ iri

71	a) d:u 'go' i	s:udu		
	b) t:d:u	s:udu		
	c) tawada (tiwadiwin)			

72	a) g:ru 'be last' i	sg:ru			
	b) t:g:ru	sg:ru			
	c)				
	d) ang:aru (ing:ura) tang:arut: (ting:ura)				
		a) msg:ru*			
		b) t:msg:ru			
73	a) šmu 'smoke' ma t	š:mu			
	b) t:šm:u ~ šm:u	š:mu			
	c) lšmiyt				
	d) ašm:ay ; * f				
74	a) ʕd:u 'abound' ar i	sʕd:u			
	b) t:ʕd:u	sʕd:u			
75	a) ili 'exist, be' i				
	b) t:ili				
76	a) ini 'say t		myini		
	b) t:ini		t:myini		
77	a) iri 'want' n		myiri		
	b) t:iri		t:myiri		
	c) tayri				

* 'agree'

List of Verbs (Ayt Ayache)

A. Unablauted

A.i.1. fa, šk:a, štka, dawa, fuk:a

1.	dawa	'cure'	ar	t
2.	ḍr:a	'do harm'	ar	t
3.	fa	'yawn'		i
4.	fafa	'wake up'		i
5.	fḍ:a	'finish'	ar	t
6.	fuk:a	'undo, get someone out of trouble'	ar	t
7.	hn:a	'be peaceful'	ar	i
8.	hr:a	'tickle'	ma	t
9.	ḥada	'touch'		t
10.	ḥd:a	'end'	ar	i
11.	ḥn:a	'pity'	ar	i
12.	ḥš:a	'cut grass'	ar	t
13.	q:la	'fry'	ar	t
14.	qṛ:a	'confess'	ar	i
15.	ṛaˤa	'look at'	ar	t
16.	ṛb:a	'educate'	ar	t
17.	sqsa	'ask'	ar	t
18.	šk:a	'doubt'	ar	i
19.	štka	'complain'	ar	i
20.	šq:a	'disturb'		t

21.	wala	'be near'		t
22.	warya	'dream'		t
23.	wṣ:a	'advise'	ar	t
24.	xṣ:a	'be necessary'	ar	i
25.	ʕf:a	'be disgusted'	ar	t
26.	ʕl:a	'ascend'	ar	t
27.	ʕz:a	'console'	ar	t
28.	γṛ:a	'tempt'	ar	t
29.	γš:a	'cheat'	ar	t

A.i.2 sal, šib, ʕum

30.	ḍur	'turn'	ar	i
31.	ḥuf	'jump on'		i
32.	k:us	'inherit'		t
33.	lum	'blame'	ar	t
34.	mun	'accompany'		i
35.	n:aγ	'fight'		i
36.	q:is	'tell stories'	ar	t
37.	sal	'ask'	ar	t
38.	sul	'remain'		i
39.	sus	'shake off'		t
40.	ṣuḍ	'blow'		t
41.	šal	'buy grain'	ar	t
42.	šib	'become white-haired'	ar	i

43.	š:ar	'share'		t
44.	zur	'be fat'		i
45.	ẓur	'visit holy places'	ar	t
46.	ʕum	'swim'	ar	i
47.	Ɣal	'think'		i
48.	ɣus	'be burnt'		i

A.i.3. xtar, slil, gzul

49.	an:ay	'see'		t
50.	arid	'be washed'		i
51.	aẓum	'fast'	ar	t
52.	aɣul	'go back'		i
53.	bxin	'be black'		i
54.	drus	'be little in quantity'		i
55.	fsus	'be light'		i
56.	gzul	'be short'		i
57.	iẓil	'be nice'		i
58.	iɣiy	'be able'		i
59.	lwiɣ	'be tender'		i
60.	mẓiy	'be small'		i
61.	mɣur	'grow up'		i
62.	sdid	'be thin'		i
63.	slil	'rinse'		t

64.	smun	'collect'		t
65.	ṣmiḍ	'be cold'		i
66.	šḍin	'be short'		i
67.	ṭšar	'make dirty'		t
68,	wṛaγ	'be yellow'		i
69.	wsir	'be old'		i
70.	xṭar	'choose'	ar	t
71.	zwar	'to precede'		t
72.	zwiγ	'be red'		i
73.	γ̣zif	'be tall'		i

A.ii. hadr, d:irz, hudr

74.	d:irz	'step back'		i
75.	d:uk:l	'make friends'		t
76.	ḍ:iqs	'burst out'		i
77.	ḥaḍr	'be present'	ar	i
78.	ḥafḍ	'keep'	ar	i
79.	ḥaṛẓ	'forbid'		t
80.	ḥaṛṣ	'prevent'	ar	t
81.	ḥasb	'count'	ar	t
82.	ḥawl	'take one's time doing something'	ma	i
83.	ḥudr	'bend, be low'		i

84.	kašf	'foretell'	ar	i
85.	q:abl	'take care of'		t
86.	safr	'travel'	ar	i
87.	samḥ	'forgive'	ar	i
88.	saʕd	'help'	ar	t
89.	saʕf	'be patient'	ma	t
90.	s:udm	'kiss'		t
91.	s:ufs	'spit'		n
92.	s:uk:f	'uproot'		t
93.	s:urf	'stride over'		t
94.	šawr	'consult'	ar	t
95.	ṭalb	'demand, apply'	ar	t
96.	walf	'get accustomed'	ar	t
97.	wažb	'answer'	ar	n
98.	xabr	'inform'	ar	t
99.	xaḍr	'risk'	ar	i
100.	xaṣm	'quarrel'	ar	i
101.	xatr	'be old'		i
102.	xulf	'differ'	ar	i
103.	zawg:	'ask protection'	ma	i
104.	zayd	'add'	ar	t
105.	zuz:r	'winnow'		t
106.	ẓawḍ	'throw away'		t
107.	ẓ:uɣr	'drag'		t

108.	žaḥd	'compete with'	ma	t
109.	žawb	'answer'	ar	n
110.	žawr	'be neighbor'	ar	t
111.	ʕaḍ:r	'meet'		i
112.	ʕawd	'repeat'	ar	n
113.	ʕawn	'help'	ar	n
114.	ʕayd	'go back'	ar	i
115.	γawl	'hurry up'		i

B. <u>Ablauted</u>

B.i.l. frh, fs:r

116.	bdr	'mention'		t
117.	bd:l	'change'	ar	t
118.	bḥ:t	'investigate'	ar	t
119.	bl:γ	'deliver'	ar	t
120.	bry	'grind'		t
121.	br:ḥ	'announce'	ma	i
122.	bṛ:m	'turn'	ar	t
123.	bš:r	'give good news'	ar	i
124.	bx:r	'burn incense, do harm'	ar	i
125.	bzy	'be wet, proud'		i
126.	bʕd	'be far'	ar	i

127.	bγḍ	'hate'	ar	i
128.	dbγ	'dye'	ar	t
129.	db:r	'manage'	ar	i
130.	dhn	'rub ointment'	ar	t
131.	dhš	'faint, become dizzy'	ar	i
132.	dlš	'massage'	ar	t
133.	dw:x	'become dizzy'	ar	t
134.	ḍhr	'appear'	ar	i
135.	ḍlm	'oppress'	ar	t
136.	ḍl:ʕ	'flatten bread'		t
137.	ḍmn	'guarantee'	ar	t
138.	ḍr:ʕ	'scream'		i
139.	ḍʕf	'be weak'	ar	i
140.	ḍʕn	'stab'	ar	t
141.	ḍγṣ	'lie down'		t
142.	fḍḥ	'reveal a secret'	ar	t
143.	fḍr	'take lunch'	ar	i
144.	fhm	'understand'	ar	t
145.	flḥ	'succeed'	ar	i
146.	fly	'tear'		t
147.	fl:ḥ	'to live on agriculture'	ar	i
148.	frḍ	'sweep'		t
149.	frḥ	'be happy'	ar	i

150.	frs	'attack'	ar	t
151.	fry	'build a fence'		t
152.	frγ	'be crooked'	ar	i
153.	fr:d	'change money'	ar	t
154.	fr:n	'weed'		t
155.	fr:z	'clarify'	ar	t
156.	fr:ž	'look at'	ar	i
157.	fr:γ	'pour'	ar	i
158.	fṛʕ	'break open'		t
159.	fsd	'be spoiled'	ar	i
160.	fsr	'spread'		t
161.	fsy	'melt'		t
162.	fs:r	'explain'	ar	t
163.	ftl	'roll'	ar	t
164.	gmr	'hunt'		i
165.	gz:r	'butcher'	ar	t
166.	hbl	'become silly'	ar	i
167.	hdm	'demolish'	ar	t
168.	hw:l	'trouble'	ar	t
169.	hžm	'attack'	ar	i
170.	ḥbs	'imprison'	ar	t
171.	ḥl:q	'dress up'	ma	t
172.	ḥl:s	'saddle'		t
173.	ḥml	'flood'	ma	i

174.	ḥm:m	'bathe'	ar	i
175.	ḥr:f	'carry'		t
176.	ḥr:š	'shake, move something'	ar	t
177.	ḥṛm	'be forbidden'	ar	i
178.	ḥṛš	'be sharp'	ar	i
179.	ḥšm	'govern, judge'	ar	i
180.	ḥš:m	'be polite'	ar	i
181.	ḥz:m	'wear a belt'	ar	i
182.	kmz	'scratch'		t
183.	krz	'plough'		t
184.	lˁb	'play'	ar	t
185.	mdy	'set a trap'		t
186.	mgr	'harvest'		t
187.	mry	'rub'		t
188.	ndm	'regret'	ar	i
189.	ndr	'moan'		i
190.	nḍl	'bury'		t
191.	nfḍ	'throw'	ar	t
192.	nfḥ	'sniff tobacco'	ar	t
193.	nq:l	'transplant'	ar	t
194.	nq:r	'shake off'	ar	t
195.	nq:z	'jump'	ma	i
196.	nṣb	'make stew'	ma	i

197.	nṣḍ	'blow one's nose'		t
198.	nšr	'saw'	ar	t
199.	ntf	'depilate'	ar	t
200.	ntl	'hide'		i
201.	nzl	'spur'		t
202.	nzγ	'pull'	ar	t
203.	nžm	'escape'	ar	i
204.	nžr	'sharpen'	ar	t
205.	nʕl	'curse'	ar	t
206.	qdr	'be able'	ar	i
207.	qḍʕ	'register a marriage'	ar	i
208.	ql:b	'check'	ar	t
209.	ql:q	'be worried'	ar	i
210.	qr:b	'be near'	ar	i
211.	qṛ:ṛ	'decide'	ar	i
212.	qṛ:š	'bite'	ar	t
213.	qsḥ	'be solid, strong'	ma	i
214.	qṣd	'intend, go toward'	ar	t
215.	qṃ:ṛ	'gamble'	ar	i
216.	rbḥ	'succeed, gain'	ar	t
217.	rdm	'demolish'	ar	t
218.	rḍl	'loan'		t

219.	rgl	'close,lock'		t
220.	rgm	'insult'	ar	t
221.	rḥl	'move'	ar	i
222.	rḥm	'have mercy on'	ar	t
223.	rkm	'boil'		i
224.	rkz	'tread'		i
225.	rẓm	'open'		t
226.	ṛẓṇ	'be patient'	ar	i
227.	ṛžm	'throw stones at'	ar	t
228.	ṛʕb	'be amazed at'	ar	i
229.	sb:b	'trade'	ma	i
230.	sḥ:r	'perform magic'	ar	i
231.	sl:k	'give a reasonable price'	ar	t
232.	sl:m	'greet'	ar	i
233.	sn:d	'lean against'	ar	i
234.	srm	'peel, have diarrhea'		t
235.	sr:ḥ	'liberate'	ar	t
236.	sty	'filter'		t
237.	ṣbṛ	'be patient, wait'	ar	i
238.	ṣfḍ	'wipe'		t
239.	ṣm:r	'nail'	ar	t

240.	ṣrf	'spend money'	ar	t
241.	ṣr:f	'change money'	ar	t
242.	ṣṛḍ	'swallow'		t
243.	ṣxḍ	'curse'	ar	i
244.	ṣy:ḍ	'hunt'	ar	t
245.	ṣy:f	'harvest summer crops'	ar	i
246.	šb:r	'cling to'		i
247.	šf:r	'steal'	ma	t
248.	šk:m	'denounce'	ma	i
249.	šḳr	'praise'	ar	t
250.	šm:l	'finish'	ar	t
251.	šm:t	'cheat'		t
252.	šnf	'roast'		t
253.	šnʕ	'be prevalent'	ma	i
254.	šrf	'tie'		t
255.	šrm	'shrivel up'		i
256.	šṛḍ	'comb, stipulate'	ar	t
257.	šṛh	'envy'	ar	t
258.	šty	'recall'		t
259.	šṭḥ	'dance'	ma	i
260.	šṭ:b	'sweep'	ma	t
261.	ṭfṣ	'fold'		t
262.	ṭṛẓ	'embroider'	ar	t

263.	wḥl	'get tired'	ar	i
264.	wk:l	'appoint as representative'	ar	t
265.	wq:r	'respect'	ar	t
266.	ws:x	'make dirty'	ar	t
267.	wx:r	'go back'	ar	i
268.	wzn	'weigh'	ar	t
269.	wžd	'be ready'	ar	i
270.	wʕr	'be hard'	ar	i
271.	xdm	'work'	ar	n
272.	xdʕ	'deceive'	ar	t
273.	xḷ:ṣ	'pay for'	ar	t
274.	xmž	'smell bad'	ma	i
275.	xm:m	'think, worry'	ar	i
276.	xr:f	'harvest fall crops'	ma	t
277.	xsr	'fail, be spoilt'	ar	i
278.	xw:n	'steal'	ar	t
279.	xzn	'store,hide'	ar	t
280.	zdm	'collect wood'		t
281.	zdr	'sink'		i
282.	zdɣ	'dwell'		t
283.	zgl	'miss'		t
284.	zrb	'hurry'		i
285.	zry	'leave,pass'		t

286.	zrʕ	'sow'	ar	t
287.	zw:q	'color'	ar	t
288.	zʕf	'get mad'	ma	i
289.	žbr	'come back'	ar	i
290.	žhd	'be strong'	ar	i
291.	žrḥ	'injure'	ar	t
292.	ʕbd	'worship, adore'	ar	t
293.	ʕbr	'measure, weigh'	ar	t
294.	ʕdl	'repair'	ar	t
295.	ʕd:b	'torture'	ar	t
296.	ʕm:r	'fill'	ar	t
297.	ʕnq	'try hard without success'	ma	t
298.	ʕq:d	'tie, start a fire'	ar	t
299.	ʕq:l	'remember'	ar	t
300.	ʕrḍ	'invite'		t
301.	ʕrm	'know of something'		i
302.	ʕs:s	'guard'	ar	n
303.	ʕšq	'love'	ar	t
304.	ʕṭ:r	'be late'	ar	i
305.	γly	'pass over'		i
306.	γml	'become rotten'	ma	i
307.	γms	'cover'		i

308.	γns	'wear'		t
309.	γṛḍ	'stretch leg'		t
310.	γṛf	'to flatten bread'		t
311.	γṛm	'indemnify'	ar	t
312.	γṛṣ	'slaughter'		i
313.	γṛy	'abort'		i
314.	γ̣fr	'forgive'	ar	t
315.	γ̣l:f	'wrap'	ar	t

B.i.2. amẓ

316.	adr	'bury'		i
317.	afḍ	'be sent'		i
318.	agl	'hang'		t
319.	agm	'bring water from a well'		t
320.	akz	'recognize'		t
321.	aly	'climb'		t
322.	amn	'believe'	ar	n
323.	amr	'order'	ar	i
324.	ams	'paint'		t
325.	amẓ	'take'		t
326.	anf	'open'		t
327.	arf	'pop popcorn'		t
328.	arm	'taste'		t

329.	arw	'give birth'	t
330.	asy	'carry'	t
331.	ašr	'steal'	t
332.	ašy	'be aware'	i
333.	awḍ	'reach'	n
334.	awl	'get married'	t
335.	awy	'take away'	t
336.	azn	'send'	t
337.	aẓḍ	'stretch hand'	t

B.i.3. f:r

338.	b:y	'cut'	t
339.	ḍ:ḍ	'suckle'	t
340.	f:r	'hide'	t
341.	f:γ	'go out'	i
342.	g̣:d	'be frightened'	i
343.	g̣:z	'descend'	t
344.	k:r	'get up'	i
345	k:s	'take out'	t
346.	l:m	'spin'	t
347.	l:γ	'lick'	t
348.	m:γ	'get wet'	i
349.	n:ḍ	'stick'	i
350.	q:d	'burn'	t

351.	q:l	'wait'	i
352.	q:n	'shut'	t
353.	q:s	'prick'	t
354.	t:l	'roll'	t
355.	t:r	'ask'	t
356.	ṭ:f	'keep'	t
357.	z:r	'depilate'	t
358.	ẓ:y	'milk'	t
359.	ẓ:ʕ	'dismiss'	t
360.	ž:y	'recover from an illness'	t

B.ii.1. af, aš:k, rar

361.	adž	'let'		t
362.	af	'find'		t
363.	ar	'be empty,empty'		i
364.	as:	'tie,bind'		t
365.	aš:k	'be lost'		i
366.	az:l	'run'		i
367.	g:al:	'swear'		i
368.	lal	'be born'		i
369.	rar	'return, give back'		n
370.	ẓ:aḷ:	'pray'	ar	t

B.ii.2. g, g:, ls, bd:, gr

371.	bd:	'stand up'	i
372.	fẓ:	'chew'	t
373.	g	'be,do'	n
374.	gm	'grow'	i
375.	gn	'sleep'	i
376.	gr	'throw away'	t
377.	g̣:	'knead'	t
378.	ks	'tend sheep or cattle'	t
379.	k:	'pass,visit'	t
380.	ls	'get dressed'	t
381.	ns	'spend the night'	i
382.	nz	'be for sale'	i
383.	nγ	'kill'	t
384.	ṛẓ	'break'	t
385.	ṛγ	'warm oneself'	i
386	sl:	'hear'	i
387.	sγ	'buy'	t
388.	š	'give'	i
389.	šl	'spend a day'	i
390.	ṭṣ	'laugh'	i
391.	zl	'lose'	t
392.	ẓḍ	'grind'	t

393.	ẓḍ	'weave'		t
394.	ʕz:	'be dear'	ar	i
395.	γṛ	'read, call out'		n
396.	γz	'dig'		t
397.	γẓ:	'crunch'		t

B.ii.3 d:u, g:ru, bdu, ʕd:u, iri

398.	bdu	'begin'	ar	t
399.	bḍu	'cut, share'		t
400.	bnu	'build'	ar	t
401.	dʕu	'pray for, prosecute'	ar	i
402.	d:u	'go'		i
403.	fru	'pay debts'		t
404.	ftu	'dictate'	ar	t
405.	f:u	'dawn'		i
406.	gnu	'sew'		t
407.	g:ru	'be last'		i
408.	hdu	'give a present'	ar	t
409.	ḥḍu	'watch over'		t
410.	ḥfu	'be, become dull'	ma	i
411.	ḥlu	'be nice'	ar	i

412.	ḥmu	'be hot weather'	ar	i
413.	ḥr:u	'be hot (food)'	ar	i
414.	k:u	'cut grass'		t
415.	mḥu	'erase'	ar	t
416.	qḍu	'accomplish'	ar	t
417	qwu	'be fat'	ar	i
418.	rḍu	'bless'	ar	i
419.	rṣu	'be quiet'	ar	i
420.	ršu	'be dirty'	ma	i
421.	rzu	'look for'		t
422.	ržu	'hope'	ar	t
423.	r:u	'win'		t
424.	sxu	'be generous'	ar	i
425.	s:u	'make the bed'		t
426.	ṣfu	'be clean, clear'	ar	i
427.	ṣḥu	'be healthy'	ar	i
428.	šḍu	'smell'		t
429.	šmu	'smoke'	ma	t
430.	šnu	'kneel'	ar	i
431.	šru	'rent'	ar	t
432.	šwu	'be sharp'		i
433.	xlu	'ruin'	ar	n
434.	xwu	'be empty'	ar	n

435.	x:u	'be mean'		i
436.	zwu	'be dry'	ar	i
437.	ẓ:u	'plant'		t
438.	žru	'happen'	ar	i
439.	ʕd:u	'abound'	ar	i
440.	ʕfu	'forgive'	ar	i
441.	ʕmu	'be blind'	ar	n
442.	ʕnu	'undergo'	ar	t
443.	ʕṣu	'disobey'	ar	t
444.	γbu	'be deep'		i
445.	γlu	'be expensive'	ar	i
446.	γmu	'paint'		t
447.	γnu	'be rich'	ar	i
448.	ili	'exist, be'		i
449.	ini	'say'		t
450.	iri	'want'		n

Verb Sample Appendix B (Ayt Seghrouchen)

	Unaugmented	Augmented		
		Causative	Reciprocal	Passive
1	a) safr 'travel' ar i			
	b) t:safar			
	c) s:frt			
	d) amsafr			
2	a) sal 'ask' arn		m:sal	t:usal
	b) t:sal		t:m:sal	t:usal
3	a) samḥ 'forgive' ar i		msamaḥ	
	b) t:samaḥ		t:msamaḥ	
	c) lmusamaḥa			
4	a) sawm 'ask for the price' ar t			
	b) t:sawan			
5	a) tṛžm 'translate ar t	s:tṛžm		
	b) t:tṛžam	s:tṛžam		
	c) atṛžm			

6	a)	t:u	'forget'	i	s:t:u		
	b)	t:t:u			s:t:u		
7	a)	wžd	'be ready'	ar i	s:užd		
	b)	t:užid			s:užid		
	c)						
	d)	mıžud					
8	a)	zrbš	'scratch'	ar i	s:xrbš		
	b)	t:xrbaš			s:xṛbaš		
9	a)	ẓ:ʕ	'chase'	t			t:waẓ:ʕ
	b)	t:ẓ:ʕ					t:waẓ:ʕ
10	a)	žn	'sleep'	i	s:žn		
	b)	džan			s:žan		
11	a)	ʕfu	'forgive'	ar i			
	b)	ʕf:u					
	c)	lʕfu					
12	a)	ʕma	'be blind or blind'	ar n		m:ʕma	
	b)	t:iʕma				t:mʕma	
	c)	lʕma					
13	a)	ɣba	'lie deep'	ar i	s:ɣba		
	b)	t:iɣba			s:ɣba		

14	a) γm	'dye'	t			
	b) γm:					
15	a) γẓ:	'crunch'	t		m:γẓ:	t:uγẓ:
	b) t:γẓ:				t:mγẓ:a	t:uγẓ:a

Sentences

This section lists examples of the different structures of Tamazight. The examples consist of 157 pairs of sentences. When a certain structure or sub-structure is discussed, it is usually followed by one or more pairs of sentences to exemplify the occurrence of such structure. The first member of each pair of sentences is from Ayt Ayache, the second from Ayt Seghrouchen.

Sentences

Introduction

The discussion of sentences in Tamazight includes

A. The Verbless Sentence
B. The Verbal Sentence.

Each of these two types of structure can have any of the following modes:

1. Affirmative
2. Interrogative
3. Negative
4. Negative-Interrogative

The structures mentioned above (A.1 - A.4 and B.1 - B.4) as well as Imperative structures which are grouped under C, will be found in the following examples. The examples include 157 pairs of sentences from the two dialects (i.e. 157 from Ayt Ayache and 157 from Ayt Seghrouchen). When examples of a certain structure or sub-structure are cited, usually one or more pairs of sentences follow a short discussion. The first sentence in each given pair is in the dialect of Ayt Ayache, the second is in the Ayt Seghrouchen dialect.

A.1 Verbless: Affirmative

Examples of such sentences are:

1. (A.A.) isminw muḥa .
   (A.S.) isminw muḥa .

   My name is Mohamed.

2. (A.A.) lˤmṛinw tlatin ˤam .

   (A.S.) lˤmṛinw tlatin ˤam .

   I am 30 years old.

A Verbless Affirmative structure may occur with /γur/ A.A. or /γr/ A.S. 'particle of possession.' Examples:

3. (A.A.) γuṛs yut trbat: .

   (A.S.) γrs išt ntrbat: .

   He has a girl.

4. (A.A.) γuṛi ṛbˤa ntfunasin .

   (A.S.) γri ṛbˤa ntfunasin .

   I have four cows.

or structures having the 'presentational particles' /ha/, /han/ A.A., /ha/, /han:/ A.S. Examples:

5. (A.A.) ha n:ˤnaˤ .

   (A.S.) ha n:ˤnaˤ .

   Here is the mint.

6. (A.A.) han ataynš .

   (A.S.) han: at:ayn:š .

   Here is your tea.

or with the help of /d/, 'particle of assertion.' Examples:

7. (A.A.) muḥa dargaz nimru waḥd .

(A.S.) muḥa daryaz n:imirwaḥd .

Mohamed is in fact an excellent man.

8. (A.A.) lḥusayn dargaz .

(A.S.) lḥusayn daryaz .

Lahoucine is indeed a man.

or as a greeting or a response to a greeting. Examples:

9. (A.A.) s:alamuˁlik:um .

(A.S.) s:alamuˁlik:um .

Hello. (to a man by a man)

10. (A.A.) ṣbaḥ lxir amuḥa .

(A.S.) ṣbaḥ lxir amuḥa .

Good morning, Mohamed.

A.2 <u>Verbless</u>: <u>Interrogative</u>

Such sentences may occur in structures similar to the above with an interrogative tome to them. Examples:

11. (A.A.) lwašun labas ?

(A.S.) lwašun labas ?

How is the family?

12. (A.A.) γurs sbˤa išir:an ?

(A.S.) γrs sbˤa l:wašun ?

Does he have seven children?

13. (A.A.) šg: dmi ?

(A.S.) wak:d šk: ?

You (ms) and who else?

or with the interrogative particle /is/ before such structures as the following:

14. (A.A.) is γurš šal lwašun ?

(A.S.) is γrš šal lwašun ?

Do you have children?

They also occur with question words. Examples:

15. (A.A.) mismnš ?

(A.S.) mismn:š ?

What is your name (ms) ?

16. (A.A.) šḥal ylˤmrnš ?

(A.S.) mšḥal ilˤmṛn:š ?

How old are you (ms) ?

17. (A.A.) šḥal taqb:ut:a ?

(A.S.) mšḥal itqb:ut:u ? ~ mšḥal taqb:ut:u ?

How much is this djellaba?

18. (A.A.) mani muḥa ?

(A.S.) mani muḥa ?

Where is Mohamed?

A.3 Verbless: Negative

These structures occur with /ur-/ 'negative particle' in A.A. and A.S. or /urid:-/ 'It's not' in A.A. and A.S. Examples:

19. (A.A.) urγuri lflus .

(A.S.) urγri lflus .

I have no money.

20. (A.A.) urid: am: wa .

(A.S.) ulid: am wu .

It is not like this (ms).

21. (A.A.) urid: ḥm:u .

(A.S.) ulid: ḥm:u .

It's not Ḥammou.

22. (A.A.) urid: nt:a .

(A.S.) ulid: nt:a .

It's not him.

23. (A.A.) urid: šg: .

(A.S.) ulid: šk: .

It's not you.

A.4 Verbless: Negative - Interrogative

Such structures are achieved with the use of /isur-/ Negative - Interrogative particle in both dialects. Examples:

24. (A.A.) isur γurs lflus ?

(A.S.) is urγrs lflus ?

Doesn't he have money?

25. (A.A.) isurid: ḥšuma γifš ?

(A.S.) isulid: ḥšuma xš ?

Aren't you (ms) ashamed?

26. (A.A.) isurid: nt:a ?

(A.S.) isulid: nt:a ?

Isn't that he?

27. (A.A.) isurid: taqduḥtns ayn:a ?

(A.S.) isulid: taq:nuštn:s adin ?

Isn't it his pot over there?

B.1 <u>Verbal</u>: <u>Affirmative</u>

B.1.1 <u>Sentences having one verb</u>. Examples:

28. (A.A.) tl:a da .

(A.S.) tl:a da .

She is here.

29. (A.A.) tl:a ytxamt .

(A.S.) tl:a ytxant .

It (f) is in the tent.

30. (A.A.) td:u γr txamt .

(A.S.) tṛaḥ γr txamt .

She went to the tent.

31. (A.A.) q:imn yfas .

(A.S.) q:imn dy fas

They stayed in Fez.

32. (A.A.) dayxd:m muḥa yṛ:bad .
    (A.S.) l:ayxd:m muḥa yṛ:baḍ .

Mohamed works in Rabat.

33. (A.A.) ha muḥa id:ad .
    (A.S.) ha muḥa iṛaḥd: .

Here comes Mohamed.

34. (A.A.) išas ʕli lflus imuḥa .
    (A.S.) yušas ʕli lflus imuḥa .

Aly gave Muha money.

35. (A.A.) iwḍnn: ʕari axatar .
    (A.S.) iwḍnn: lʕri amq:ṛan .

They reached (there) the high mountain.

36. (A.A.) dat:lʕabn lwašun k:u ṣbaḥ .
    (A.S.) l:at:lʕ:abn lwašun kul: ṣ:baḥ .

The kids play every morning.

37. (A.A.) imun muḥa dfaḍma saḥidus .
    (A.S.) imun muḥa dfaḍma ɣruḥidus .

Mohamed and Fatma went to the dance.

38. (A.A.) adid:u γr tad:artns .

(A.S.) adiṛaḥ γr tad:artn:s .

He will go home.

Notice that the word order of sentences consisting only of a verb and its subject is preferably:

Verb + Subject [in Construct State]

but sometimes can be:

Subject [in Free State] + Verb

Compare members of the following pairs:

39. (A.A.) if:γ umaziγ .

(A.S.) if:γ umaziγ .

The Berber went out.

and

40. (A.A.) amaziγ if:γ .

(A.S.) amaziγ if:γ .

The Berber went out.

41. (A.A.) iswa urgaz atay .
(A.S.) iswu uryaz at:ay .

The man drank tea.

and

42. (A.A.) argaz iswa atay .
(A.S.) aryaz iswu at:ay .

The man drank tea.

43. (A.A.) zṛiγ argaz t:mḍ:ut: .
(A.S.) ẓṛix aryaz t:mṭ:ut: .

I saw the man and the woman.

and

44. (A.A.) zṛiγ tamḍ:uṭ: durgaz .
(A.S.) ẓṛix tamṭ:ut: duryaz .

I saw the woman and the man.

45. (A.A.) ttša tafunast duγyul .
(A.S.) ttšu tafunast duγyul .

It (f) ate the cow and the donkey.

and

46. (A.A.) itša uγyul t:funast .
(A.S.) itšu uγyul t:funast .

The donkey and the cow ate.

If any of the moveable affixes (i.e. object pronominal affixes or particles of proximity, /d/ in A.A. and /d:/ in A.S., and remoteness, /n/ in A.A. and /n:/ in A.S.) occur, they are post verbal if the sentence does <u>not</u> have any temporal or modal prefixes, prepositions or conjunctions, and pre-verbal if any of the above elements does occur in the sentence. (See Pronominal Systems III.3.)

Examples:

47. (A.A.) išat:id .

(A.S.) yušast:d: .

He gave it (f) to him (nearer).

48. (A.A.) išastid .

(A.S.) yušastid .

He gave it (m) to him (nearer).

49. (A.A.) iγṛfastid .

(A.S.) iγṛfastid .

He threw it (m) at him (nearer).

50. (A.A.) dastidit:awy .

(A.S.) l:astidit:awy .

He is bringing it (m) (nearer) to him.

51. (A.A.) yiwyastid .

(A.S.) yiwyastid .

He brought it (m) to him (nearer).

52. (A.A.) isɣad muḥa xmsṭaˤš ntfunast .

(A.S.) isɣud: muḥa xmsṭaˤš: ntfunast .

Mohamed bought fifteen cows (nearer).

53. (A.A.) tsɣad faḍma ṛbˤa yful:usn .

(A.S.) tsɣud: faḍma ṛbˤa y:aẓiḍn .

Fatma bought four chickens (nearer).

54. (A.A.) argaz n:a disɣan irdn aya .

(A.S.) aryaz din d:isɣin irdn ayu .

This is the man who bought wheat (nearer).

(Also see #73, 75, 81, 105, 106, 107, 108, and many others.)

The verb 'to be', /g/ in A.A. and /iž/ in A.S., occurs in many structures preceded by /ay/ 'who, which, what'. Examples:

55. (A.A.) taxamt urgaz ay tga

(A.S.) taxant uryaz aytžu .

This is the man's tent.

56. (A.A.) iy:is ntslit ag:a .

(A.S.) yis ntslit: ag:žu .

This is the bride's horse.

57. (A.A.) šg: bulḥm:am ay tgid .

(A.S.) šk: bulḥm:am ay tžit .

You are the public bath attendant.

58. (A.A.) ayt ʕy:aš taq:bilt taxatart ay tga .

(A.S.) ayt ʕy:aš taq:bilt tamq:ṛant ay tžu .

Ayt Ayache is a big tribe.

59. (A.A.) nḳ:ni inslmn ay nga .

(A.S.) ntšni imslmn ay nžu .

We are Moslems.

60. (A.A.) nḳ:ni tarwa nmulay dris ay nga .

(A.S.) ntšni dar:a nm:ulay dris ay nžu .

We are the offspring of Mulay Dris.

61. (A.A.) muḥa argaz iẓiḷ: ag:a .

(A.S.) muḥa aryaz iʕdln ag:žu .

Mohamed is a nice man.

62. (A.A.) t:lawt iẓiḷ: ayt tga .

(A.S.) t:lawt iʕdln ay tžu .

This is a nice song.

B.1.2 Sentences having two verbs.

Expressing English 'to, in order to' is achieved by the use of two verbs where the second is in the future form. Examples:

63. (A.A.) id:a adixdm .

(A.S.) iṛaḥ adixdm .

He went to work.

64. (A.A.) id:a adign .

(A.S.) iṛaḥ adižn .

He went to sleep.

65. (A.A.) d:an lahl l:ʕil ad:s:utr: tarbat: ilahlns .

(A.S.) ṛaḥn lahl w:rba ads:utrn tarbat: ilahln:s .

The boy's parents went to ask for the girl's hand from her parents.

66. (A.A.) ikžmd adisl:m xf ʕm:is .

(A.S.) yudfd: adisl:m xunuži .

He came in to greet his uncle (paternal).

67. (A.A.) riγ add: uγ γr s:uq: .

(A.S.) bγix adṛaḥx γr s:uq: .

I want to go to the market.

68. (A.A.) riγ aditrard γr tmazirtinw .

(A.S.) bγix aditr:t γr tmurtinw .

I want you to take me back to my country.

69. (A.A.) tra at:d:u γr ʕt:is .

(A.S.) tbγa at:ṛaḥ γr ʕt:is .

She wants to go visit her aunt (paternal).

The use of conjunctions necessitates two verbs. Examples:

70. (A.A.) ʕd:an win:a days:an lq:hwa imalik:an .

(A.S.) g:utn idin is:n lq:hwa imarikan .

There are a lot of people who drink coffee in America.

71. (A.A.) nḳ:ni tarwa nmulay dris n:a ynḍln
yfas ay nga .

(A.S.) ntšni dar:a m:ulay dris udin inḍln
di fas aynžu .

We are the offspring of Mulay Dris who is buried in Fez.

72. (A,A.) imyu:san muḥa dˤli yṛ:baḍ n:a
yžmˤn .

(A.S.) imyus:an muḥa dˤli ir:baḍ dindi
žmˤn .

Muha and Aly got acquainted in Rabat where they met.

73. (A.A.) art:mšawar: mimš ašt:g:an
at:nγin .

(A.S.) alt:mšawaṛn mism asγažn
at:nγn .

They were consulting how to manage to kill him.

74. (A.A.) ad:ay nra ang atay dans:naw aman
bˤda .

(A.S.) ad:ay nbγa an:ž at:ay l:ans:naw aman
bˤda .

When we want to make tea, we boil water first.

75. (A.A.) ad:ay yawḍ lˤil xf yiwl , dast:xṭ
ayt uxamns tarbat: n:as it:iˤžibn .

(A.S.) ad:ay yawḍ urba γyiway , l:asṭ:xtaṛn
ayt uxamn:s tarbat: din asit:iˤžibn .

When the boy reaches the age of marriage, his family chooses the girl he likes.

76. (A.A.) art:waryaɣ am:i l:an sbʕa itran .

(A.S.) l:at:iržitx am:ani l:an sbʕa ytran .

I dreamt of seven stars.

77. (A.A.) art:waryaɣ is l:an sbʕa yiyun .

(A.S.) l:at:iržitx is l:an sbʕa yfunasn .

I dreamt that there were seven oxen.

78. (A.A.) iɣal is tga tamḍ:uṭ: iẓil: .

(A.S.) in:a is tžu tamṭ:ut: iʕdln .

He thought that she was a nice woman.

79. (A.A.) l:iy t:isal xf inmdi tn:as ur ɣuṛi l:in .

(A.S.) zg:a t:isal ximmdi , tn:as urɣri l:in .

When he asked her about wheat, she told him that she has none.

80. (A.A.) iq:im al:iy iwḥl .

(A.S.) iq:im azg:a yuḥl .

He stayed until he got tired.

81. (A.A.) d:an al:iy n:iwḍn ʕari axatar .

(A.S.) ṛaḥn azg:a n:iwḍn lʕri amq:ṛan .

They went until they reached (far) the high mountain.

Conditional sentences have two verbs also and occur with the conditional particles:

mš (A.A., A.S.)	if (possible, probable)
mr (A.A., A.S.)	if (impossible, contrary to fact)
mšur (A.A., A.S.)	if not (possible)
mrid: (A.A.)	if not (impossible, contrary to fact)
mlid: (A.S.)	if not (impossible, contrary to fact)

Examples:

82. (A.A.) mš iwta wnẓaṛ urt:f:q: .

(A.S.) mš iwtu wnẓaṛ urt:f:x: .

If it rains I will not go out.

83. (A.A.) mš qbl: , dat:d:un adqḍᵊn .

(A.S.) mš qbln , l:ag:um adqḍᵊn .

If they agree, they go register the marriage.

84. (A.A.) mš trid at:g:anid al: ask:a .

(A.S.) mš tbɣit at:ṛžit , al:utša* .

If you want to wait, let it be tomorrow.

85. (A.A.) mš ḍhṛ: isignaw , adiwt unẓaṛ .

(A.S.) mš ḍhṛn isinaw , adiwt unẓaṛ .

If clouds appear, it will rain.

* al + dutša

86. (A.A.) mš šyaɣ ša , td:ut at:an:ayt
aḍbib .
(A.S.) mš šyuɣ ša , tṛaḥt at:ẓṛt aḍbib.

If you are sick, go and see the doctor.

87. (A.A.) mš qbl: , dat:dun lˤil t:rbat:
dlahlnsn ɣl lbiru adqḍˤn .
(A.S.) mš qbln , l:ayg:ur urba t:rbat:
dlahln:sn ɣl lbiru adqḍˤn .

If they agree, the boy and the girl and their parents go to register.

88. (A.A.) mšur astidiši adastis:utr .
(A.S.) mšur astidiwši adastis:utr .

If he does not give it (m) to him (nearer), he will ask him for it (m).

89. (A.A.) mšurdid:i ask:a add:uɣ ɣr midlt .
(A.S.) mšur d:iṛaḥ dutša adwaˤdx midlt .

If he does not come tomorrow, I will go to Midelt.

90. (A.A.) mšur dtd:i faḍma as:a , and:u
ad:ɣifsnk: ask:a imidlt .
(A.S.) mšurd:tṛaḥ faḍma iḍu , an:ṛaḥ
ad:xsnk: dutša imidlt .

If Fatma does not come (here) today, then we go and visit her (together) in Midelt tomorrow.

91. (A.A.) mr γuri l:in lflus iḍl:i , l:asγiγ
igran nʕli .

(A.S.) mr γri l:in lflus iḍn:at: , l:asγix
ižran nʕli .

If I had the money yesterday, I would have bought Aly's fields.

92. (A.A.) mr it:n:id adasiniγ aditntidiš .

(A.S.) mr it:n:it l:anixas aditntid:iwš .

Had you told me, I would have asked him to give them (f) to me.

93. (A.A.) mrid: isuridawa ḍ:alb lʕil l:aym:ut .

(A.S.) mlid: isuridawa ṭ:alb arba l:aym:ut .

Had the Sheikh not cured the boy, he would have died.

94. (A.A.) mrid: istẓṛiγ iḍl:i , l:ašiγas lḥžab .

(A.S.) mlid: is tẓṛix iḍn:at: l:awšixas lḥžab .

If I had seen him yesterday, I would have given him the amulet.

95. (A.A.) mrid: isurḍhiṃ isignaw iḍl:i urik:at
unẓar as:a .

(A.S.) mlid: isurḍhiṃ isinaw iḍn:at: uritšat
unẓaṛ iḍu .

Had clouds not appeared yesterday, rain would not have fallen today.

96\. (A.A.) mrid: isurastidiši , adastis:utr .

(A.S.) mlid: isurastidiwši , adastis:utr .

Had he not given it (m) to him (nearer), he would have asked him for it (m).

97\. (A.A.) mrid: ša yaḍn urt:it:awy sql: mn st:my:at ryal .

(A.S.) mlid: ḥd: ḍnin , urt:it:awy sql: mn st:my:at ryal .

If it were somebody else, I would not have sold it (f) for less than 600 Rials.

The use of Aorist in narration to denote a perfective, imperfective or future action (i.e. past, present or future) is exemplified in the following sentences.

98\. (A.A.) iḍl:i id:a muḥa γr s:uq: isγ sk:ṛ day iˁayd: γr tad:art .

(A.S.) iḍn:at: iṛaḥ muḥa γr s:uq: isγ sḳ:aṛ day iˁid γr tad:art .

Yesterday, Moha went to the market, bought sugar, then came back home.

99\. (A.A.) k:u ṣ:baḥ ad:ay tk:r g:iṭṣ dats:aγa lˁafit day ts:nw aman day tˁm:ṛ atay day tls iˁban: l:xdmt day td:u sigran .

(A.S.) kul: ṣ:baḥ ad:ay tk:r zg:nud:m , l:at:saɣa lʕafit , day ts:nw aman , day tʕm:r at:ay , day tirḍ iʕban: l:xdnt day twaʕd ižran .

Every morning when she wakes up, she makes a fire and boils water, then makes tea, then puts on work clothes and then goes to the fields.

100. (A.A.) ask:a adid:u ɣr s:uq adiz:nz imndi , isɣ yut tqb:ut: , iʕdl iduša day iʕayd: ɣr tad:art .

(A.S.) dutša adiṛaḥ ɣr s:uq: adiz:nz imndi isɣ išt ntqb:ut: , iʕdl iduša day iʕidd: ɣr tad:art .

Tomorrow he will go to the market to sell wheat, buy a djellaba, repair shoes, and then go back home.

B.2 Verbal: Interrogative

This is achieved by the use of this interrogative particle /is-/ prefixed to a verb in the past (A.A. and A.S.) or the interrogative particle /id:-/ (A.A.) or /isd-/ (A.S.) prefixed to a verb in the future. Examples:

101. (A.A.) is ifṛḥ muḥa ?

(A.S.) is ifṛḥ muḥa ?

Is Mohamed happy?

102. (A.A.) is iʕm:ṛ s:uq: maduhu ?

(A.S.) is iʕm:ṛ s:uq:u mad ihi ?

Is the market full or not?

103. (A.A.) isdats:am atay ytmazirtn:un mad uhu ?

(A.S.) ists:m at:ay itmurtn:un mad ihi ?

Do you (mp) drink tea in your country or not?

104. (A.A.) id:adimʕawan muḥa dʕli ?

(A.S.) isdadimʕawan muḥa dʕli ?

Will Mohamed and Aly help each other?

Notice that the use of the particles mentioned above causes the moveable particles to be pre-verbal. Examples:

105. (A.A.) isastiγṛf ?

(A.S.) isastiγṛf ?

Did he throw it (m) at him?

106. (A.A.) isastidiša ?

(A.S.) isastidyušu ?

Did he give it (m) to him (nearer)?

107. (A.A.) isast:iša ?

(A.S.) isast:yušu ?

Did he give it (f) to him (nearer)?

108. (A.A.) isastidit:awy ?

(A.S.) isastidit:awy ?

Is he bringing it (m) to him (nearer)?

Two verbs might occur in such constructions. Examples:

109. (A.A.) istrid at:dud γr s:uq: ?

(A.S.) is tbγit at:ṛaḥt γr s:uq: ?

Do you want to go to the market?

110. (A.A.) isaš in:a adid:u ?

(A.S.) isaš in:a dad:iṛaḥ ?

Did he tell you that he will go?

111. (A.A.) isd:an adqḍˤn ?

(A.S.) isṛaḥn adqḍˤn ?

Did they go to register the marriage?

112. (A.A.) id:ad:d:un adγifnγk:n ?

(A.S.) isdad:ṛaḥn adixnxk:n ?

Will they come to visit us (nearer)?

The use of question words in interrogative sentences is exemplified by the following.

113. (A.A.) maγr id:a ˤli ?

(A.S.) maniγr iṛaḥ ˤli ?

Where did Aly go?

114. (A.A.) mag:a s:uq: as:a ?

(A.S.) mag:žu s:uq: iḍu ?

How is the market today?

115. (A.A.) may γuṛun did:an ?

(A.S.) wid: γrun iṛaḥ ?

Who came to your (mp) house?

Sentence #116 below shows that the moveable particle /-aš-/ 'to you' is preverbal in the environment of the question word /ma/ 'what':

116. (A.A.) maš tga ṣ:aḥt ?

(A.S.) maš tžu ṣ:aḥt ?

How are you (ms) ?

B.3 Verbal: Negative

This is achieved by the negative prefix /ur-/ in A.A. and A.S. before verbs in the past or /ur-/ in A.A. and /ul:i-/ in A.S. before habitual stems. Examples:

117. (A.A.) uryan:ay ag:d yun bnadm .

(A.S.) urizṛi ulad idž nbnadm .

He did not see a single person.

118. (A.A.) urtyan:ay ag̣:d yun bnadm .

(A.S.) urtiẓri ulad idž nbnadm .

Not even a single person saw him.

119. (A.A.) urdžin: an:ayɣ am: wa .

(A.S.) urɣmṛi ẓṛix am wu .

I never saw some {one / thing} like this.

120. (A.A.) urdžin: d:iɣ ɣr s:uq: nmidlt .

(A.S.) ur ˁmṛi ṛaḥx ɣr s:uq: nmidlt .

I never went to the Midelt market.

121. (A.A.) ur:iɣ ad:uɣ ɣr s:uq: .

(A.S.) urbɣix adṛaḥx ɣr s:uq: .

I {do / did} not want to go to the market.

122. (A.A.) urdayit:iˁžib t:f:aḥ .

(A.S.) ul:iyiyt:iˁžib t:f:aḥ .

I don't like apples.

123. (A.A.) urdat:d:uɣ ɣr s:uq: nmidlt .

(A.S.) ul:ig:urx ɣr s:uq: nmidlt .

I never go to the Midelt market.

The occurrence of the negative particles /ur-/ or /ul:i-/ causes the moveable particles to be preverbal. Examples:

124. (A.A.) urdtd:i γr s:uq: as:a .

(A.S.) urd:tṛaḥ γr s:uq: iḍu .

She did not come to market today.

125. (A.A.) urn:t:d:u γr s:uq: ask:a .

(A.S.) urn:tg:ur γr s:uq: dutša .

She will not go (far) to the market tomorrow.

126. (A.A.) urtidniwy .

(A.S.) urtidniwy .

We did not bring it (m) (nearer).

127. (A.A.) urn:id:i γr s:uq: , urixdim g:granns .

(A.S.) urn:iṛaḥ γr s:uq: , urixdim g:žrann:s .

He neither went (far) to the market nor worked in his fields.

128. (A.A.) urastidiši .

(A.S.) urastidyuši .

He did not give it (m) to him (nearer).

B.4 Verbal: Negative-Interrogative

This structure is achieved by the prefixation of /isur-/ to a verb. /isur-/ also causes the moveable particles to be preverbal. Examples:

129. (A.A.) isurastiši ?
     (A.S.) isurastiwši ?

     Didn't he give it (m) to him?

130. (A.A.) isurast:idiši ?
     (A.S.) isurast:d:yuši ?

     Didn't he give it (f) to him (nearer)?

131. (A.A.) isurast:idit:awy ?
     (A.S.) isurast:d:it:awy ?

     Isn't he bringing it (f) to him (nearer)?

132. (A.A.) isurixdim muḥa as:a ?
     (A.S.) isurixdim muḥa iḍu ?

     Didn't Mohamed cook today?

C. Imperative Structures

An imperative structure can occur without a verb, e.g. (A.A.) the use of the particle /awra/ 'Come! '

133. (A.A.) awra .

(A.S.) awru .

Come!

Other than that, all imperative structures include a verb. Imperative structures directed to second person may contain one or more verbs. Examples of such imperatives with one verb are

134. (A.A.) xdm !

(A.S.) xdm !

Work!

135. (A.A.) xdm amuḥa !

(A.S.) xdm amuḥa !

Work, Mohamed!

136. (A.A.) xd:m asidi !

(A.S.) xd:m asidi !

Do work, Mister! or Get in the habit of working, Mister!

137. (A.A.) ns ylman .

(A.A.) ns ylman .

Good night.

138. (A.A.) ini nʿam imayš .

(A.S.) ini nʿam iym:aš .

Answer your mother.

Notice that habitual stems can occur to express an energetic Imperative. Example:

139. (A.A.) xd:m .

(A.S.) xd:m .

Do work! Or Get in the habit of working.

Examples of Imperatives having two verbs in the imperative:

140. (A.A.) d:u xdm !

(A.S.) sir xdm !

Go work!

141. (A.A.) d:ut munat .

(A.S.) sirm munm .

Go together.

Examples of sentences having one verb in the imperative and another verb in the future to express such ideas as "go in order to work" are

142. (A.A.) q:is ša yzlan imuḥa adis:ɣd .
(A.S.) q:is ša yzlan imuḥa adis:ɣd .

Sing some songs to Muha so that he can hear you.

143. (A.A.) ad:ud atsl:md xf unbyi .
(A.S.) awru at:sl:mt xunuži .

Come greet the guest.

144. (A.A.) d:uyat at:z:nzm irdn .
(A.S.) sirm at:z:nzm irdn .

Go (mp) to sell the wheat.

145. (A.A.) d:uyat at:sl:mm xf muḥa .
(A.S.) sirm at:sl:mm xmuḥa .

Go (mp) and say hello to the young man.

Second person Imperative structures could be expressed without the use of an imperative form. Examples here use /ixs:a/ 'It's necessary, you have to' followed by a verb in the future form.

146. (A.A.) ixṣ:a aditinid lḥq: .
(A.S.) ixṣ: adinit lḥq: .

You have to tell me the truth.

147. (A.A.) ixṣ:a aditidtawid adan:ayγ .

(A.S.) ixṣ: aditit:awit at:ẓṛx .

Bring him here so that I see him.

148. (A.A.) ixṣ:a aditṛẓmd tawaryit:a .

(A.S.) ixṣ: aditṛẓmt tiržit:u .

You must explain that dream for me.

Negative Imperative (second person) structures are realized by the use of /adur-/ before a habitual stem. Notice /adur-/ causes the moveable affixes to be preverbal.

149. (A.A.) adurdt:lˤab da .

(A.S.) adurd:t:lˤab da .

Don't play (nearer) here.

150. (A.A.) adurastidt:awy .

(A.S.) adurastidt:awy .

Don't bring it (m) nearer.

151. (A.A.) adurastidtak:at dγi .

(A.S.) adurastidttšitšt durṭ:x

Don't give it (m) to him (nearer) now.

First person imperatives (i.e. hortatory or cohortative constructions expressing an exhortation or suggestion for first person) occur with verb /k:r/ 'to get up' or the particle /yaḷ:ah/ 'let us'. Examples:

152. (A.A.) yaḷ:ah answ atay ,

(A.S.) yaḷ:ah answ at:ay .

Let us (go and) have (drink) tea.

153. (A.A.) yaḷ:ah and:u answ:q: .

(A.S.) yaḷ:ah an:ṛaḥ an:sw:q .

Let us go and shop.

154. (A.A.) k:raγ and:u γr s:uq: .

(A.S.) k:rax an:ṛaḥ γr s:uq: .

Let us (mp) go to the market.

155. (A.A.) k:raγ and:u t:afad an:awḍ zik: answ:q: .

(A.S.) k:rax an:ṛaḥ t:af an:awḍ ziš an:sw:q .

Let us (mp) go so we will be there early and stop.

156. (A.A.) k:rntaγ and:u γr tad:art .

(A.S.) k:rntax an:ṛaḥ γr tad:art .

Let us (fp) go home.

The Aorist may be used after an imperative form to express second person imperative. Example:

157. (A.A.) d:u ɣr ʕari tẓdmd: šay sɣaṛ: tgd
lʕafit tssnud aksum iwnbyi .

(A.S.) sir ɣl lʕri tzdntd: šay sɣaṛn , tžt
lʕafit , ts:nut aysum iwnuži .

Go to the mountain, collect (nearer) some wood, make a fire and cook meat for the gucst.

* * *

INDEX

Comparative Notes:
on Numerical System in A.S.,33
on Phonology in A.S.,19-20
on Pronominal System in A.S.,77-85
on the Noun,126-130
on the Verb, 216-239
Conjuctions:
of Ayt Ayache,141-143
of Ayt Seghrouchen, 143-145
Consonants:
alveolar, 2
alveo-palatal, 2
bilabial, 2
dental, 2
emphatic, 8
flat, 5, 7
fortis, 11
glottal, 2
labialized, 5, 7, 8
labio-dental, 2
lax, 2, 11
lenis, 11
list of, 2
non-emphatic, 8
palatal, 2
pharyngeal, 2
post-palatal, 2
pronunciation of, 5
/s/, tongue position for, 10
/s/, tongue postion for, 10
syllabic, 11
/t/, tongue position for, 9
/t/, tongue position for, 9
table of, 4
tense, 2, 7, 11
uvular, 2
velar, 2
voiced, 2
voiceless, 2
Noun:
affixes
masculine singular, 93-94
masculine plural, 94-95
feminine singular, 95-96
feminine plural, 96-97
augmentative, 116
collective
plural, 117
singular, 116
composed, 118
construct state
masculine nouns, 119-120
feminine nouns, 120-121
conditions for, 121-126
definite, 92
diminutives, 115-116
gender, 89, 92, 93
indefinite, 92
number, 89, 93
plural
feminine external, 109-111
feminine internal, 111-112
feminine mixed, 112
masculine external, 97-104
masculine internal,104-107
masculine mixed, 1o7-109
with /ayt/, 115
with different roots, 115
with /id-/,/ist:/, 114-115
stems
basic, 88-92
derived, 92, 182-185
unity, 117
Numerical System:
cardinal, 22-29
fractions, 31-33
ordinal, 29-31
Particles:
conditional, 150
derivation of, 200-207
interrogative (A.A.), 132-136
interrogative (A.S.), 137-141
presentational, 149
vocative, 150
Prepositions:
Ayt Ayache, 145-147
Ayt Seghrouchen, 147-149
Pronominal Affixes:
direct object of verb
affirmative, 49-52

interrogative, 61-63
negative, 55-58
negative-interrogative, 66-69
indirect object of verb
affirmative, 46-49
interrogative, 58-61
negative, 52-55
negative-interrogative, 63-66
Pronouns:
affixes (see Pronominal)
demonstrative, ha, han, 71
demonstrative, singular, 69
demonstrative, plural, 69
demonstrative, pron. suffixes, 69-71
indefinite, every, each, 76
indefinite, proximate, 74-75
indefinite, remote, 75-76
personal, emphatic, 35
personal, independent forms, 35
possessive, independent set, 36-37
possessive, pronominal suffixes, 37-44
relative, object, 74
relative, subject, 72-74
Semi-Vowels:
table of, 4
pronunciation of, 5
see also Vowels and Consonants
Sentences:
imperative structures, 315-320
verbal:affirmative, 293-308
verbal:interrogative, 308-311
verbal:negative, 311-314
verbal:neg.-interrogative, 314-315
verbless:affirmative, 287-289
verbless:interrogative, 289-291
verbless:negative, 291-292
verbless:neg.-interrogative, 292-293
Syllable:
structure of, 15
stress of, 17
Verb:
affixes
fixed discont. morpheme, 158=160
fixed prefix, 155-157
fixed suffix, 158
movable, 154-155
derivational processes
causative stem, 179
future tense, 195-197
habitual VH of unaug. stem, 176-178
imperative structures, 187-192
participles, 200-202
passive verb stem, 181-182
past tense, 192-195
present tense, 197-200
reciprocal verb stem, 179-181
list of(A.A.), 262-282
morphophonemic sketch
examples, 210-215
general rules, 207-210
sample appendix A, 240-261
sample appendix B, 283-285
stems
ablauted, 160-173
basic, 153
conjugations, 170-173
derived, 153, 182-185
metathesis in, 165-166
unablauted, 160, 167-171
Vowels:
list of, 2
table of, 4
rules for allophones, 13
table of allophones, 12

Made in the USA
Monee, IL
07 April 2023

31489568R00195